Biblical Foundations in Theology

General Editors

JAMES D. G. DUNN
Professor of Divinity, University of Durham

JAMES P. MACKEY
Thomas Chalmers Professor of Theology,
University of Edinburgh

Meaning and Truth in 2 Corinthians

BIBLICAL FOUNDATIONS IN THEOLOGY

General Editors
James D. G. Dunn   James P. Mackey

New Testament Theology in Dialogue
James D. G. Dunn and James P. Mackey

Jesus and the Ethics of the Kingdom
Bruce Chilton and J. I. H. McDonald

Meaning and Truth in 2 Corinthians
Frances Young and David F. Ford

Biblical Foundations in Theology

General Editors
JAMES D. G. DUNN   JAMES P. MACKEY

MEANING AND TRUTH IN 2 CORINTHIANS

Frances Young

and

David F. Ford

First published in Great Britain 1987
SPCK
Holy Trinity Church
Marylebone Road
London NW1 4DU

227·3

British Library Cataloguing in Publication Data

Young, Frances M.
Meaning and truth in 2 Corinthians.—
(Biblical foundations in theology).
1. Bible N.T. Corinthians, 2nd—
Criticism, interpretation, etc.
I. Title II. Ford, David F. III. Series
227'.306 BS675.2

ISBN 0-281-04317-5

Printed in Great Britain by
the University Press, Cambridge

Contents

Editors' Foreword

The aim of this series is to bridge the gap between biblical scholarship and the larger enterprise of Christian theology. Whatever the theory or theology of the canon itself, Christian theologians have always seen in the Bible their ultimate court of appeal, and exegetes have rightly expected their work to contribute directly to a better theology for each succeeding century.

And yet the gap remains. Theologians from the beginning, the greatest as well as the least, have been guilty of forcing their preferred conclusions upon a biblical text which they could have better understood. And the more professional biblical scholars, too anxious perhaps for immediate theological impact, have often been tempted to produce Old or New Testament theologies which in the event owed too little to the rich variety of their authoritative texts, and too much to prevailing theological fashions. Co-operation between a critical scholar of the texts and a critical commentator on theological fashions was seldom evident, and few individuals have ever been able to combine both of these roles successfully.

Biblical Foundations in Theology attempts to address this problem by inviting authors from the disciplines of Biblical Studies or Systematic Theology to collaborate with a scholar from the other discipline, or to have their material reviewed in the course of composition, so that the resultant volumes may take sufficient account of the methods and insights of both areas of enquiry. In this way it is hoped that the series will come to be recognized as a distinctive and constructive contribution to current concerns about how, in the modern world, Christianity is to be lived as well as understood.

JAMES D. G. DUNN

JAMES P. MACKEY

Preface

We owe debts of gratitude for help with this book to far more people than we can name, as it has been developed through more than six years of discussions, seminars and correspondence. We specially thank each other and our families. We also thank Dan Hardy, John Eaton, Abraham Malherbe, Margaret Thrall, Werner Jeanrond, Wayne Meeks, Hans Frei, George Lindbeck, David Kelsey, Gillian Weston, Andrew Mayes, Mícheál Ó Siadhail, Peter Hocken and the postgraduate seminar in which we first tried out our ideas, and which so often sharpened up the questions for us. We have been grateful too for the encouragement of the staff of SPCK during this long process, and their efficiency in its eventual production. Elnora Ferguson deserves special mention for her speedy and cheerful work on the Index.

Introduction

This joint study of a particular biblical text, involving a systematic theologian and one trained in the disciplines of scholarly exegesis, arose out of apparent coincidence. Yet in the doing of it there has been deepening conviction that it was appropriate to the present state of theology. It has also proved to be challenging, exciting and 'overflowing' in its potential. We have felt compelled by it, as if here we had a 'vocation'. We have not always felt adequate: who is sufficient for these things? But if others are fired by the task that will be enough.

We can articulate three starting-points: (1) a sense that systematic theology and biblical studies were finding it more and more difficult to act as dancing partners, each following its own agenda, unable to synchronize their steps or even grasp what the other was about; (2) a fear that biblical criticism was becoming isolated and undervalued in the context of the wider theological spectrum, not to mention the Church, and consequently suffering from a failure of nerve as it spawned 'canon criticism' and 'structuralist exegesis'; (3) a conviction that hermeneutical theory had little effect upon practising exegetes because it remained abstract and theoretical and was not engaged with the practical realities of interpreting particular texts. What we aim to do is to think through these problems by undertaking this co-operative exercise in practical hermeneutics.

It is usually helpful in trying to characterize a situation to have at least an outline awareness of how the situation arose. The historico-critical method of biblical interpretation, as it is usually described, evolved as part of a liberation movement. Philology was embraced as a way of taking the text absolutely seriously. Before its advent at the time of the Renaissance (though in certain respects it was anticipated in some patristic exegesis), the text had become a vehicle for dogma: if the words did not fit, the interpretation ensured that they did and difficulties were circumvented by the use of allegory. Now, however, the text itself was to be the criterion of interpretation. The intention was so to focus a searchlight on the text that its message would be plain, unclouded by the dogmatic presuppositions of ecclesiastical tradition or the personal prejudices of the individual interpreter. The text was to be viewed 'objectively', given its own independence, and studied in its earliest linguistic forms. The excitement of philological discovery can be sensed if one simply handles a volume of the London Polyglot published in the 1650s. This ideal of objectivity was reinforced by the developing tradition of scientific investigation. Both were movements critical of the tyranny of preconceived ideas. Freed from its incubus, the world of nature, the text of Scripture, could speak for itself. So in the latter case, it would become the living Word of God, active and cutting as a two-edged sword, piercing to the division of soul and spirit, joints and marrow. The critic would be one who sat in awe and wonder and joy before the truth revealed. It was assumed that Scripture had one true meaning and that that true meaning was its original meaning.

But this hope has not been realized. There is now a widespread feeling that biblical studies have reached an impasse. The historico-critical method, it is said, has not been able to yield any hermeneutic: it has simply produced a deep gulf between use of the Bible in the community of the Church, and specialist investigation into its background and language in the academic community. More and more voices are heard criticizing what is now regarded as the 'traditional' historicism and advocating new methods and approaches. Some borrow from the psychologizing or structuralist techniques of current literary studies, others assert that hermeneutics must begin from the present situation and find biblical support for a political programme or 'praxis'. This whole 'post-critical' movement has something to teach us, though it is often over-belligerent and less than honest about its debt to criticism. It also betrays a failure to grasp the importance of those values, and the validity of those methodological techniques, which are enshrined in the philological method – not to mention its theological import. We surely dare not sacrifice what has been gained, even if we acknowledge some lack of vision, some narrowness, some distraction into the wrong preoccupations.

The philological method instigated a tremendous effort of critical examination: of manuscripts to find the original wording, of the Greek language to find the original meaning, of the religious and cultural background to find original connotations. It is not altogether surprising that discussion and debate focused on establishment of the facts. The apologetic element in the origins and practice of criticism aided and abetted this evolution, and it was accentuated by the nineteenth-century conflict between emerging science and biblical narratives hitherto unquestioned, not to mention the advent of 'positivism'. This concern with the 'facts' had a distorting effect on much biblical study: it turned exegesis into a kind of archaeological study, more concerned with distinguishing the layers of deposit than listening to what the text had to say; it made a kind of idolatry of the facts and distracted from the possibility of resonances and layers of meaning in a text which might point beyond its original sense and its immediate historical context; it ignored questions about the potential meaning and truth of the biblical text for readers in other cultures and historical periods – the possibility of transcendence; and it appeared to make the critic the judge and master of the text, with the authority to determine what it was about.

Of course this is something of caricature, but there is enough truth in it for some of the charges to stick. Debate in specialist circles has revolved around the correctness of this or that reconstruction of the original form or context of the text. Novel theories have been canvassed and differing hypotheses tested at the bar of evidence and of other people's scholarship. And all this has contributed to the divorce so often noted between critical study and use of the Bible in worship and devotion. So has the evident tension between so-called 'conservative' and 'radical' scholars, who though apparently sharing the same methods, find themselves producing different exegeses and different reconstructions of history. The realization has dawned that no one is 'objective', all come to the task with presuppositions if not vested interests. 'So much for objectivity!' goes up the cry. 'There is an inevitable hermeneutical circle whereby we find in the text what we are looking for.' Thus the whole basis of the endeavour is brought into disrepute. 'Objectivity' has come to be regarded as unattainable, appeal sometimes being made to some contemporary philosophy of science to justify this epistemological claim.

Now the more sober, of course, agree that conclusions in historical research and in the interpretation of texts can only be provisional – there are no 'assured results'. But this does not mean, in our view, that we are trapped in a hermeneutical circle of the kind described. If we only ever found in texts what we were looking for and never learned anything, there would be no point in reading them. It is a common experience that reading Homer or Plato, Shakespeare or Goethe, has an effect upon the reader. The reader brings a good deal to the reading, but also takes away something. In fact there is a hermeneutical spiral, because consciously or unconsciously a kind of dialogue is going on between the text and the reader. The text is not a *tabula rasa* on which the reader can draw his own pictures unrestrained, but a communication to which the attentive reader has to pay attention. Furthermore, to deny all objectivity is to capitulate to the extreme relativism of some contemporary intellectuals. It fails to do justice to the fact that everything is not subjective, and that it is possible to acquire competence, and improve one's understanding. There is an external world and an external text that impinges upon us, and to which our models of understanding approximate. The approximation can always be improved. Furthermore, questions of meaning are not private but belong to the public domain, because language belongs to a public. Structuralism has something to teach us here: humankind is not only a creator of significations, but significations are imposed upon human beings. In other words an author's creativity is constrained by the structures of the language being used, and the possibilities of meaning are limited by what the text actually says. Some debates about meaning are capable of being settled. To reach definite agreement about the meaning of an ancient text in an unfamiliar language is bound to be more complex than reaching agreement about what the Prime Minister said/meant this morning, but some debates have been settled by using the philological method to uncover the constraints of linguistic structure and 'cultural codes' within which the author inevitably operated at the time of writing. Other debates about meaning have been opened up because such procedures have produced greater awareness of possibilities of meaning. We refuse to accept that disciplined search for the meaning intended or assumed by the author is not the proper starting-point for exegesis, especially in the case of a text which is so clearly the product of a particular set of circumstances in the past as is 2 Corinthians.

But that is not to say that we are satisfied with the archaeological approach to the biblical text. That approach has given rise to another notorious problem, namely that of the 'hermeneutical gap' between our situation and the totally different cultural situation of the text now distanced from us through its treatment in a purely historical manner. How can the Word of God in Scripture be appropriated? How can a biblical text contribute to systematic theology? This matter has received a great deal of theoretical treatment, and the theoretical discussion will be taken up in due course. It does not seem to us that taking the philological method seriously precludes the possibility of meanings beyond what the author intended. A literary text may be – in fact, must be – interpreted, re-interpreted, clarified by new insights, read in new ways, in one generation after another, and these new readings are not necessarily illegitimate. This is not to open up a multiplication of meanings beyond constraint or to validate any and every interpretation. It is not to give free rein to the subjectivity or vested interests of the interpreter(s). It is simply to acknowledge the possibility of latent meanings discernible only within a subsequent perspective, and to recognize the mutual interaction of worlds involved in reading and responding to a text. There is no insuperable hermeneutical gap, any more than there is for a classical scholar reading Euripides or an English don reading Jane Austen. There is the possibility of something new emerging from the encounter with what is strange and yet familiar.

Furthermore, we suggest that the supposed problem of the hermeneutical gap reflects a theological inadequacy, a failure to embrace within systematic theology the consequences of the critical method. The systematic theologian rightly has his preoccupations, just as the biblical critic has his own agenda, but systematic theology is inevitably dependent in some sense upon Scripture and tradition. To the biblical scholar, the theologian sometimes seems to sit very lightly to the foundation documents of the faith, or to be perpetuating a naive and uncritical use of the Bible. On the other hand, the biblical scholar appears to the systematic theologian to be preoccupied with irrelevant details or to be immersed in unsettlable debates, reluctant to raise questions about the fundamental truths to be found in the texts being dealt with. So the theologian loses patience with the scholar's failure to give him dependable results and rather arbitrarily adopts what seems to be the respectable or 'consensus' view; while the scholar is impatient with the systematic theologian for sitting lightly to the reality of the historical problems, uncertainties and debates which are the critic's preoccupation.

The question we pose here is whether there might not be a creative way out of this impasse which denies neither the concerns of the biblical critic nor those of the modern systematic theologian, but brings them fruitfully together. If anything is an 'assured result', it is that the Scriptures are not a collection of theological statements in an eternally unchangeable and permanently valid form. They are documents arising out of particular events and particular situations, then subject to the changes and chances of textual transmission, deeply affected at every point by the contribution of fallible human agents, their sins of commission and their sins of omission. They are texts which pose historical jigsaw puzzles, reveal human weaknesses, texts bounded by particularity. Has theology taken seriously enough the fact that God has submitted himself to the changes and chances of human history and the fallibilities of humanity, not just through the incarnation, but in the very mode of his self-revelation in Scripture? In our view it is precisely this discovery about the nature of God which is potentially theologically fruitful, and coherent both with Paul's theology of the cross expressed in 2 Corinthians, and with those movements of modern theology which seek to smash the idolatries of 'theism'.

So our exercise in practical hermeneutics is intended to throw light on a number of issues in contemporary theology. By focusing on a particular text, we hope to articulate and reflect upon what is involved in the process of interpretation, sometimes perhaps seeming to state the obvious, but always with the aim of showing up the inadequacy of some ill-informed claims or proposals. Our aim is to enable readers to re-read or 'perform' the text with heightened awareness. We do not claim to produce the definitive work – indeed, we would suggest such a work would be impossible. There are many present 'performances' of 2 Corinthians, there have been others in the past, and there will be others in the future. Some performances are more convincing than others, but there is no 'final' statement of it which brings out its whole meaning. Its meaning is related to what Paul intended when he wrote it, but that does not exhaust it, even if it were possible to ascertain precisely what that meaning was. We seek to move in a disciplined way through what Paul meant to an apprehension of the truth he potentially communicates.

Perhaps our aim may be elucidated by reference to Buber. As is well known, Buber alerted his readers to the need to go beyond analysis and objective scientific study of a thing – say a tree – to a genuine encounter or relationship with it, describing the difference between these two approaches as 'I-It' and 'I-Thou'. Precisely what Buber meant, whether he had some mystical idea in mind, has been much discussed, but for our purposes it is important to notice that Buber did not dismiss the 'I-It' out of hand. It is an indispensable element in our grasp of the world. There is a sense in which criticism has got bogged down in the 'It' of the text, and what people are looking for is a way of meeting the 'Thou'. This will not be achieved, we suggest, by abandoning or denigrating the 'It' approach, for the 'It' approach should ideally release the dead language of the text from its chains and enable the encounter with the 'Thou'. But meeting the 'Thou' is the end of exegesis. Unless we are changed by response to the text, our reading is inadequate.

Let us delay no longer and anticipate no more. It is time to get down to the business of studying 2 Corinthians. What follows has emerged from work in which both of us have been involved at every stage. The translation we wrestled with together, and much else is the result of the discussions that exercise stimulated. However, Chapters 1–4 are attributable to the pen of Frances Young, and Chapters 5–9 to that of David Ford. Inevitably there are differences of style and approach. But we hope that that is an enrichment rather than a defect.

1

Discerning the Thrust of the Text

It has been said that all exegesis is an extension of translation. We would agree with those who object to this definition on the grounds that it implies too narrow an understanding of all that is involved in the interpretative process; yet at the same time, when one is dealing with a text written in a language other than one's own, in practice the attempt to understand it must begin with the discipline of translation, an exercise which not only brings one into creative engagement with the text as one tries to re-express what it says in a new medium, but also brings out all the potentialities of meaning and all the problems of understanding which exegesis is concerned to unpack as far as possible. What are these problems?

(1) One particular word in one language usually does not convey precisely the same sense as one particular word in another. The process of playing with different possible renderings alerts one to the variety of possible meanings that might be involved. To translate a word in one context, may mean exploring its use elsewhere, trying to decide whether it is used in different ways and in different senses in different contexts, or whether there is a consistency of idea, however difficult it is to find an equivalent word to use consistently in translation. In other words, the sheer practical necessities force one to be aware of the need to understand the thrust of the text as a whole in order to discern the force of individual statements and render them appropriately.

(2) Words in any given language have resonances deriving from the culture and society of those who speak it. In different

cultures and societies, ways of thought and forms of logic differ. It is often difficult, therefore, to translate in a way that makes perfect sense, and usually impossible to find perfect verbal equivalents. The translator is constantly aware of the need to be as immersed as possible in the world of the text. The text may derive from an 'in-group' which has developed its own peculiar linguistic habits or which shares a common tradition to which allusions are made. It may have arisen from a particular situation, the details of which can only be discerned from allusive clues, but knowledge of which is essential for complete understanding. The author may use language in an idiosyncratic way. All of these things have to be taken into account in the process of translation, and while background knowledge is vital, so is some insight into the thrust of the text as a whole if its peculiarities are to be discerned.

(3) Different languages have different structures, and to render a sentence word for word may on occasion, not merely obscure the sense, but even reverse it. It is not only knowledge of linguistic usage which is important here, but also careful attention to the context and flow of thought. Sometimes a preconceived idea of how the argument runs can cloud one's perception of what one element in it is really driving at. Even more serious, jumping to conclusions about what the text refers to may distort one's whole approach to a particular sentence. This then affects the proposed translation. Understanding sentences depends on understanding coherences, and once again the discipline of translation forces one to engage at a deeper level with the meaning of the whole.

(4) In the case of a biblical book, all kinds of prejudgements are built into the text as it is presented to us. I refer here not simply to the inbuilt knowledge of traditional translations and exegeses which years of even superficial familiarity tend to leave engrained, but the fact that a text which was originally continuous comes divided into chapters and verses, that modern editors have determined paragraphing – indeed, a long succession of scribes and editors have made contributions to the tradition of how the text is to be read. Originally it would even have been without punctuation or word divisions. A fresh read-

ing of the text may imply a search for underlying coherences which all these prejudgements have obscured.

(5) But it is not just a case of scribal prejudgements, there are also the problems arising from scribal error, or alteration. Decisions about exactly what words actually belong to the text cannot be avoided, and may make a crucial difference to the meaning. The discipline of translation means that one has to face up to the uncertainties, but also that one is aware of possibilities that tradition may have rejected or obscured. The importance of reaching some kind of overall perspective about the meaning of the whole becomes apparent when decisions have to be taken about the content in specific small instances. This is not to ignore the importance of technical text-critical skills for establishing the best reading, but it is to stress yet again the inter-relationship between careful attention to detail and a grasp of the entire thrust of the text with which one is concerned.

(6) Texts belong to literary genres. To read a novel as a bio-graphy or vice versa is to misunderstand the text. To grasp the thrust of the text depends upon correct identification of genre, and this in turn will affect the way in which particular elements in the text will be translated. A statement in one kind of genre is more likely to be ironical than in another; language used in one genre is more likely to be used in a technical sense than language used in another, and so on. The process of translation makes one vividly aware of even these wider issues of interpretation.

This book is an attempt to invite the reader to join in an enter-prise, and to become conscious of all that is involved in that enterprise. The enterprise is reading 2 Corinthians. It is an enterprise in which we have been jointly engaged for some time, and it is not possible to show all the workings which have gone into it. We have not attempted to include a commentary, even though creating one has been an essential part of the process of wrestling with the text. Every interpreter needs to create their own, and in doing so every interpreter will be dependent upon all other interpreters, both for what they borrow and for what they reject and react against. But our aim is not to do all the work for people, certainly not to give the impression that we can provide the definitive work on 2 Corinthians, but rather to indicate what is involved and reflect upon the process and its results.

We have, however, included the translation which has been the result of our common endeavour. Those who have the competence to check it may feel we have made mistakes; certainly they will notice some unusual features. Those who have no Greek will make similar observations if they compare it with any standard translation. This is because it reflects the conclusions we have reached about how to interpret this letter. Our understanding of the whole has affected our choices of words, our endeavours to keep or not keep a consistent vocabulary in translating certain words or phrases, the way we have divided up the text into paragraphs, or construed sentences, even at times the form of text we have chosen to follow. Our understanding of the whole has affected the parts as we have tried to convey the meaning of the text in a different language – I say tried, because the results are always inadequate and one is never wholly satisfied. Be that as it may, the aim of this chapter is to try and spell out, at least in a preliminary way, the overall thrust that we have discerned, and show how the parts contribute to it. In succeeding chapters the crucial questions of genre, presuppositions, allusions, social and cultural context, and so on, will be explored.

1 WHAT THE LETTER IS ABOUT

The letter is about two closely related things. One of these, is the glory of God, the other is the reputation of Paul. Crucial to the whole is the relationship between these two themes, and perhaps it is no accident that the Greek word *doxa* means both reputation and glory. It is of course important to know the circumstances which have occasioned the letter if we are to understand why these themes figure as they do. But it is doubtful whether the precise reconstruction of the circumstances is vital for interpretation – it is only too obvious that Paul's reputation is at stake, and that is sufficient, at any rate to begin with.

The Greek word *doxa* means in the first place, 'opinion', and so 'glory' in the sense of high reputation among men, with its consequent status and pride, the sort of glory people vied for in Greek society, what the Greek Fathers would later call *keno-doxia*, vainglory, empty glory. However, Paul only once uses the word to refer to his own reputation (6.8). What Paul is concerned about is the glory of God, or the glory of Christ, and his usage has been affected by the connotations of *doxa* in the Scriptures.

In Hebrew the word *kabōd* originally had connections with 'weight', and by being used to describe a 'weighty' person came to connote a person with reputation, not unlike the Greek word eventually used to translate it. (Was Paul aware of this when he spoke of 'an eternal weight of glory' in 5.17?) But when used of God, the word acquired connotations of splendour and radiance, and is usually associated with what Old Testament scholars call 'theophanies'. So for Paul, the glory of God is sometimes the glory given to him by the praises of men, his reputation, the hallowing of his name (1.20; 8.19), and sometimes the glory imparted by God (2 Cor. ch.3 *passim*) through his self-revelation. That is the true glory, the glory that made Moses' face shine, however temporarily,[1] and which transforms those who believe in Christ so that they reflect the glory of God which is revealed in his image, in the face of Jesus Christ (see Chapters 4 and 9 below). That is the kind of glory Paul claims, rather than the empty glory imparted by human society. That is why the issue of his reputation is closely interwoven with his profoundly theological discourse about the glory of God. It is also the basis of his claim to authority (see Chapter 8).

Usage of the particular word *doxa* is largely to be found in 2 Cor. 3 and 4; and there are none after 2 Cor. 8. That should not, however, mislead us into thinking that it is a mistake to treat this as the central theme. Throughout the epistle we find the verb *kauchōmai* and the related nouns *kauchēsis* and *kauchēma*; these are now usually translated 'boast' but the AV used 'glory', John Wesley used 'rejoice', and we would prefer to use 'exult' or 'take a pride in'. It has been claimed that these words are used in a slightly different sense in the last four chapters than in the first part of the epistle, but we are not convinced. It is possible to 'boast' appropriately or inappropriately, to take an appropriate or inappropriate pride. In the early part of the epistle, Paul uses the words positively for the most part; in the last four chapters he is sensitive to their negative possibilities.

But throughout, what he is after can be summed up in the text
he quotes in 10.17, which we translate: 'Let him who prides
himself on anything, pride himself on the Lord.' The same
issue is at stake: namely the right kind of 'glorying', and the
contrast between what usually goes on and what Paul claims for
himself, and urges upon other apostles.[2]

Proper pride depends upon being dependent on God and
operating 'according to the Spirit'; improper pride arises from
glorying in one's own achievements, operating 'according to the
flesh', that is according to human norms. Even though Paul
acknowledges that we cannot help being human, and even our
knowledge of Christ originated at the human level, he cannot
accept any compromise with the human techniques of ensuring
or claiming success, human wisdom though it be. Simply because it is self-dependent and not the result of single-minded
concentration on God, it is a form of cheating and deception,
and not the way to proclaim the gospel of the new covenant in
the Spirit.

The so-called 'opponents' of Paul are foils to bring out this
fundamental contrast, the kind of glory sought among men and
the kind of glory imparted by God. We suggest it is possible to
understand a good deal of what Paul is saying without ascer-
taining the exact 'charges' against him, or the identity of these
shadowy figures. Since much of Paul's language has a certain
conventionality, deductions from it may not be reliable. His
target is a stereotype (see Chapters 2 and 3 below) whose main
purpose is to help make Paul's point about the character of his
own mission. Paul's way of going about things had a certain
idiosyncrasy, and did not conform to norms in contemporary
society. He did not seek patronage, or offer teaching for money.
On the other hand, he was now trying to get money out of them
for one thing and another, and his extreme caution about not
handling the cash himself (8.20) suggests that suspicions sur-
rounded this. There were other reasons for suspecting him of
being two-faced: his constant protestations that he was coming
to Corinth and his repeated failure to turn up. There is a deep
crisis of confidence in the relationship between Paul and his
converts in Corinth. That is clear. The entire letter is concerned
with re-establishing mutual confidence. But Paul is more concerned to convey his own understanding of his own role and

woo back the doubters, misled by others or not, than to attack any specifically identifiable 'opponents'.

This is true even in the final four chapters of the letter. In spite of being almost indoctrinated with modern critical theories which dissect the epistle, we have become more and more suspicious of them as we have read and re-read the text. There is a coherence of theme and vocabulary, of circumstances presumed, of fundamental aim that demands to be taken seriously. There is nothing in the textual tradition to suggest that this has ever been anything other than a unified document. We believe that this view makes better sense of the text, and our case will progressively emerge during the course of our study. This presumption not only affects our understanding of the whole, but even makes quite a difference to the way certain sentences are read.

Throughout, Paul's fundamental aim, in the face of suspicions of his double-dealing, is to assert his utter transparency and openness and his single-minded commitment to his vocation. The focus is on the God who empowers him, as he tries to play down any powers of his own. Human wisdom and God's grace are contrasted over and over again as Paul ranges from appeal to cajoling, warning, anguish, anger, love and longing in his efforts to get across to his perverse children. At one level he is indulging in an emotional self-justification; at another he is proclaiming a high theology of the cross – for God's glory and power are there supremely revealed in weakness, and it provides the model for his own pattern of ministry. In the end it is not a case of justifying himself, but of pleading with them not to forgo the salvation they received through his ministry – everything is for their sake, and their future is at stake if they refuse to be reconciled with the spokesman of God, in other words, Paul.

Over the whole letter hovers a sense of urgency arising from the reality of God's final judgement. Then the truth will out. But what Paul is most anxious to achieve is mutual support and recognition when it comes to that appearance before God. The real sign of his apostleship is the community of the new covenant which he has formed. So he depends on them, just as they depend on him. A web of partnership, collaboration and interdependence is both affirmed and threatened in this letter, and it is this which makes the emotional tone both intense and alternating. Crises of confidence are most painful when they arise within the most intimate relationships. Furthermore, the need to persuade, a need both personal and pastoral, would imply skilful manipulation of mood to provoke the required reaction. The author's intention is to evoke a response, and one way to do that is to play upon the feelings of the 'audience' in an appropriate way. Like a parent Paul switches from compliment and encouragement to threats and warnings; the stick and the carrot can both be effective.

Paul's reputation is at stake, and yet 'everything is for your sake, so that grace abounding through more and more (of you) may cause thanksgiving to overflow to the glory of God' (4.15). In this way the theology and circumstances cohere: the response of the community is important both for the reputation of Paul and for the glory of God, two things which are themselves indissolubly linked.

2 AN OVERVIEW OF THE WHOLE TEXT

To write a commentary involves carving up the text into manageable units, and sometimes it seems that this dissecting process obscures the flow of the whole. Having stated what we believe to be what the letter is all about, let us work through the text to get some feel for the overall flow. More detailed issues of meaning will be tackled at a later stage (see below Chapter 4), even though such questions are in the end inseparable from what we attempt here, and much of what we say at this stage depends upon what will be argued in detail later on.

Paul as usual opens with a greeting which both utilizes and modifies contemporary conventions, Jewish and Greek, and fills them with particular Christian significance. Whether or not precedents existed, the way he addresses his churches would be recognized as somewhat unconventional, and he apparently creates a Christian 'in-language' which becomes standard for Christian correspondence.[3] The standard Greek greeting word (*chairein*) is replaced by the highly charged 'grace' (*charis*), and linked with the Hebrew 'peace' (*shalōm*). He introduces himself with the significant description 'apostle through the will of God'; and speaks of the grace and peace which he wishes them as coming from God the Father and Lord Jesus Christ. In important ways these features prepare for what is to come. The greeting is followed by a thanksgiving. Again, (see below Chapter 2) Greek convention opened letters with thankful invocation of the gods, and Paul has taken this up and used it for his own purpose; but the language is that of Jewish synagogue worship, and the content anticipates the theme of God's power effective in weakness.

For Paul's subject is not consolation whenever things go badly, as so many translations almost suggest by using the word 'comfort': in modern English this word has been emasculated and its connection with 'fortify' has been forgotten. We have chosen to translate with the word 'encourage', partly to bring out this stronger sense, but also in an endeavour to find a word that could cover a similar range of meaning in English to that covered by the Greek words *parakalō* and *paraklēsis*. These words reappear at crucial points in the epistle, often meaning 'appeal' or 'exhort'. The work of Christian prophets seems to have been particularly characterized by these words, God appealing, exhorting, chiding and encouraging through their messages.

Which is precisely what Paul is doing all through the epistle, claiming that he is God's spokesman, and appealing, exhorting, chiding and encouraging. The epistle begins in thankful mood, celebrating the fact that God is the source of encouragement in the most dreadful circumstances – indeed the One who gives life when death alone seems the likely outcome, and opening up the picture of the life of a Christian community in which God's encouragement overflows onto others and into more and more thanks and praise. In important ways this community is the partner and collaborator of the apostle and of his Lord. The mood is one of confidence in the face of disasters, and while at first there seems no cloud over the mutual relationship of Paul and the church he founded, in fact the content anticipates much that is to come as these difficulties are faced.

The whole point is that total confidence be put in God, and self-confidence abandoned. The shadows between Paul and the Corinthian church begin to emerge, as he insists upon the fact that he has conducted himself in the world with the single-minded commitment (literally, 'simplicity' or 'purity' – the

text is uncertain)[4] and straightforwardness of God, and by implication counters the charges of inconsistency or double-dealing.
The sequence of thought in 1.15–22 is not easy to discern, partly
because no English translation, we believe, has correctly construed v.17b. When Paul speaks of making plans 'according to
the flesh', we believe he is contrasting those who operate according to human wisdom (cf.1.12) with those who may act
unpredictably because they are subject to the promptings of the
Spirit: it does not rest in Paul's hands that yes be yes and no be
no. He is single-minded in carrying out the will of God, even if
that means not being a good businessman and keeping to his
schedules. The fact that he did not go to Corinth when expected
is admitted in 1.23. But that does not mean that either he or God
is inconsistent or unfaithful. Those who treat 18–22 as a digression have failed to see the thrust of the text[5] (see also below,
Chapter 4).

Paul admits, then, that he did not come to Corinth as he
promised, but attempts to put the whole thing in a different
light: he is a man under authority, and can act only in God's
grace. This kind of single-minded commitment he hopes they
will recognize and acknowledge in the end (1.12–14). But there
was also another motive, a motive grounded in the authority
delegated to him to build them up, not tear them down (10.8). It
was to spare them that he wrote instead of visiting them. He
hastens to assure them that his role is that of servant rather than
lord, and that damage to their mutual relationship is what he
was and remains primarily concerned to avoid. But the word
'spare' anticipates the dire warnings and appeals that will come
later.

Here Paul is anxious to stress his love for them and their
mutual responsibility in the face of disruptive influences in the
community. His motivation for writing and not coming lay in
his desire both to avoid disastrous conflict (or worse, as we shall
see), and to test their response. He seems to imply that they have
responded as he demanded in the case of some offender, whose
identity and offence is far from clear, and he now urges restraint,
forgiveness, and a return to mutual fellowship. It seems, however, that relationships are still not altogether right. Unless
forgiveness can flow from one to another, there is still the
possibility of Satan taking advantage of the community (2.11).

Nevertheless here Paul is anxious to express his profound love for them, and consequent anguish when their mutual understanding is under threat: he was on tenterhooks waiting for Titus' news, and his concern for them actually took priority over a possible opening for mission. But this pain and concern for the churches is part of the agony of apostleship (11.28). It is God who determines where he will go, and he is like a captive dragged around helpless in a victory procession.

The coherence of the second chapter of 2 Cor., suggested in the previous paragraph, is often missed. Commentators tend to suggest that Paul is expressing his joy and relief at the news received from Titus, that the passage presupposes that the quarrel has been made up, that there is an inexplicable hiatus in the narrative – 2.13 being taken up again in 7.6 – and therefore the intervening material comes from somewhere else. We suggest that there is no 'narrative' as such. Rather the reference to Titus and Paul's anguished waiting for him is intended to reinforce his expression of concern, and the mood is one of continuing anxiety. Expressed in an outburst of thanksgiving, 2.14 is not a sudden break with what has gone before, but a celebration of the fundamental point Paul tried to make in the previous chapter, namely that he is the prisoner of God and not responsible for his own actions. The complex metaphor also carries an implicit warning: those who refuse to accept Paul, the martyr whose sacrificial incense rises wherever he goes, will find themselves among the perishing. His gospel is discriminatory in the sense that people are divided and judged by their response to it. Paul will make this even plainer in 2 Cor. 6 when he appeals to them not to forgo the salvation they have received, but to open their hearts to him.

There is an indissoluble link between responding to Paul and responding to God. Paul himself is overawed by the responsibility that that puts on him. Who is adequate? No one who relies on anything less than God's grace. That is why Paul does not resort to the conventional means of advancing his cause. He does not trade in God's word, earning his living by it and therefore tempted to preach what his patrons want to hear (2.17; 4.2). Nor does he require letters of commendation to introduce him to new patrons. The results of his mission are his only commendation. In fact the Corinthians are themselves his letter of commendation. Slipping from image to image, from idea to idea, Paul proceeds to argue in a way that our kind of logic finds difficult to follow (for further discussion see Chapter 4), and which depends entirely upon allusion to key prophecies and narratives of what we call the Old Testament. The contrast between a written letter and a letter written on hearts suggests the difference between the Mosaic covenant written on tablets of stone, and the new covenant written on hearts by the Spirit. But the nub of Paul's argument concerns what true glory is. By implication he rejects the glory sought by most travelling preachers, the glory accorded by popularity and patronage.

Paul has no adequacy of his own. He is simply the slave who delivered the letter, the servant of God who brought them the new covenant. Even the old covenant, the covenant which brought judgement and condemnation and death, had something of the true glory, the glory of God, but Moses had to veil it. Paul suggests that the veil was to conceal the fact that it was fading, reading the idea into the text of Exodus 34.[6] It was fading because it pointed beyond itself and would therefore become obsolete (we would suggest that *telos* in 3.13 is ambiguous and means both 'end' and 'fulfilment'; we translate 'outcome'). But this outcome, the real glory of God, is still veiled when Moses is read, and it is only when people turn to the Lord (an Old Testament phrase for repenting and returning to covenant-loyalty) that the veil is removed. Paul interprets that turning to the Lord as receiving the covenant of the Spirit imparted through Jesus Christ. Then the veil is removed, and complete openness is possible.

Unlike Moses Paul can boldly exercise the power of free speech. His gospel is not veiled. He and other genuine apostles reflect the glory of God in the face of Christ and are being transformed into that self-same image (see further Chapters 4, 8 and 9). He has nothing to conceal. Faced with suspicion of double-dealing, Paul asserts his utter transparency. And it all comes from his utter dependence upon God. Yes, there are those who react against him, there are those who are unfaithful (or unbelieving), and they are among the perishing, their eyes blinded. Perhaps he implies that the Corinthians had better beware in case they find themselves among that number. But the whole point is that Paul does not preach himself, or depend upon himself: his very weakness and sufferings indicate his own powerlessness and God's power to bring life out of death (4.7–14; cf. 1.8–11).

Two things are at the heart of Paul's intentions: the salvation of the Corinthians themselves ('everything is for your sake'), and the glory of God (4.15). For the sake of these he will never give up. Paul and all those in Christ live at two levels: they are still struggling with the trials of their present earthly existence, but all the time they are being re-created and prepared for quite another future. The downpayment on this is their life in the Spirit. The afflictions of the present are nothing compared with the eternal weight of glory for which they are destined. So Paul will never give up, and he knows that in the end all will be made absolutely clear on judgement day. This is simply the interim, a time of struggle; but the new creation is anticipated in Christ. This means that as an apostle he cannot use the dubious techniques that might bring worldly success, least of all self-commendation, but must act solely under the direction of God and in fear of him. Paul desperately hopes that the Corinthians will understand, and will take a pride in him rather than succumb to the blandishments of those who commend themselves.

Through Christ God has reconciled the world to himself by a powerful exchange, turning into sin one who was sinless so that sinners could be turned into righteousness. Paul has already insisted that his ministry depends upon God's mercy (4.1); now he indicates that the message he is commissioned to deliver as God's ambassador is the fact that God has reconciled us to himself through Christ and no longer counts our sins against us. But the emphasis at the end of 2 Cor. 5 is upon Paul's role as ambassador. He is the one with the message, and if they do not respond to his appeal to be reconciled with God, a real question-mark hangs over their salvation. Paul reinforces the appeal with words from Scripture, and a catalogue of the signs that confirm his apostleship, by which he means his commissioning by God (6.1–10).

A real question-mark hangs over their salvation if they do not respond to Paul. Already Paul has implied this (2.14; 4.3). The faithful who become unfaithful are among the perishing (this makes 4.3 much clearer than the assumption that *apistoi* means unbelievers). With terrible force Paul quotes the Scriptures as he appeals to the Corinthians not to let that happen. Apostasy is the worst imaginable sin. It is a kind of idolatry, a kind of adultery (6.14–18). Seen in this light, these verses belong to Paul's appeal, and there is no more reason to abstract them from the text than the scriptural warnings used by the author of the Epistle to the Hebrews. To get across his point, Paul moves from encouragement and hope to dire warning, but it does not come out of the blue. It has been anticipated and will be reinforced later (see further Chapter 2).

There is still a possibility that things may not come right. But Paul has dawning hopes that they will. The basis of his encouragement is the news from Titus, which really confirms what he liked, but hardly dared, to expect from them. We are now told how overjoyed he was to hear how they had reacted to his demands. At one level he deeply regrets having hurt them with his letter; but at a deeper level he knows it was a good thing. They were hurt under God, and repentance was the result. It is very difficult to piece together what has happened, because Paul has no need to explain to outsiders. But it seems that someone has somehow hurt Paul himself, and the Corinthians have responded to the demand that he be disciplined. One suspects that the person concerned lies at the root of the crisis of confidence between Paul and the church. Taking the hints in chapters 2 and 7 together it seems that Paul now hopes for forgiveness and reconciliation with the offender, but still fears for his divisive influence upon the community. Hence the urgency of his continued appeal. The purpose of that 'testing' letter was to clarify their real feelings about Paul, and it has apparently succeeded.

But there is still an area of possible suspicion. Paul wants money. At one time the church was enthusiastic to support his collection for the saints, as outlined towards the close of 1 Corinthians, but their doubts about him seem to have intervened. It is not surprising that Paul has gently shifted the mood from dire warning to hopeful encouragement and confidence in them before approaching this delicate subject. Nor is it surprising that he approaches it in a somewhat roundabout way, trying to provoke them into response by praising others. He relates this ministry, like his own, to fundamental theological realities. Finance and dedication are part and parcel of the same thing, and they should 'overflow' with both, just as the riches of God's grace have overflowed in Jesus Christ (cf. 1.5). All this should not distract us from noticing how careful he is to avoid actually handling the money (8.16ff.). There are built-in safeguards to ensure that no suspicions can be entertained.

But of course, he really doesn't need to mention it – the standard way of ensuring that one does and appealing to the pride of hearer or reader! He is a bit afraid they will let themselves down, however, and that would be a pity in front of people for whom they have been an example. There's nothing like playing one lot off against the other! Paul uses the tactics of persuasion, a sure sign that one of the principle areas of uneasiness lies precisely here. But for all that, Paul keeps firmly in view the ultimate aim of it all, which is the ascription of glory to God through the thanksgiving and mutual support of the churches.

All along the undertones of conflict have darkened the letter, and Paul's love and joy have elements of anguish. At times the seriousness of the situation has broken through in dire warnings. Now as he reaches the climax of his appeal Paul pulls out all the emotional stops. It remains an appeal for their response rather than an assertion of authority, and the word is *parakalō*. They all remember a visit which ended in Paul's humiliation. No doubt Paul himself is only too aware of the contrast between his weak presence and his absurdly threatening letters. He may or may not be responding to reported reservations. He reasserts the position he has taken all along: his campaign is God's campaign, and that means he cannot be expected to use normal human techniques. Nor will they find him weak if he is forced to exert his authority, for everything is to be brought under the obedience of Christ. It really is Christ who speaks in him, whatever they think (cf. 13.1–3).

Paul has authority, authority which he must exercise for their good, to build them up not tear them down; given that, he will not be shamed into pretending that he did not intend to terrify them with his letters. It was, as he has already said in chapter 7, a good thing for them to be hurt under God. This seems to us to make better sense of 10.8–9 than attempts to translate which are informed by the supposition that this sentence belongs to a different letter, possibly the missing previous letter to which Paul has referred in chapters 2 and 7. Paul asserts that whatever happened before, he will bring the severity of judgement and condemnation if necessary next time he comes (cf. 13.1–3), and he is not going to be trapped into any comparisons with other so-called apostles.

Throughout the letter Paul has superficially contradicted himself: he doesn't commend himself (3.1); he does commend himself (4.2); he doesn't commend himself (5.12)....Now the point is clarified. The person approved is not the one who commends himself but the one whom the Lord commends, and Paul only commends himself as one who single-mindedly carries out the mission to which God has called him. How are the Corinthians to know that that is the case? By the very fact that he first evangelized them. If others come along, they are taking advantage of his work, and their self-commendation, perhaps their possession of introductory letters of commendation, makes them suspect. He takes a proper pride in what he has done as God's apostle, but no pride in himself: Let him who prides himself on anything, pride himself on the Lord. All this links closely with what he said at the beginning of 2 Cor. 3 about the Corinthians themselves being his letter of commendation.

Paul's aim is to reach the limits God has set, and overflow beyond them – perhaps he drops a hint here that if their relationship had been right, he would have expected to be sent on by them in future missions beyond – that is, that they would provide finance as he launched into virgin territory, just as the Macedonians had provided the finance for their own evangelization, with the result that he had never been a financial burden to them (cf. 11.7–9). The question of finance is as sensitive as ever in these concluding chapters. But meanwhile Paul seems by implication to get drawn into an emotive comparison with someone else, who has apparently poached on his territory. He is worried that this is having the effect of seducing the church, and undermining their commitment, their betrothal to Christ. The extent of his fears for them finally pours out, and the notion that they are subject to a kind of seduction links with the implied analogy with the harlotry of Israel already suggested in 2 Cor. 6. This, coupled with strife and factionalism and rebellion against his authority is the sin he fears he will find when he comes (12.20–1).

So once again disloyalty to Paul is coupled with disloyalty to Christ. The glory of God and the reputation of Paul are indissolubly linked, and the question of proper pride and proper commendation is to the fore. It seems there must have been some outsider(s) ironically referred to as 'superapostles'. He/they must have somehow been a catalyst of discontent against Paul. Perhaps the person who has turned up is the one who has offended Paul, and for whose forgiveness he pleaded early on. But the failure of the Corinthians to take Paul's part, his fear that they have been so unsettled that their relationship is persistently endangered, has lurked under the surface all along, and now comes pouring out.

There seem to be some clues to the identity of such interlopers in these chapters – Jewish Christians not sticking to the Jewish mission, perhaps (though see further Chapter 2). But the focus remains Paul's understanding of his own vocation, and the proofs of his call which he regards as valid – the fact that he is entirely dependent upon God, and the fact that God's power is evident in his weakness. The Corinthians need to beware of being taken in by frauds and cheats who masquerade as apostles, and Paul will be relentless in exposing anyone who relies on himself: he will chop down their base so that they are forced to rely only on God as he does. This we suggest (see further Chapter 4) is the implication of 11.12, which should be interpreted in the light of Paul's own key text from Scripture: Let him who prides himself on anything, pride himself on the Lord (10.17).

Just as the epistle opened with a celebration of reliance on God and God alone, so Paul's climax affirms his pride in the things that reveal his weakness – a point that has punctuated the letter (cf. 4.7ff.; 6.3ff.), and culminates in the catalogue in 11.21ff. Paul is prepared to affirm the fact that he has genuine access to the counsels of heaven, the mark of a true prophet of God, yet this is not something he makes much of since it is not something public – it is an area where he cannot be transparent to them. The really important point is that God's grace is sufficient, and Paul has had to learn that the hard way at a very personal level. The exact implications are not clear from Paul's very metaphorical language. The point is that he is powerful because he has the power of God, but this is only clear because in himself he is weak and humiliated. He delights in his weaknesses because it means that the power of Christ is pitched over him like a tent. With frequent recollection of points made earlier, Paul urges them to watch out, because he really is coming, and contrary to their expectations, he will act with God's power against them should they fail to receive him.

For all its mood-changes, we suggest that this text is to be read as a whole, that the cross-references to Titus, to other letters and visits, are all consistent with this reading, and that even in the final words the anguish of Paul's love and concern for his rebellious children coheres with all that has gone before. Given the need for persuasive tactics the oscillation between protestations of anger, of love, of appeal and warning is entirely explicable, and the coherence of the fundamental argument is clear.

NOTES

1 A. T. Hanson, 'The Midrash in II Corinthians 3: a reconsideration', *JSNT* 9 (1980), 2–28 is a fascinating treatment of this extremely difficult section, but it has not changed our view of the sequence of thought in this text. See further Chapters 3 and 4.

2 See Eric Fuchs, 'La faiblesse, gloire de l'apostolat selon Paul (Étude sur 2 Cor. 10—13)', in *Études théologiques et religieuses* 55 (1980), 231–53; Stephen Travis, 'Paul's boasting in 2 Cor. 10—12', in *Studia Evangelica* vi, ed. E. A. Livingstone, TU 112 (1973), 527–32; and C. Forbes, 'Comparison, Self-praise and Irony: Paul's Boasting and the Conventions of Hellenistic Rhetoric', in *NTS* 32 (1986), 1–30.

3 See Judith M. Lieu, '"Grace to you and peace": the apostolic greeting', *BJRL* 68 (1985) 161–78.

4 M. E. Thrall, '2 Cor. 1.12 ΑΓΙΟΤΗΤΙ or ΑΠΛΟΤΗΤΙ?', in J. K. Elliott, ed., *Studies in New Testament language and text*, Novum Testamentum Supplements 44 (Leiden 1976).

5 F. M. Young, 'Note on 2 Corinthians 1.17b', *JTS* NS 37 (1986), 404–15.

6 This seems the most natural reading of the text despite Hanson, art. cit.

2

Paul's Case for the Defence

We have suggested that this text is to be read as a whole, contrary to the prevailing critical opinion. Such a position will need to be defended. Interestingly enough, an argument which goes beyond the mere 'instinct' expressed in the last Chapter was provided by our search for the proper genre of this letter.

In 2 Cor. 12.19 Paul suggests that his readers might think he had been making his apology. In 1 Cor. 4.3, he had already shrugged off being judged by those he is addressing or any other human court; and in 4.5 he had appealed to them not to prejudge the issue, for everything would be brought to light when the Lord comes. Nevertheless in 1 Cor. 9.3, he had introduced some points of self-defence by stating, 'My apology to those condemning me is this.' In 2 Cor. 1.14 he looks for their mutual recognition and pride in one another on judgement day, and later in 5.10ff. associates the disclosure of all the truth before the judgement seat of Christ with the hope that the Corinthians will be persuaded of his transparent integrity. The law-court metaphor pervades his dealings with the Corinthians, and while he purports to be disinterested in their judgement in view of the final judgement of God, clearly he is anxious to convince them as well.

These are some of the indications that point towards the conclusions of this Chapter, namely that 2 Corinthians is to be construed as Paul's apology in the quasi-technical sense of a 'speech for the defence', an *apologia in absentia* for Paul's style of mission. If this correctly identifies the genre, then we believe it also suggests an overall structure which demonstrates the unity of the epistle. On the basis of these conclusions, maybe we shall be able to discern enough about the situation in Corinth to appreciate the reasons for this impassioned plea, and so come to a better understanding of the text. As has been hinted in the last paragraph, there are strong reasons for thinking that the situation which called for this response already existed in Corinth when Paul wrote the first letter. If fresh interlopers, people not mentioned before the final chapters of 2 Corinthians, did arrive at some point, they merely exacerbated an already existing failure in mutual understanding. We think identifying them precisely is less important for understanding the epistle than would appear in most recent work on these epistles. They largely provide a foil for Paul's exposition of his own style of apostleship. In 2 Corinthians, the issue is Paul himself. The letter is a letter of self-defence.

So our positive argument is that the genre of 2 Corinthians, together with its structure, is that of an apologetic letter, and this demonstrates its unity. But first we must review and assess the strength of the case for partition.

1 ARE THE OBJECTIONS TO THE UNITY OF THIS LETTER COGENT?

The fundamental problem we face is that our view contradicts the consensus. While standard introductions to 2 Corinthians accept Pauline authorship without question, they are usually sceptical about its unity. Most students of the epistle therefore look at it with the weight of scholarly consensus affecting their attitude, not only because of its apparent authority, but because of its initial plausibility. There are a number of places where breaks in thought or mood seem to demand an explanation.

It is therefore important to remind the reader again that there is no textual evidence for partition theories, and the epistle was always treated as a unity until modern critics sharpened their tools. Furthermore, we may now be misled by the fact that most editions in which we read the text organize the material in such a way that the apparent breaks in sequence are reinforced. In fact the situation addressed appears to be the same throughout, and the themes and vocabulary also make the presumption of unity a natural starting-point. It is often the case that assumptions made at the start affect the reading of the text, and our contention is that it has been worth seeing whether the assumption of unity makes sense. We believe the last Chapter justified that assumption: the text has a unified thrust.

Yet so strong has been the attack on unity that the burden of proof appears to be on those who would defend it. It is therefore necessary to examine the particular arguments advanced with some care. Are the arguments against unity really cogent?

(i) 2 COR. 10—13

The most generally agreed view has been described as the 'four chapters hypothesis'. 2 Cor. 10—13 seem markedly out of tune with all that has gone before. Whereas in 2 Cor. 2 and 7 Paul seems, at least at first sight, to be overjoyed that the breach with the church has been made up, in 2 Cor. 10—13 he is clearly in the thick of controversy, and he writes with great pain and passion. A so-called 'stern letter' which we apparently do not possess, is referred to in 2 Cor. 2.9 and 7.8. So, it is suggested, is it not likely that the final four chapters in fact belong to an earlier stage in the controversy and can be identified with this 'stern letter'? Others detect problems with this view, and suggest that Paul's optimism in the letter containing 2 Cor. 2 and 7 proved groundless, and 10—13 belong to a subsequent letter. Certainly some explanation for the change of mood is demanded, and Lietzmann's suggestion that Paul had a sleepless night is hardly sufficient to meet the case, quite apart from its speculative character.

The fundamental difficulty has been reinforced by the discovery of (a) alleged contradictions between 2 Cor. 1—9 and 10—13; by the claim that (b) particular words are used in different senses in the two parts of the epistle; by the suggestion that (c) certain passages in the early part of the letter presuppose the contents of the final chapters; and by the assertion that (d) a different situation is presupposed. These points have been subjected to careful examination by Bates and Stephenson,[1] and it is hardly necessary to go over all the ground again. Let us just review each area of debate.

(a) The claimed contradictions prove to be very slight, and most of them fall into the category of verbal contradictions which need not be fundamental, but simply the outcome of the change in mood, which is admitted. Paul is quite capable of self-contradiction at the surface level of the text, even if coherence can be discovered at a deeper level: e.g. in Romans 3 he appears to say a Jew has an advantage but a few verses later claims that the Jew has no advantage whatsoever; and in Romans 2 he claims that all are judged according to their deeds, which appears to contradict the thrust of the rest of his argument concerning justification by faith. Likewise in precisely that section of 2 Corinthians whose integrity is not generally questioned, we find the implication in 3.1 that he does not commend himself, the statement in 4.2 that he does, the statement in 5.12 that he does not, and the statement in 6.4 that he does. To apply strict logic to the fluctuating reactions of Paul (or indeed anyone else under pressure) is not satisfactory exegesis. The only fundamental contradiction remains the apparent words of approval in the early part of the letter and the severities of the last four chapters, but the seriousness of this can be exaggerated, and in any case, it only confirms the fundamental objection to integrity. It does not reinforce it.

(b) The main example of words used in a different sense in the different parts of the epistle is the word 'boasting'. It is used favourably in the first part of the epistle to express legitimate pride – the apostle's legitimate pride in the church and the church's legitimate pride in him; whereas in the last chapters the words are used in an unfavourable sense, and Paul claims to boast reluctantly. Again, if this is right, the change in mood is simply being confirmed. However, it is possible to dismiss this also on the grounds that it is scarcely an independent argument, and also to suggest that it misrepresents the facts, as we have already noted in the previous Chapter. Paul's use of the 'boasting' and 'exulting' terminology is a particularly fascinating aspect of his whole discussion, and we certainly will not be leaving it on one side as our study proceeds. Suffice it to say here that even in 2 Cor. 10—13, Paul uses it in favourable as well as unfavourable senses, notably at 10.17 and 11.18, where Paul clearly intends the quotation from Scripture to imply 'proper pride', and the contrast he draws is between exultation in worldly success and exultation in God.

(c) The argument that some parts of 1—9 presuppose the

contents of 10—13 is hard to sustain. Some who favour partition would certainly not wish to press this point, as noted above. A typical example that has an initial plausibility is the following:

> 13.10: I write these things in my absence, so that when I'm present I may not act drastically....

> 2.3: I wrote that (notorious letter) to avoid coming and being hurt by those who should make me rejoice....

But there is no necessity to think that each of these statements refer to the same letter. Most of the examples look convincing if the partition theory is already decided for, but they would not convince on their own. The references to Titus' movements are another source of argument, perhaps suggesting that 10—13 must belong to a subsequent letter; but 12.18 need not necessarily be a back reference to 8.16ff.; for there Titus is apparently to be accompanied by two other brothers, not one, and if we take the letter as a unity, 12.18 can easily refer to the trip Titus took which is mentioned in 2 Cor. 2 and 7. Most of the points raised are inconclusive.

(d) The final argument concerning the fact that a different situation is presupposed, refers not to the situation in Corinth itself, which everyone agrees has not changed between one part of the letter and another, but to Paul's location. The first part of 2 Corinthians was written from Macedonia (7.5ff.), but from a geographical point of view, 10.16 reads more naturally if written from Ephesus. Paul expresses an interest in going to the 'parts beyond you' to evangelize, presumably referring to Rome and Spain, at least if one correlates this with what he says at the end of Romans. Not much confidence can be placed in this kind of argument given the extreme vagueness of the text, and the hypothetical nature of any statements about the so-called 'severe' letter. Ultimately, then, the only serious argument is the psychological one to which we will return.

(ii) OTHER SUSPECTED DISLOCATIONS

Careful study of the text has proved that arguments based on presumed psychological or logical disconnections cannot stop here. Convinced by that first partition, critics have gone on to find more, imagining this is the only way to deal with the difficulties. A useful account of the history of criticism is provided by Francis Watson.[2] The difficulties may be presented as follows:

(a) 6.14—7.1 appears uncompromising, presupposes a sharp dualism involving hostility to unbelievers, is inconsistent with attitudes Paul expresses elsewhere (in 1 Corinthians for example), and does not fit the context. These verses contain an exceptionally high number of *hapax legomena* (words that occur only once in Paul's writings), and parallels with Qumran have sharpened the question whether these verses might not even be Pauline.[3] It is generally agreed that a satisfactory explanation of their position here in 2 Corinthians has not been so far advanced. They are usually treated as an insertion.

(b) 2.14—7.4 are suspect, partly because 2.13 appears to be picked up in 7.5 and the intervening material seems digressive if not unrelated, but also because these chapters presuppose continuing tension between Paul and the church, whereas peaceful reconciliation is the obvious background of 2 Cor. 2 and 7. This section is not so violent as 10—13, but it is certainly controversial: Chrysostom notes the 'covert rebukes' here. Collange assumes that this is a separate letter and in his study concentrates solely upon it. In Bultmann's scheme it is treated with 2 Cor. 10—13 as Letter C, the interim letter.

(c) 2 Cor. 8 and 9 constitute the other notorious problem. Is not one or the other redundant? 2 Cor. 9 begins by suggesting that it is superfluous to write about the collection, when Paul has apparently been writing about it for some time, and slightly different stages in the saga of the collection seem to be presupposed. For Bultmann, 2 Cor. 9 belongs to Letter C, and 2 Cor. 8 with the rump of 1—7 constitutes Letter D.

So the more tests of coherence are stressed as arguments for disintegration, the more the epistle falls apart. The multiplication of partitions weakens the fundamental case if it is after all possible to discover an underlying coherence which superficial examination of the text has missed. As will have been apparent in the previous chapter, it seems to us that such a coherence can be discovered in the epistle as a whole. Further exegetical backing for this view will emerge in Chapter 4, but meanwhile let us briefly consider each case in turn:

(a) Suppose this passage has nothing whatever to do with marriage to outsiders. The reference could be to the bad practice of yoking incompatible draught animals, say an ox and an ass, as forbidden in Deut. 10.22. It is true that the LXX version of that text does not use *heterozugos*, whereas it is used in Lev. 19.19, a prohibition on mating different kinds of animals. Even so, it is conceivable that this passage is a kind of catena of scriptural proofs that those who are not for us are against us. Paul is warning against association within the community with those who are disloyal. Does it not then follow directly on the previous appeal of Paul in 6.1, 11? This connection is obscured by the paragraph divisions in most texts, but it makes sense. The loyal and the disloyal cannot pull together.

Suppose we further connect this with Paul's terrible claim in 2.15–16 that his gospel divides people into the saved and the damned whether he likes it or not. It then fits into the whole argument of the epistle which is fundamentally about the necessity of accepting Paul or else.... Suppose the reference here and in 4.4 is not to unbelievers, but to the unfaithful. Are not the unfaithful in the Scriptures regarded as idolaters and adulterers? Does not that idea fit with Paul's statement in 11.1–3: 'I am jealous for you with God's own jealousy; for I engaged you to one man, to give you away to Christ as a pure virgin; but I fear that just as the serpent deceived Eve with his cunning, so somehow your minds may be distracted from their single-minded commitment and dedication to Christ'? Could it not be that the sin Paul fears to find when he comes is the sin of apostasy, and that the problems of strife, jealousy, passions, disputes, slanders, tale-bearing, posturing, rebellion, impurity, adultery and perversion, which he anticipates in 12.20–1, fundamentally stem from their failure to receive Paul as the spokesman of God? This does not rule out the possibility that literal sexual offences have been committed – 1 Corinthians certainly presupposes that that is the case. But all this perversion may well have been seen by Paul as the natural result of apostasy (cf. Romans 1). It is not at all inconceivable that the actual idolatry implied in 1 Cor. 8—10 was related in Paul's mind to a failure in loyalty.[4]

In these verses Paul pulls together his challenge and backs it up with Scripture: either they respond to him or else they are unequally yoked to the unfaithful. There is no possibility of communion between righteousness and wickedness. They have become the righteousness of God (5.21); but if they do not respond to his appeal, then they are destined to revert to the old order which is passing away. They will find themselves among the perishing. It is as serious as that. True apostles reflect the light of God's glory (3.18) and communicate knowledge of it (4.6); so opponents belong to the realm of darkness. Those on Paul's side are a temple of the living God; the others are effectively idol-worshippers. This may be an idiosyncratic way of understanding 'pollution', but it is not inconsistent with the warnings of the Old Testament prophets, nor with statements Paul makes elsewhere.

What about the unpauline character of the vocabulary, and the Qumran connections? Surely the question is whether we are in a position to judge that Paul could not have written such a passage on the basis of the evidence we have. In fact Michael Newton[5] has argued for its essentially Pauline character: 'Paul's Temple has no specific location but exists wherever the "saints" are assembled together. Unlike Qumran, Paul does not consider that contact with outsiders conveys impurity, but he warns, in a manner which is similar to the Qumran covenanters, that contact with believers who have become impure is to be avoided.' Newton does not believe the passage belongs here, but it is far more difficult to give a sensible account of why this passage is in all the texts we possess if it were not there originally, than it is to suppose that Paul composed or borrowed this catena of biblical texts and allusions to apocalyptic writings to serve his purpose in this context. We suggest that the passage bears a profoundly relevant meaning in the context in which it is found.

(c) As for the last case, the chapters on the collection, suppose one of the fundamental problems between the church and Paul revolves around the financing of his mission. There is plenty of evidence in both 1 and 2 Corinthians to support such a view: 1 Cor. 9; 2 Cor. 11.7–9; 12.16–18. Paul is clearly defensive when it comes to the question of money, and in these chapters he is careful to distance himself from handling the cash (see 8.20ff.; 9.3–5). To suggest that it is superfluous to discuss it is a typical rhetorical trick, just as our 'not to mention' is a deliberate device for mentioning it. It was recognized as such by Chrysostom, himself a professionally trained rhetorician. It is possible to read these chapters as a coherent entity without a sense of doing violence to the text, and if finance was one of the chief bones of contention, it is hardly surprising that so much space is devoted to it.

(b) There remains 2.14—7.4 for discussion. This largely depends upon the argument that in 2 Cor. 7 Paul continues the narrative about meeting Titus which is abruptly left off in 2 Cor. 2, and it is therefore an intrusion. But even if we remove this section we are not left with a continuous narrative – in fact it is not a narrative at all. At each stage Paul draws attention to a particular point in the build-up of his argument. In 2 Cor. 2, the mention of his desire to meet Titus is offered as proof of his love and concern for the church; in 2 Cor. 7, he is reinforcing his appeal with expressions of confidence in them, confidence which rests upon good grounds given the news Titus has brought. (Watson makes similar, though not identical points.)

The sequence of thought from the journey to Macedonia in 2.13 to God's dragging him around in triumph in 2.14 can be explained in the light of a coherent exegesis of 1.15ff.: introducing that journey takes him back to the fundamental point that in his travel plans he is not his own master, but entirely in the hands of God, the point of 1.17bff. according to our understanding. This sequence was outlined in the last Chapter, and will be explored further in Chapter 4. It is interesting that Bultmann notes that the phrase which begins 2.14 (Thanks be to God...), usually refers to what directly precedes, but because of his partition theories he has to say that here there is no such reference, since the context is lost. We believe that it does refer back to the immediately preceding material, and there is no break here, as so often supposed.

Once this is admitted, namely that the sequence of thought is not impossible, indeed is clear, then the shakiness of the whole partition approach becomes apparent. There are many connections between this section and 2 Cor. 10—13: e.g. the weakness of the apostle (4.7ff. and 12.5ff.), preaching and its effects, the justification of his apostleship and its style, 'boasting', self-commendation, etc., including a contrast with other apostles implied or overt. Indeed it is possible to argue (as Bates does) that 10—13 is a reiteration of what has gone before. In fact, 12.19 (whether we read *palin* or *palai*) refers to previous statements or arguments, and suggests that an earlier apologetic has been advanced which is now repeated. This implies that 10—13 is not the 'severe letter', but the end of 1 Corinthians.

Besides, even in the glowing chapters Paul is advancing justification for his behaviour, and the whole epistle seems to be written against a background of misunderstanding rather than total undoubted reconciliation. This is basically Bates' case: the whole letter is one of strife and contention. Even the 'apology' for having hurt them with his intervening letter does not give an inch. Bates explains the apparent break between 2 Cor. 9 and 10 by a parallel with Galatians, arguing that Galatians 5 and 6 summarize in a more hard-hitting way the substance of what has gone before, perhaps being Paul's 'autograph' over against the work of his secretary. In the same way, 2 Cor. 10—13 is a recapitulation of 2 Cor. 1—9, and the epistle is a unity. Fundamentally we accept this assessment of the function of 10—13, but we believe we have a better explanation of its presence.

2 WHAT IS THE GENRE OF 2 CORINTHIANS?

So far then we have suggested that the arguments for partition are not conclusive, even if they have an apparent cumulative force; rather it is possible to read the epistle as a unity, and it is justifiable since there is no textual evidence for partition. Now we wish to suggest a positive case for treating the epistle as a unity, a case based upon a theory as to its genre, structure and purpose.

Since Deissmann's famous *Light from the Ancient East* (1910), it has been generally assumed that Paul's letters are letters and not epistles – that is, non-literary occasional documents written in the heat of the moment, not public artificial literary productions. We do not question one aspect of these assumptions, namely that a letter like 2 Corinthians had an occasion, and that there are circumstances behind it known to Paul and his readers which are not readily accessible to us; to that extent it was a private letter not intended for publication. But we have come to the conclusion that the assumed corollaries of that do need to be questioned. The analogies to 2 Corinthians are not the brief non-literary paypyri to which Deissmann drew attention, but certain 'epistles' which he distinguished from those un-selfconscious products.

The closest analogy is in fact a letter purporting to be written by Demosthenes (*Ep.* 2). Whether it is a genuine letter or the product of someone in the rhetorical schools does not really matter: it is in genre and structure similar to 2 Corinthians, and certainly existed at a date prior to Paul. We do not suggest that Paul knew this particular letter, but rather that it is typical of the kind of model which Paul could have had in mind as he wrote.

Demosthenes' letter is an apologetic speech in epistolary form. He is (or is supposed) to be in exile on the island of Calauria in 323 BC, and he writes to the Council and people of Athens to plead for his own restoration. The striking thing about it is that he begins by commending the Athenians and treating his position as an exception to their usual scrupulous attention to evidence and fairness in judgement. Indeed, they owe it to themselves to reconsider his case. He goes on to speak of his own services to the city and to Greece in general – though with hesitation. He reviews the events which led to the present situation and enumerates points in his favour. He then answers the points against him. Finally he sums up his plea in far more passionate terms then he has dared to use earlier in the letter, appealing to the Athenians to save him, stressing his wrongs and pulling out all the stops.

Superficially there is a striking resemblance to 2 Corinthians. Both are epistles, both are from men appealing to have their case reviewed, for both their case revolves around their relationship with and services to the community addressed – that is, they are apologetic appeals, in the ancient and proper sense of apology. Both begin by focusing on common ground, respect, mutual recognition assumed as the basis from which to make the case, both go over points for and against the pleader, reminiscing about services rendered, answering charges; and, assuming that 2 Corinthians is a unity, each ends with a passionate review of the material covered, in which tact and politeness gives way to hard-hitting emotion.

Now the supposed, or perhaps genuine, letter of Demosthenes

is a superb little example of the standard form of forensic speech
in epistolary form. Whether you turn to Aristotle's *Rhetoric*, the
Lysias of Dionysius of Halicarnassus, or Quintilian's *Institutio
Oratoria*, you find the same structural outline. Aristotle, of
course, long predates Paul, Dionysius functioned in Rome from
30 BC, so slightly predates Paul, Quintilian wrote his large edu-
cational handbooks sometime later and was a younger contemporary of Paul. We do not suggest Paul knew of the writings
of any of them, but still these authors testify to the continuity of
rhetorical conventions in the Greco–Roman culture of Paul's
world. The common structural outline was as follows:

(a) Introduction or exordium (*prooimion*)
Here it was regarded as important to win the attention and
sympathy of the audience. Prejudices need to be removed, goodwill elicited, the speaker must present himself as more fair-
minded than the opposition (Dionysius). But direct appeal at
this stage would suggest a 'bad case' (Aristotle). The aim is to
ensure attention and perhaps outline the salient points of the
case, preparing the way for what is to come. The minds of the
hearers are to be subtly influenced, so as to be stirred to an
appropriate reaction, whether it be excitement, hope, fear or
sympathy.

(b) The narrative (*diēgēsis*)
Usually, though not invariably, an account of the events leading
to the court case would follow, and witnesses might be introduced to substantiate the version given. But this was not necessarily to be a consecutive or connected account – just enough to
make the facts clear and demonstrate the standpoint of the
speaker. He may admit the facts but seek to put them in a
different light (Aristotle), indicating that his purpose has been
misunderstood. Anyway the intent is to persuade the hearer
to the speaker's point of view. The narrative may not be
included – it all depends what is appropriate in a given case;
or it may shade into the proof.

(c) The proof(s) (*pistis*)
The proofs are regarded as the meat of the speech and would
usually be backed up by witnesses in an actual court case. Proofs

should demonstrate. They also include refutations, replies to charges. It is not good form to enumerate points – indeed Quintilian gives the impression that flexibility is what makes a good orator, for a good orator knows the rules in order to play around with them. Digressions can be a useful diversion where the case is shaky. Aristotle, however, was more determined to ensure that proofs were logical, true and convincing. Dionysius distinguishes factual, emotional and moral proofs: by the first he meant deductions from facts, arguments from probability, the use of examples, etc., a whole collection of ways by which the actual evidence could be elevated to the status of positive proof; the emotional proofs were designed to arouse pity, exaggeration not being condemned; and the moral proofs were testimonies to character, past actions, principles, etc., which should make it implausible that the particular charges can be made to stick to the particular character charged.

(d) The peroration
The conclusion is always contrasted with the exordium in emotional tone. It is basically a recapitulation of the principal points deliberately geared to excite emotion, to raise the sense of injustice, anger, jealousy, etc., and involves invocation of the gods, entreaties, tears, deliberate display and the excitement of passion in speaker and audience.

What we suggest is that 2 Corinthians as a unity has essentially this structure. It begins with a tone of thanksgiving and emphasis on mutual encouragement. The body of the letter reviews the points over which there has been misunderstanding, and tries to put them in a different light. Factual, emotional and moral proofs are offered, and the language varies from appeal to threats to confident hope with clear and appropriate attention to the required effect on the 'audience'. 2 Cor. 10—13 is the emotional peroration recapitulating the proofs and arguments laid out in the body of the epistle. It is clear that 'apologetic letters' were a recognized form in the period in which Paul wrote; for quite apart from the analogy with the letter of Demosthenes, Demetrius, writing on letter types about the first century BC or AD, lists twenty-one of which the eighteenth is described thus: 'The apologetic is the one which brings against charges the opposite arguments with proof.' 2 Corinthians, we suggest, is an apologetic letter, and as a whole conforms to the structure that such a letter would be expected to take, provided we accept its unity.

3 CAN OBJECTIONS TO THIS THEORY BE MET?

Certain objections to this proposal can be foreseen. Firstly there are Paul's disclaimers: he is not a good speaker, not wise according to the wisdom of this world, nor does he use worldly techniques of persuasion (2 Cor. 10.10ff.; cf. 1 Cor. 1.18ff., especially 2.4). In 11.6 he describes himself as an *idiōtes* in speech – which is usually taken to mean that he sees himself as a 'layman' when it comes to the techniques of rhetorical speech-making.

Paul does admit, however, that his letters are impressive, even if his personal presence was not (2 Cor. 10.10). Perhaps this implies that those who read his letters out were able to make a more impressive rhetorical show than Paul could in person;[6] but at least that means the letters were well enough written for that effect to occur. Besides 2 Cor. 12.19 does suggest that they might deduce from his letter that he was offering an apology in the technical sense of defending himself (...*apologoumetha*). In his commentary, John Chrysostom, who at least up to a point seems to have recognized in Paul a fellow-rhetorician, comments: 'having seated them on the judgement-seat he placed himself in the role of advocate...'; and at one point suggests that Paul makes a particular point because it is his '*prooimion*'. Several times in the commentary he suggests that Paul seems to be making his apology, and as we have already noted, he draws attention to the rhetorical trick at the beginning of 2 Cor. 9. The fact is that Paul uses a number of the rhetorical conventions of his day – syncrisis or comparison, irony and parody, at least.[7]

Paul's language, though not striving for the stylistic polish of contemporary rhetoric, with its cadences, rhythms, figures of speech, etc., is nevertheless the language of someone trying to create an effect, full of antitheses, repetitions, the language typical of public address, whether political or evangelistic. It had rhetorical power, as the Fathers recognized, even as they accepted Paul's self-assessment, a 'layman in speech' – this after all made its power all the more remarkable and attributable to the Holy Spirit! But it was not simply supernatural. Indeed, we have chosen to translate 11.6, 'If my speech is idiosyncratic', believing that the root meaning of *idios*, 'peculiar to oneself', may be the sense more appropriate to the context. Commentators have long recognized the tricks and conventions of the diatribe in his Epistle to the Romans.[8] Even his disclaimers have parallels in Hellenistic rhetoric[9] and philosophy – Betz has argued that here is a *topos* taken over from the Socratic tradition; certainly they are connected with Paul's argument. He cannot admit to using worldly techniques, whether they be those of commerce or propaganda. His wisdom is foolishness in the eyes of the world. So he cannot own up to using rhetorical skill. He just cannot help doing so. It is part of the cultural air he breathes.

Or is it? A second objection might go like this: there is no sign in Paul's epistles that he received a classical *paideia*, no references to classical literature, no hints he had any but Jewish schooling. This is true, but the force of these observations can be exaggerated.

In the first place, Quintilian admitted a certain natural inevitability in rhetorical structure which meant it was reflected in the speeches of barbarians and the uneducated. George Kennedy, a specialist in classical rhetoric, argues that rhetoric is universal,[10] and what the Greco–Roman rhetoricians did was simply to develop its theory to a high level of self-consciousness. Even if entirely unexposed to the influence of professional Greek educators, Paul could still have produced letters structured in a rhetorical way. But in fact, much recent scholarship points to the likelihood that Paul had some considerable grasp of the Greek culture in the midst of which he moved. We are becoming more and more aware of the fact that even Palestine was affected by Hellenizing influences, and even if Paul was sent to Jerusalem for his entire education, the pupils of Gamaliel received instruction in the wisdom of the Greeks.[11]

Whether Paul reached the higher levels of Greek education or not, he lived in an atmosphere in which there was a good deal of 'filter down' effect. Untrained people were used to hearing speeches, and were as good judges of skill in this regard as untrained listeners now may be good judges of a performance of classical music. There is plenty of evidence that Paul had picked up the tags of Hellenistic literary culture.[12] Furthermore he employs classical rhetorical comparisons, the athlete in 1 Cor. 9.24ff., for example, and the military analogy of 2 Cor. 10.3–6. True, there are reasons for thinking that these did not come to him direct, but through the medium of Hellenistic Jewish commonplaces.[13] But we should not underestimate the extent to which the synagogue had been influenced by the Hellenistic schools, nor the extent to which 'models' were adopted by partly-Hellenized alien groups like the Jews and filled with Jewish rather than pagan content. Ezekiel the Tragedian had after all used the dramatic form and language of Aeschylus and Euripides to tell of the Exodus from Egypt.[14]

Studies of Paul's own epistolary conventions reveal how daringly he adopted and adapted standard motifs. The greetings possibly follow earlier Semitic precedent,[15] yet they echo the conventional Greek *chairein* and the conventional Hebrew *shalom* in the phrase 'grace and peace', while being filled with Paul's Christian emphases.[16] The thanksgivings that regularly appear at the beginning of Paul's letters have been shown to conform to Hellenistic epistolary convention, while being Jewish in their language[17] – indeed, to be Hellenistic in structure while the contents were influenced by Jewish thought.[18] Why should this sort of thing not be true of the structure of the epistle as a whole? 2 Corinthians, not unlike other Pauline letters, emerges as a fascinating example of Semitic and scriptural motifs (see below, Chapter 3) finding expression in the Greek language and, we would argue, in a Greek form. Paul, like other Jews, has taken over the language and genre from the dominant Greek culture, but filled the conventional structures with allusions to the Bible rather than Homer. We would suggest that everything points to a remarkable confluence of cultural forms and language having contributed to Paul's idiosyncratic writing.

This confluence is further illustrated by the combination of stereotyped phrases Paul uses to characterize his opponents. In the following chapter we shall explore the Jewish contribution. Here we note a passage from the works of Dio Chrysostom which almost uncannily parallels what we have discovered to be Paul's way of characterizing his own vocation in contrast to that of others: 'But to find a man who with purity and without guile speaks with a philosopher's boldness, not for the sake of glory, nor making false pretensions for the sake of gain, but who stands ready out of goodwill and concern for his fellowman, if need be, to submit to ridicule and the uproar of the mob – to find such a man is not easy, but rather the good fortune of a very lucky city, so great is the dearth of noble independent souls, and such the abundance of flatterers, charlatans and sophists. In my own case I feel that I have chosen that role not of my own volition, but by the will of some deity...'[19] Even in his most fundamental self-understanding Paul reflected the ideals of his time, as well as biblical models (see further the next chapter).

In fact, since developing our own view of the genre of 2 Corinthians, we have become aware of the considerable amount of work that has been done, particularly in the United States, which is consonant with this theory, H. D. Betz[20] pioneered the 'rhetorical criticism' of Paul with his work on Galatians. Already he had suggested that 2 Cor. 10—13 is an apology in the Socratic tradition, in which Paul defends himself against classic changes against false philosophers and sorcerers. Much of the material Betz adduces is of interest and relevance to our case. More recently George Kennedy has assembled a kind of review volume called *Rhetorical Criticism and the New Testament*:[21] this work offers useful assessment of the work of Betz and others. But what Betz and Kennedy failed to appreciate is that this kind of approach might revolutionize our understanding of the structure of 2 Corinthians as a whole. Both are too wedded to the critical consensus. 2 Cor. 10—13 are not so distinct in flavour or situation as Betz thought. That Bates noticed the similarity in the structure of Galatians and 2 Corinthians, and Betz made a similar case about Galatians, encourages us to believe that our theory about the structure of 2 Corinthians has a high degree of probability. It is also in line with J. P. Sampley's initial study of Paul's self-defence and Roman legal practice.[22]

Our conclusion is not that Paul was a Jewish Demosthenes, but that 2 Corinthians was self-consciously conceived as an apology according to the norms of the day. This theory accounts for the changes in emotional tone within the epistle, for it was written with a view to producing certain effects on the reader/listener. It was aimed at persuading, and uses the arts of persuasion. Read in a linear way (Kennedy stresses the importance of reading ancient texts as speeches, and thus being able to appreciate their linear quality), the rhetorical shape of the whole can be observed. The fact that it opens with a tone of approval, in spite of underlying tensions which progressively emerge, fits with this fundamental purpose; so does the emotional ending. The spiralling arguments of the body of the letter can very easily be analysed into a series of apologetic proofs which conform to Quintilian's view that they should be presented in a flexible sequence not according to some rigid enumeration. 2 Corinthians was written as an apologetic letter, and the text is a unity.

Now this conclusion confirms the generally accepted view that the letter was written to defend Paul's apostleship. This implies that charges had been brought against its validity. To what extent is it possible to reconstruct the situation that occasioned its composition, and how crucial is it to make that reconstruction if we are to understand this epistle?

4 WHAT WAS THE SITUATION WHICH GAVE RISE TO THIS APOLOGY?

Clearly the need for this apology arose out of a particular situation. Allusion is made to the situation in the course of Paul's argument. If the full meaning is to be understood we need to know what it is to which the text refers. This is why attempts to reconstruct the situation are not irrelevant to the process of exegesis. We cannot avoid the standard critical questions so often discussed in relation to the Corinthian epistles by claiming to focus on the text rather than its background, because the text poses the questions.

At the same time, it is important to admit ignorance if ignorance is all we have. A great deal of exegesis falls into the trap of circularity: the text is used to reconstruct the situation and then the situation is used to interpret the text. In reaction against this, we have endeavoured to look at what Paul was saying and not be too concerned to deduce a precise reconstruction of what lies behind it. We have also come to the conclusion that a number of factors affected the way Paul perceived the situation and led him to characterize it in certain stereotyped ways. This reduces the possibility of drawing conclusions about the reality behind the text from the descriptions we find in

Paul's letters. And indeed, for the purpose of interpreting this text, it may be more important to understand how Paul saw the situation than to grasp what it really was. All too often scholars have been so preoccupied with reading between the lines for clues as to what was going on that they have failed to engage with what Paul has to say.

For all these reasons we do not propose to go into elaborate discussion of the situation behind these epistles, but simply to try and draw out the minimum required to understand why Paul wrote to the church in the way in which he did, even if it means doing little more than stating the obvious, or even reverting to precritical commonsense positions. Nevertheless we recognize that at least this is essential. The text demands that the particularities of the situation be taken seriously. To find here 'timeless truths' is to be unfaithful to the character of the text with which we have to deal. Even precritical commentators recognized that Paul is engaged here in a particular profound controversy, and found it necessary to determine what the 'stern letter' was, who was the offender in 2 Cor. 2, etc., in order to explain what was going on in the text.

To get some perspective on what was going on in Corinth, it is essential, we believe, to note the intimate connections of theme and language between the two Corinthian epistles. Standard commentaries now seem to have reached a consensus that a radical change has taken place between the situation in 1 Corinthians and that in 2 Corinthians. The chief reason for this seems to be that everyone begins with 1 Corinthians, and faced by all the passages discussing various ethical and doctrinal points, deduces that the Corinthians were distracted by views of a gnostic kind. They then turn to 2 Corinthians and discover that rival apostles who do not appear to be gnostic but rather Jewish and conservative (Judaizers?) are maligning Paul's apostleship and elevating their own authority. A new situation is thus deduced. However if we reverse the procedure and read 1 Corinthians in the light of 2 Corinthians the position appears very different.

In 2 Cor. 10.7, Paul comments that if anyone claims to be 'of Christ' he should remember that he, Paul, is too. Turning back to 1 Corinthians we find this anticipated: for the first issue he tackles is the fact that different people in the church are claiming to be of Paul, or of Apollos, or of Cephas, or of Christ. This surely implies that Paul's personal ascendancy in a church which he was responsible for founding, is already under attack, and that the names of other apostles, and even of Christ, are being appealed to against him. It need not imply that parties already exist, nor need it imply that any of these other apostles were actually present in Corinth, or had been, though Paul does seem to suggest later that Apollos had built on his foundations. What it does imply is that rumours were floating around in Corinth that Paul's status and methods were inferior.

Clearly contacts between Christians were frequent. Probably many of the early converts were involved in trade, like Aquila and Priscilla; and many more were part of the 'Jewish network' with which Paul remained in close contact (Sanders has questioned the Acts record that he operated through it, believing that the agreement reported in Galatians was ethnographic rather than geographic; yet he stresses that Paul would not have received the thirty-nine lashes from synagogue authorities if he had not tried to remain a Jew – an apostate would be beyond the jurisdiction of the synagogue courts[23] (see further Chapter 7 below)). It seems likely that through such contacts the Corinthians had begun to fear for their own position in relation to the wider Christian mission. In spite of the impression created by Acts, early missionary activity was not solely in the hands of Paul – the major churches of Antioch and Rome were founded by others. That Paul's position was suspect in the wider Christian network is surely proved by the existence of the Epistle to the Romans, as well as passages in all the other genuine epistles, and hints in the book of Acts.

The Corinthians, having been converted by Paul, now find themselves contrasting him with the rather different style of Apollos, and begin to hear disturbing rumours of his lack of acceptance elsewhere. Cephas (Peter) is rumoured to be the real authority. Yet some remain loyal to Paul. Others, perhaps, try to transcend these personalia by claiming to be 'of Christ'. What may well have crystallized these divisions in loyalty was a debate in the church about certain ethical and doctrinal differences in which it was proposed that an 'official' letter be sent to Paul to enquire for his advice. Promptly alternatives were canvassed: Apollos is wiser and more reliable – why not write to him? The real authority is Peter – why not write to him? We've

got the Spirit, why don't we work it out for ourselves? (See
1 Cor. 3.1–4, 18–23; 4.8,10, etc.) Apparently Paul's supporters
won the day, and Stephanas and others take the letter to Paul
(1 Cor. 7.1; 16.15–18). But Chloe's people (of whom we know
nothing but who have been the subject of much imaginative
speculation) have informed Paul of the debate. So before he
answers the 'official' letter, he has to clear the ground – a delicate matter, since he cannot simply back his own supporters
without endangering the unity of the church.[24]

Already, then, Paul's authority and style of apostleship is
being questioned. Some people do not expect him to return to
Corinth (1 Cor. 4.18). Certainly they seem to have doubts about
his standing in comparison with others. Also they contrast his
lack of skill in public speaking with the competence of others
(Apollos?), and his earning his own living as an artisan with the
usual practice of travelling teachers who expected patronage, a
practice adopted by other apostles who claimed hospitality and
support on the strength of Jesus' instructions as recorded in the
mission discourses of the Gospels (Cephas? or some claiming
to be 'of Christ'?).[25] 1 Cor. 1—4 and 9 anticipate a remarkable
number of themes picked up again in 2 Corinthians: these we
summarize in the appendix to this chapter. Paul does not yet feel
he has to produce a full-blown apology; rather he handles the
situation more obliquely, grateful that they have consulted him
while pained at what is happening in the church.

The root of the difficulties in Corinth is pride and jealousy.
Paul's insistence upon mutual respect, love and unity throughout the first epistle suggests that the real problems are to do
with people priding themselves on spiritual achievements and
looking down on those without the same insights. There does
not really seem to be a coherent doctrinal opposition of one sort
or another. Some of the disagreements may well have arisen
from Paul's own gospel of freedom from the law. Others may
have emerged in different 'house churches'. What Paul has to
say suggests that he had not given strict guidance about ethical
matters – we shall see why Paul has no 'halakah' in the next
chapter. His converts were to discover for themselves what
living by the Spirit meant in terms of day-to-day practice.
Social and ethnic differences, however, tended to undermine
Paul's idealism (see further Chapter 6). In practice all kinds of

realities 'at the human level' (*kata sarka*) impinged upon their attempts to live 'according to the spirit' (*kata pneuma*). We believe that Chrysostom was right to discern in Corinth not doctrinal problems, but moral and spiritual problems, a lack of humility, too much self-assertion, too little regard for the scruples of the 'weaker' brethren.

In these circumstances Paul subtly introduces as a model of mutual respect his own relationship with Apollos. The Corinthians may have set up unfortunate comparisons, but Paul refuses to exploit them to his own advantage. There are not to be divisions and jealousies among them. Chrysostom notes that in 4.6 Paul says: 'These things I have transferred in a figure to myself and Apollos, that you may learn from us to live according to Scripture and not be puffed up in favour of one against the other,' and suggests that this is a deliberate device. He avoids mentioning the rude dividers of the church, concealing them, as behind masks of a sort, with the names of the apostles. Chrysostom has perhaps seen something easily overlooked, even if his principal interest is to avoid imputing unseemly conflicts to the apostles he idealizes. Paul does not in the first epistle overtly defend himself, but seeks to move the community to greater mutual respect as well as to recognition of his own apostolic status, whatever his idiosyncrasies. His primary concern is to deal with the church's internal disputes. But already the matters which will occasion the apology of 2 Corinthians are clouding his own relationship with the community.

Now if this is right, and it has at least the merit of being based on the many observable anticipations of 2 Corinthians in the text of 1 Corinthians, then there are two consequences of great importance. Firstly, the suspicions of Paul and his need to apologize were not necessarily occasioned by the later arrival of interloping false apostles whom we eventually meet in 2 Corinthians 10ff. Whoever these people were, they were either already around at the time 1 Corinthians was written, or they were simply an irritant to an already existing situation. That there must have been interlopers of some sort becomes clear when finally Paul pulls out all the stops, apparently accusing others of poaching on his territory; but their importance lies in the threat they pose to the Corinthians' relationship with Paul himself, rather than any discernible differences of doctrine. Although their effect upon the Corinthians is described in somewhat similar terms to the effect the Judaizers had on the Galatians, there is nothing to suggest that they were Judaizers, no hint of debate about the key issues of circumcision and law.[26] The 'false apostles' remain veiled behind stereotyped language, much of which has the purpose of contrast with Paul's methods and claims. Whoever they were, the threat to Paul's acceptance in Corinth was apparently already around at the time 1 Corinthians was written.

Another curious observation one may make is that in the attacks at the end of 2 Corinthians, Paul oscillates between the singular and the plural. It is possible that one interloper is being 'generalized'. So perhaps the threat came from Cephas. Paul had after all fallen out with him in Antioch, according to Galatians, and the story of the conversion of Cornelius in Acts suggests that Peter may well have been a rival apostle to the Gentiles, in spite of the agreement reported by Paul that the 'pillars' would concentrate on the circumcision while the gospel to the uncircumcised was entrusted to Paul. This agreement may well lie behind the awkward passage about 'limits' in 2 Cor. 10. It is understandable that Paul would endeavour to avoid outright conflict between himself and Peter for as long as possible. The unity of the Church was a matter which greatly exercised him. Certainly until 2 Cor. 10—13 direct confrontation with the opponent(s) is avoided, even in 2 Corinthians. Up to that point Paul builds upon the foundations already laid by 1 Corinthians: he is their 'father in Christ', the founder of the community, and no one else can possibly claim that relationship. They have accepted his lead over the discipline of the offender. He can appeal to a basis of mutual belonging and support, even as he tries to respond to criticisms. Perhaps the reason for the anguish and the mystery is that the rival is no less than Peter. Perhaps he uses Apollos 'in a figure' in 1 Corinthians to avoid facing the real challenge. (Barrett has traced all the specific clues that Peter may be the problem.)[27]

In 2 Corinthians there are hints in what Paul claims for himself which may illuminate what his rival(s) claimed. They must have been Jews. They may well have been Palestinians. It is plausible to suggest that they knew the historical Jesus (11.22ff.; 5.16 perhaps). They probably had letters of recommendation, and probably depended upon patronage and hospitality, unlike Paul. Some of this would fit the suggestion that Cephas is the interloper, as would the implication that someone has poached on Paul's territory. However, it is equally possible that they are unknown travelling Christian preachers from Palestine who were claiming to be living in accordance with the instructions of Jesus (unlike Paul), while actually exploiting the Christian hospitality network, and therefore all the more likely to poach on already established communities rather than launching into new areas of mission. Certainly the later *Didache*, and other writings like Lucian's satire, *Peregrinus*, presuppose the existence of travelling apostles dependent upon hospitality, which was a prime Christian virtue, easily abused.[28] Such could well be the object of Paul's attacks.

It is possible that outsiders of this kind have exacerbated the rift between Paul and the church he founded in Corinth. It is possible that they have succeeded in turning Paul's initial defence (as outlined in hints in 1 Corinthians) against himself. For in 1 Corinthians Paul contrasts himself and his way with the wisdom of the world, wisdom at the human level (*kata sarka*); whereas in 2 Corinthians the charge of acting *kata sarka* seems to be directed at Paul himself (10.2; 1.17b). This seems odd, since it appears to be Paul's terminology in the first place. Perhaps it is Paul's way of characterizing the charges against him which he imputes to the Corinthians, rather than their terminology. But it could be that the tables have been turned on Paul by the interlopers.

Furthermore, in 1 Corinthians Paul claims apostleship indirectly by appealing to his vision of the risen Christ and placing himself alongside legitimate apostles like Cephas in the process. He does admit he is not sufficient to be called an apostle, and speaks of Christ appearing to him as to one untimely born (15.8–9), an amazing admission compared with remarks in 2 Corinthians (e.g. 2.17; 3.5); yet he confidently speaks of this vision and of the revelation he has received (1 Cor. 1.7; 2.9–10). No one else seems to be concerned about visions in 1 Corinthians. But in 2 Corinthians Paul hesitates to 'boast' of his visions and revelations. He is finally compelled to, but recognizes that they are not 'public'. He now prefers to take a pride in weaknesses which are obvious to all (12.5–7).

Now according to Acts, the qualifications for an apostle (met by Matthias who replaced Judas among the Twelve) consist in having been amongst those who accompanied Jesus during his ministry, from the time of the baptism to his death, and also being a witness to the resurrection. Maybe these qualifications reflect a later perception, but it is curious that Paul seems to be up against people who suggest that he qualifies on neither count. Perhaps Paul has realized that claiming special revelations did not begin to persuade when others could claim the qualifications alluded to.[29] Paul has to appeal to other 'signs of an apostle' in 2 Corinthians, and play down his former reliance on claims to revelation because the argument was not effective, and had been turned against him by the interlopers. Thus it is that in 2 Corinthians he concentrates upon the outworking of death and resurrection in his ministry (also already anticipated in 1 Cor. 4.9–13) as the principal sign of his genuine vocation to apostle-ship and reliance upon God. The claim to revelations originally comes, it seems, not from Paul's opponents, but from Paul himself.

Now if these observations are correct, we may summarize our conclusions as follows – though the alternative proposed above might equally well be true: the interlopers claim to be Hebrews, Israelites, descendants from Abraham and servants of Christ (2 Cor. 11.22). They may come from Palestine, though not necessarily – they may simply be Jews. Paul does regard them as having poached on his territory (2 Cor. 10.12ff), and to be making invidious comparisons. It is possible that they claim to have known Jesus whereas Paul did not, thus fulfilling the one qualification which was not open to Paul (2 Cor. 5.16 perhaps). It is plausible that they were carrying out their mission in accord-ance with the instructions of the gospel mission discourse tradition and that found in the *Didache*, moving from place to place expecting hospitality and living on trust (i.e. 'by faith' and 'according to the spirit', not 'according to the flesh'; though it should be noted that this terminology appears to be Paul's, so either it was common Christian terminology about which the interpretation was being disputed, or it has been skilfully poached and turned against its originator). It is also possible that they claim to be 'of Christ' in the sense of Mark 9.41:[30] Paul needs to assert his own claim to be 'of Christ'. But if so they must already have been around when 1 Corinthians was written, being the occasion of Paul's remark about those claiming to be 'of Christ' at that stage.

There does not seem to be any need to link these interlopers with any particular doctrine, or with any particular anti-Pauline Judaizing movement. They are casual, and possibly as false as Lucian's *Peregrinus*: Paul may not have misjudged the situation after all! They are a personal embarrassment to Paul, coming as they did into an already problematical situation.

But how much do we really know about them? In Thessalonica he had already contrasted his own mode of operation with that of less scrupulous teachers (2.3–12), perhaps anticipating the sort of difficulties which did materialize in Corinth, though the implications of his remarks are far from clear. We have no reason to think there were interlopers in Thessalonica, and the 'rivals' really do appear to be simply a foil for Paul's call to appreciate and imitate his style of commitment. In both situations they are described in language traditional to conflict between 'true philosophy' and 'false' or 'sorcerous' or 'sophistical' rivals, cheating, watering down the wine, anxious to please.[31] Paul also sees them in terms of the 'tricksters' condemned in the Psalms (see the next chapter).

In Corinth there do seem to be real competitors, whatever the situation in Thessalonica, and however stereotyped the language. But really we know very little about them apart from the fact that they are particularly embarrassing because Paul needs to maintain his principle of independence, so that no one can suspect him of getting anything out of preaching the gospel, at a time when he wishes to involve the Corinthians in the collection for the poor in Jerusalem. And he wants to be sufficiently confident of their understanding and loyalty to solicit their support for missions further west (2 Cor. 10.15–16), as he had used the support of the Macedonian churches in his mission to Corinth (11.8–9). Paul's embarrassment over the financial implications of all this is evident in a number of passages (e.g. arrangements not to handle the money himself in ch. 8; and 12.14ff.). Yet even though the false apostles exacerbate this financial problem, the question of Paul's support had already arisen in Corinth (1 Cor. 9). The problems about finance and patronage were initially generated in Corinth, just as most of the other charges

against Paul were already hatching before the interlopers
appeared. The issue of Paul's eloquence, or rather lack of it,
was raised by comparison with Apollos, not by the newcomers
(1 Cor. 1—2).

Now if this close link between 1 and 2 Corinthians is right,
the second consequence is that there is no reason for positing a
lost letter between the two we possess. The previous letter
referred to is 1 Corinthians, as Chrysostom and all the traditional exegetes assumed. Already the problems in Corinth cause
Paul distress and anger, even if he deals with them diplo-
matically, as far as he can, in the letter itself. He probably made
a visit to Corinth between writing the two letters, a visit referred
to in 2 Cor. 2.1, and implied also by 12.13 and 13.1, a visit that
was by no means reassuring. Paul was somehow humiliated, and
it was possible to contrast his powerful letters with his weak presence. The person referred to in 2 Cor. 2 may well be the person
who caused that humiliation. It is possible that when Titus went
on Paul's behalf (2 Cor. 7.8), he carried a letter which we no
longer possess, but the course of Paul's relationship with the
Corinthian church is now seen in a much simpler and more
straightforward way, and we need not assume that the missing
letter is a missing link, or that 2 Cor. 10—13 must be it. Indeed,
the substance of 10—13 must follow material in 1—9, and the
unity of both epistles is more convincing than partition theories.

Yet even this minimal attempt to reconstruct the situation has
left us with most matters unsettled. There may have been a lost
letter. The offender in chapter 2 might be the interloper of
chapters 10ff., or someone who has personally offended Paul, or
possibly even the offender of 1 Cor. 5 as traditional exegetes
assumed – there is at least the connection that Satan appears in
both contexts. We have made two quite different suggestions
about the identity of Paul's opponents, each of which has a
certain plausibility. We have two possible understandings of
what it was to claim to be 'of Christ'. So how important is it to
settle these questions in order to understand the text? Which
questions really matter?

5 WHAT CRITICAL CONCLUSIONS MATTER IN ORDER TO UNDERSTAND THE TEXT?

At one level everything we can learn or deduce will increase our understanding of the text. If Paul is alluding to charges made by others and we do not detect this, we lose something. If we imagine he is when he is not, we may be misled.[32] Many details are lost to us if the reference of the text is not clear. It would help enormously if we could settle what lies behind the claim and counter-claim to be 'of Christ', for example.

On the other hand we surely have to recognize that in order to grasp the fundamental lines of Paul's self-defence, we do not in fact need to know who his opponents were or what in fact they represented. All we need to know is what Paul thought of them. They appear because they have occasioned his apologetic appeal, and because they provide a contrast to his own aims, methods, self-understanding, etc. What the text is about is Paul, not his opponents, and its thrust is discernible without precise knowledge of the situation. This is surely evident from the last chapter. It is possible to admit ignorance, and still make something of the text.

At the same time it is important to grasp the fact that the text had an occasion, and addressed itself to a particular set of circumstances. It does not even claim to be a work of general and timeless relevance, as a work of philosophy might. It is earthed in particularities. If it speaks beyond its occasion, its importance may lie precisely in its resistance to detachment from the actual situation which produced it. Whatever theological contribution it makes, it demands that theology remain attached to particularities. Christianity is worked out in the midst of living in this world and struggling with relationships.

However, one critical conclusion does seem particularly important to understanding the text. The purport of the text is enshrined in its 'genre'. It makes a real difference whether a narrative is read as a novel or a biography. For this reason we regard it as important to try and establish the unity of 2 Corinthians as an apologetic letter, even while not regarding it as vital to reconstruct the precise circumstances that occasioned it. We need to listen to the text as Paul intended it to be heard. It is quite possible that Paul misjudged his 'audience' and they did not hear it as he intended – how often that happens in our own experience! But it does seem possible to recognize Paul's fundamental intention. He wishes to persuade the Corinthians that their doubts about him are unfounded, that he really is an apostle called of God, and that their reaction to him is of life and death significance.

This in itself means that Paul will be 'heard' differently by different readers. To some he will appear to have the ultimate humility: all is of God, nothing of himself. That is how Chrysostom read the text. To others he will appear to be making the most preposterous and arrogant claims – the very claim to be God's spokesman is a terrible self-commendation, inviting suspicion. That is how Graham Shaw read Paul in his book *The Cost of Authority*.[33] Paul's appeal for recognition by the Corinthians in those particular circumstances long ago demands from readers of all time the same response. We are challenged by the text to make the same judgement: Was this man the spokesman of God as he claimed? Did he know what he was talking about? Or was he mad? This is not a question of purely historical interest. The text is earthed in historical particularities, but not confined to them. For the purpose of interpretation and response we cannot avoid the critical questions, but we can discern the fact that it is not equally important to settle every debate, especially when the establishment of plausible hypotheses distracts from what the text is really about, and involves the interpreter in inescapable circularities.

We conclude that there is much we cannot know definitely about the occasion of 2 Corinthians, but that the thrust of Paul's argument is clear, provided we take the text as a unity, and understand its genre as that of an apologetic letter.

APPENDIX: THEMATIC AND VERBAL ANTICIPATIONS OF 2 CORINTHIANS IN 1 CORINTHIANS

1 Cor. 1.1: Paul's self-designation as apostle through the will of God; cf. 2 Cor. 1.1

1 Cor. 1.5; 4.8ff.: Grace/riches imparted to the Corinthians. The apostle suffers/dies for the church to live/be rich; cf. 2.

Cor. 4.12, and the financial metaphors in 2 Cor. 8 and 9.

1 Cor. 1.7–8: Anticipation of parousia and judgement; cf. 2 Cor. 1.14. Also 1 Cor. 3.13 and 4.4ff. – the Day will reveal all; cf. 2 Cor. 5.10 etc.

1 Cor. 1.9: The faithfulness of God; cf. 2 Cor. 1.18.

1 Cor. 1.10: Appeal using *parakalō*; *passim* 2 Cor. 1.3–8 etc.

1 Cor. 1.17: Weakness of word/cross; cf. 2 Cor. 10.10 et al.

1 Cor. 1.18, 24: Division of cross: weakness/foolishness v. power and wisdom; cf. 2 Cor. 12.9–10; 4.7. Also the saved and the perishing in 2 Cor. 2.14.

1 Cor. 1.15: Weakness of God stronger than men; cf. 2 Cor. 13.3ff.

1 Cor. 1.26: Those called not wise.

1 Cor. 2.1ff.: Techniques of sophistry not used; 2 Cor. 1.17; 10.

1 Cor. 2.5: Not wisdom of men but power of God.

1 Cor. 2.6: Nevertheless, has wisdom, but not wisdom of this age; cf. 2 Cor. 11.6: has knowledge. Also 2 Cor. 4.6 etc.

1 Cor. 1.29–31: Boasting in the Lord, including Jer. quotation vs. boasting in men. Also 1 Cor. 3.21; 4.8; cf. 2 Cor. *passim*, especially 2 Cor. 10.17.

1 Cor. 1.30: Righteousness of God; cf. 2 Cor. 5.21.

1 Cor. 2.3ff.: Weakness, trembling, fear of Paul in Corinth; cf. 2 Cor. mult. loc.

1 Cor. 2.7–8: *doxa*, self-*doxa*, Lord of *doxa*; cf. 2 Cor. 3.

1 Cor. 2.9–10: Revelation through Spirit; cf. 2 Cor. 12.4.

1 Cor. 2.13: Judging the spiritual by the spiritual; 2 Cor. 3 possibly.

1 Cor. 3.3; Corinthians accused of being *sarkikoi* and walking *kata anthrōpon*; cf. the apparent charges against Paul in 2 Cor. 1.17 and 10.

1 Cor. 3.6, 7.9: Emphasis on God; cf. 2 Cor. *passim*, especially chapters 1—4.

1 Cor. 3.16: Temple of the Spirit; cf. 2 Cor. 6.16.

1 Cor. 3.8: Economy, reward, stewardship. Also 4.1ff., and reference to collection at end of first epistle; cf. 2 Cor. 8 and 9.

1 Cor. 4.3: The Corinthians judging Paul; cf. whole thrust of 2 Cor.

1 Cor. 4.10–13: Catalogue of hardships; cf. 2 Cor. 4.7ff.; 6.4ff.; 11.

1 Cor. 4.15: Paul as founder of church; cf. 2 Cor. 3.

1 Cor. 4.18: People do not expect Paul to come; cf. first criticism faced in 2 Cor.

1 Cor. 4.21: Paul coming with rod; cf. threats in 2 Cor., especially chaps. 6 and 13.

1 Cor. 5.1ff.: Paul giving judgement at a distance; cf. 2 Cor. 2 and 13.

1 Cor. 9 *passim*, especially the mention of his 'apology to those who judge him', and the defence of the policy of self-support by working with his hands. N.B. 9.15–17 includes 'boasting'. The whole of 2 Cor. is thus anticipated.

There are also comparable lists of vices in 6.9–10 and 2 Cor. 12.20ff. It is difficult to determine how far these are to be taken metaphorically, as suggested for the passage in 2 Cor. 6, i.e. as being related to the fundamental adultery of apostasy, and how far literally, given the case Paul faces in 1 Cor. 5.

NOTES

GENERAL BIBLIOGRAPHICAL NOTE

For commentaries referred to in this chapter (e.g. Barrett, Bultmann, Furnish, Lietzmann, etc.) see the list on p. 277. The Loeb Classical Library contains the texts of the classical authors referred to (Demosthenes, Aristotle, Dionysius and Quintilian). For Pseudo-Demetrius, see A. J. Malherbe, 'Ancient Epistolary Theorists', *Ohio Journal of Religious Studies* 5.3–77 (1977), where the text of the Teubner Edition of V. Weichart, Leipzig 1910, is reproduced and translated together with other relevant material, after a useful introduction.

1   W. H. Bates, 'The Integrity of II Corinthians', *NTS* 12 (1965), 56–69; A. M. G. Stephenson, 'A defence of the integrity of 2 Corinthians', in *The Authorship and Integrity of the New Testament*, SPCK Theological Collections 4 (London 1965).

2   Francis Watson, '2 Corinthians x–xiii and Paul's Painful Letter', *JTS* NS35 (1984), 324–46.

3   J. A. Fitzmyer, 'Qumran and the Interpolated Paragraph in 2 Cor. 6.14—7.1', in *Essays on the Semitic Background of the New Testament*, SBL Sources for Biblical Study 5 (Scholar's Press, 1974). On this section see also J. Lambrecht, 'The fragment 2 Cor. vi.16—vii.i. A plea for its authenticity', in T. Baarda, A. F. J. Klijn, W. C. van Unnik, ed., *Miscellanea Neotestamentica* II (Leiden 1978); M. E. Thrall, 'The problem of II Cor. vi.14—vii.1 in some recent discussion', *NTS* 24 (1977), 132–48; and Gordon D. Fee, 'II Corinthians vi.14—vii.1 and food offered to idols', *NTS* 23 (1977), 140–61.

4   Fee, art. cit., has a rather different view of this passage, but his treatment of idolatry is helpful.

5   Michael Newton, *The Concept of Purity at Qumran and in the Letters of Paul*, SNTS Monograph Series 53 (Cambridge 1985).

6   E. A. Judge, 'Paul's boasting in relation to contemporary professional practice', *Australian Biblical Review* 16 (1968), 37–50.

7   Furnish; A. B. Spencer, 'The Wise Fool (and the foolish wise). A Study of Irony in Paul', *Novum Testamentum* 23 (1981), 349–60; C. Forbes, 'Comparison, Self-praise and Irony: Paul's Boasting and the Conventions of Hellenistic Rhetoric', *NTS* 32 (1986), 1–30.

8   Bultmann; S. K. Stowers, *The Diatribe and Paul's Letter to the Romans*, SBL Dissertation 57 (California 1981).

9   Judge, art. cit.; Forbes, art. cit.; H. D. Betz, *Der Apostel Paulus und die sokratische Tradition* (Tübingen 1972).

10 George Kennedy, *Classical Rhetoric and its Christian and Secular Tradition from Ancient to Modern Times* (London 1980); apart from his other studies of rhetoric, note particularly *New Testament Interpretation through Rhetorical Criticism* (University of Carolina Press 1984).

11 Judge, art. cit.; Forbes, art. cit.; M. Hengel, *Judaism and Hellenism* (London 1974); A. J. Malherbe, *Social Aspects of Early Christianity*, 2nd enlarged edn (Philadelphia 1983).

12 Malherbe, op. cit.

13 V. C. Pfitzner, *Paul and the Agon Motif* (Leiden 1967).

14 Hengel, op. cit.

15 See the commentary by Furnish.

16 W. G. Doty, *Letters in Primitive Christianity* (Philadelphia 1973); Lieu, art. cit.

17 P. Schubert, *Form and Function of the Pauline Thanksgivings* (Berlin 1939).

18 P. T. O'Brien, *Introductory Thanksgiving in the letters of Paul*, Novum Testamentum Supplements 49 (Leiden 1977).

19 A number of the Greek words in this passage are words used by Paul in 2 Corinthians: e.g. in the phrases, *katharōs kai adolōs parrhēsiazomenon, mēti doxēs charin*; we are indebted to A. J. Malherbe, '"Gentle as a nurse": the Cynic background to I Thessalonians ii', *Novum Testamentum* 12 (1970), 203–17 for this reference.

20 H. D. Betz, 'The Literary Composition and Function of Paul's Letter to the Galatians', *NTS* 21 (1975), 353–79; *Commentary on Galatians* (Hermeneia, Philadelphia, 1979).

21 Op. cit.

22 J. P. Sampley, '"Before God I do not lie" (Gal. 1.20). Paul's self-defence in the light of Roman legal praxis', *NTS* 23 (1977), 477–81. Note also Stanley N. Olson, 'Epistolary uses of expressions of self-confidence', *JBL* 103 (1984), 585–97.

23 A. E. Harvey, 'Forty Strokes Save One: Social Aspects of Judaizing and Apostasy' in *Alternative Approaches to New Testament Study*, ed. A. E. Harvey (London 1985), 79–86.

24 N. A. Dahl, *Studies in Paul*: Theology for the early Christian mission (Minneapolis, Minnesota 1977).

25 G. Theissen, *The Social Setting of Pauline Christianity* (Philadelphia 1982).

26 *Pace* Barrett et al., this seems conclusive evidence that they were not like the Galatian Judaizers. However, the case presented by D. W. Oostendorp in *Another Jesus* (Kampen 1967) is a good one, and might lead one to revise this opinion.

27 C. K. Barrett, 'Cephas and Corinth', in *Abraham unser Vater*, Festschrift für Otto Michel, ed. Betz, Hengel, Schmidt (Leiden 1963). See also M. E. Thrall, 'Super-apostles, servants of Christ, and servants of Satan', *JSNT* 6 (1980), 42–57.

28 Theissen, op. cit.; Malherbe, *Social Aspects*, cit. sup.

29 H. J. Schoeps, *Paul* (London 1961).

30 Theissen, op. cit.

31 Malherbe, 'Gentle as a nurse...', art. cit.

32 C. J. A. Hickling, 'The Sequence of Thought in II Corinthians, Chapter Three', *NTS* 21 (1974), 380–95, is a timely warning against seeing the opponents behind everything Paul says.

33 G. Shaw, *The Cost of Authority* (London 1983).

3

The Biblical Roots of Paul's Perceptions

We have argued that 2 Corinthians is Paul's apology. The corollary is that the text's primary purpose is self-explanation. We would therefore expect to have access here to Paul's self-understanding. That is what the text is explicitly about.

But of course, what a person consciously makes explicit about himself or herself, is not necessarily the whole story: other people may perceive aspects of character of which the person is unaware, and there may be unconscious elements at work, not immediately perceived either by the self or by the observer. This is true not only in cases of direct personal encounter, but also in encounter through what a person has written. Reading 'between the lines' can sometimes be both justifiable and profitable for deeper understanding.

It is not surprising, therefore, that in this century, psychological models have been exploited to try and interpret texts, including texts from the past. Paul has been a prime candidate for speculative psychologizing, given what is known about his dramatic conversion, and the fact that apparently we have access to his mind through personal letters.

But reading between the lines may also be hopelessly erroneous. The problem about any approach to interpretation which uses models based on modern data is that it may distort material deriving from a very different culture. Models cannot simply be transferred from one culture to another because the basic presuppositions and assumptions of each may be profoundly different. Social relationships and individual self-perceptions are culturally formed. Neither Freud nor Marx, Piaget nor Weber, can be uncritically exploited to illuminate Paul and his contemporaries. The merit of Bruce Malina's book, *The New Testament World*,[1] is that it alerts us to the very different perspective needed to appreciate what New Testament texts meant in their original socio-cultural context, where for example, conscience was not regarded as an internal, psychological thing, but something to do with correct social relations: a 'dyadic personality' exists in a complex web of social interactions, rather than as an internal 'self' with its discrete story.

On the other hand, such cultural contrasts can be exaggerated. We may consciously be individualists, but we are also 'dyadic personalities', profoundly dependent upon what others think of us, and on our roles and social relationships. Paul belonged to a less individualistic culture, yet he was certainly conscious of himself as an individual with a quite specific 'call' – that is evident in the texts. Observations about cultural formation – the way in which relationships and social interaction, example and habits, the passing on of stories and the traditions of the 'tribe', universally give identity and 'socialize' the individual – may help us to 'read between the lines' in an appropriate way. So may analogous examples of cultural assimilation and cultural transformation – say, the personal tensions of a Westernized Indian. For like such a person Paul belonged to two converging worlds, and was formed by both. Paul also found himself obliged to relate to both those worlds in new ways because of his vocation and his new commitment. Consciously and unconsciously he was involved in rejecting and retaining elements from the cultures by which he was formed. It is possible to discern something of the conscious process on the surface of the text, and also the unconscious process by reading between the lines, provided we look for factors relevant to his cultural context, rather than impose modern psychological models.

In the last chapter we suggested that a remarkable confluence of cultural forms and language had contributed to Paul's idiosyncratic writing. There we were exploring the contribution of Hellenistic rhetorical structures and social norms, and we promised to explore the Jewish contribution here. This contribution can be seen at a quite superficial level. We have already noted that *shalōm*, the Jewish greeting, is added to *charis* which is derived from Greek convention. The Greek custom of invoking the gods and giving thanks at the beginning of a letter is replaced in 2 Corinthians, alone of all Paul's epistles, with a *berakah* form – the Jewish liturgical phraseology, 'Blessed be God...'.[2] God is characterized as the Father of 'mercies' or compassion, and the God of all 'comfort' or encouragement: the Greek terms, *oiktirmōn* and *paraklēsis*, are reminiscent of the lament Psalms. Already scriptural terminology is noticeably important.

Moving further into the text, we find the letter is punctuated, as are other Pauline texts, with liturgical outbursts (e.g. 2.14; 8.16; and probably liturgical material underlies such verses as 1.20–1), and quotations from Scripture. In 2 Cor. 3, if nowhere else, scriptural exegesis appears to constitute the method of argument. Scripture is not as constitutive of the argument, at least superficially, as it is in Galatians and Romans, but there is enough on the surface of the text to alert us to its importance. In 2 Cor. 6, Paul's direct appeal is made through the words of Isaiah 49.8: 'at the acceptable time I heard you and on the day of salvation I helped you'. Scriptural tags are used in the collection appeal at 8.15 and 9.9. The key text from Jeremiah, 'Let him who boasts, boast in the Lord', is quoted in 10.17. Assuming the unity of the text, there is also the concentration of scriptural quotations in 6.16–18.

What we wish to suggest in this chapter is that these examples on the surface of the text may provide the clue to a much deeper level at which Paul's entire outlook has been formed by 'living in the Bible'. If in the last chapter we tried to indicate that Paul was more Hellenistic than is generally supposed, now we want to argue that he was more 'biblical' than is generally supposed, and that this goes far beyond his explicit use of Scripture. Indeed, we would speak of Paul's 'biblical spirituality'. If Dio provides a surprising philosophical parallel to Paul's personal defence and sense of vocation, the language and content of that personal self-understanding was provided by the Psalms, the prophets, and the Wisdom literature, possibly to a greater extent than even Paul himself was aware. It is extremely doubtful whether his Corinthian converts ever realized it. But that does not mean that a deeper understanding of Paul and his meaning in this text is not accessible to someone who perceives this underlying dimension.

There have been many studies of Paul's use of Scripture and his Jewish ways of thought. W. D. Davies, *Paul and Rabbinic*

Judaism (1958), was a pioneering study. A. T. Hanson, *Studies in Paul's Technique and Theology* (1974), pursued Paul's methods of exegesis and argument, using parallels from the Targums and Midrash to illuminate the material. More recently E. P. Sanders[3] has produced a major discussion of Paul's debt to Judaism, and suggested a way of perceiving the nature of his reaction against it which is very different from the long-standing exegetical tradition that focuses on his supposed critique of 'legalism'. Paul has come to be seen as a converted Rabbi whose use of Scripture belongs to the rabbinic tradition.

Now all this is very illuminating, and it serves to highlight for us the fact that our historico-critical methods of using the Bible are profoundly different from the way Paul approached his Bible. Our introductory paragraphs, however, should have indicated that we do not propose to advance a technical argument of that kind, or to try to establish a 'hard case' which might be demonstrable in a conclusive kind of way. Rather we wish to share the insight that Paul's self-understanding and his perception of what was going on in Corinth were grounded in a deep assimilation of certain parts of Scripture and certain scriptural models. Paul is illuminated by the observation that he has 'lived in the Bible' to the point where the Bible has formed his whole outlook on how the world is and what his place in it might be. Those who idly suppose that Scripture is important only when Paul uses it in argument in Galatians and Romans have a superficial view of the situation.

1 THE IMPORTANCE OF THE PSALMS

In 2 Cor. 4.7ff. we have a crucial passage in which Paul reiterates a constant theme of the epistle: 'we have this treasure in earthenware pots, in order that this extraordinary power may be God's and not come from us.' Human weakness and mortality is to be affirmed so that there can be no doubt about the source of life and power (cf. 1.8–10; 6.9; 12.9–10; 13.3–4). Paul provides two reasons for his preposterous confidence in the face of apparent failure, struggle, weakness, persecution and so on. The first is on the surface of the text: 'knowing that the one who raised the Lord Jesus will raise us also with Jesus – for always we who live are being handed over to death for Jesus' sake, so that Jesus' life too might be made apparent in our body' (4. 8–11, 14). Paul's confidence explicitly depends upon the resurrection, as he has already indicated in 1.9, and will again in 13.4.

The second reason is hidden in the midst of the first: in v.13 Paul slips in the comment: 'having the same spirit of faith (as the Psalmist), according to the text "I believed, therefore I spoke", we too believe and therefore also speak.' Presumably Paul interprets that 'same faith' as being faith in the resurrection, since the two points are made in the same sentence, and do not appear on the surface of the text to be discrete points at all. But the quotation from the Psalm proves to be the clue to the hidden dynamic at work – Paul's confidence is the confidence expressed in the Psalms, so that the words of the Psalmist (Paul no doubt assumed one author, David) become the words of Paul himself.

We have already noted that in 2 Cor. 1 the language of the *berakah* is reminiscent of the language of the lament Psalms. Now, however, it becomes possible to see how profoundly this self-understanding underlies everything Paul has said and is going to say. There are not many direct quotations or even fairly precise allusions. It would be impossible to prove close literary dependence. But the impact of reading the Septuagint (Greek) version of the Psalms with the Greek text of 2 Corinthians in mind is quite extraordinary. Paul would no doubt have been raised on the Psalms in the synagogue, though he may have used Hebrew in that context. Be that as it may, the language of the Psalms seems to have got into his bloodstream, and putting the Greek texts side by side makes this evident.

In 2 Cor. 4.13 Paul quotes what appears in the LXX as the opening words of Psalm 115 (116.10 in Hebrew and English: all references in the following discussion will be given in the LXX enumeration): 'I have trusted (or believed), therefore I speak.' So, says Paul, we have believed and therefore we speak. Now that might appear to be that, but let us look at other phrases from the same Psalm. It goes on:

> but I was deeply humiliated (*etapeinōthēn*).
> I said in my *ecstasis*,
> Every man is false.
> I will receive the cup of salvation (*sōtērion*)
> and I will call upon the name of the Lord.

Precious before the Lord
is the death (*thanatos*) of his holy ones.
O Lord, I am your servant/slave (*doulos*).

The following points are worth noting:

(1) It is evident that Paul has experienced, and faces the possibility of again experiencing, humiliation (2 Cor. 11.7; 12.21). He knows that he appears *tapeinos* to the Corinthians (10.1). He calls God the 'one who encourages the downcast (*tapeinous*)' in 7.6.

(2) Very shortly he will affirm that 'if we were beside ourselves, it was for God' (5.13). Whether *ei exestēmen* refers to ecstasy, amazement or madness is a difficult question to settle. But there is a verbal parallel with the Psalm. What the Psalmist discerns in his *ecstasis* is the falsehood of every man. Curiously enough Paul quotes these exact words, 'every man is false', in Romans 3.4 as part of his argument that all have fallen short of the glory of God. Could it not be that Paul's *ecstasis*, his 'madness' in the eyes of the Corinthians, is precisely the singleminded concentration on God which leads him to suspect falsehood in his opponents? Like the Psalmist and Elijah he feels that he alone is left as loyal prophet and apostle.

(3) The word salvation (*sōtērion*), although not very frequent in the epistle, nevertheless appears at crucial points, notably when Paul makes his direct appeal to the Corinthians at the beginning of 2 Cor. 6, using the words of Isaiah. It was also there alongside *paraklēsis* (encouragement) in 1.6.

(4) Paul has barely escaped death (1.8), and is aware of the fact that death is at work in him (4.12). We have already noted the importance of the life out of death emphasis in this epistle.

(5) Paul does not call himself the Lord's slave (*doulos*) in this epistle, but he does use the phrase 'slave of Christ' elsewhere (Rom. 1.1; Gal. 1.10). In 2 Cor. 6.4 he will use the phrase 'servants of God' (*diakonoi*), presumably plural because 'we' in this epistle ambiguously refers to himself and his fellow-workers – the true apostles – or to himself as the typical true apostle. Whether the actual phrase is used or not, it is surely evident that the idea of being 'God's slave' is at the very basis of everything

said in the epistle, and is surely implied by such texts as 2.14, assuming – rightly, I am sure – that it refers to Paul being carried around as a captive in God's triumphal procession.

Given these observations, one might almost claim that LXX Psalm 115 is the text of Paul's second letter to the Corinthians.

But the influence of the Psalms is not exhausted by that observation. The previous Psalm (in fact, the earlier verses of the same Psalm in the Hebrew enumeration, though not the LXX) contains the verse:

> The pangs of death surrounded me.
> The dangers of Hades found me.
> I found affliction (*thlipsis*) and pain.

It goes on to speak of God 'saving my life', rescuing 'my life from death' and 'my eyes from tears'. Humiliation is again mentioned. Earlier in the epistle Paul has hinted at his humiliation, spoken of his tears, and dwelt upon the encouragement in affliction (*thlipsis*) and rescue from death which he has received from God.

If we move on, putting the Psalter and the epistle beside each other, more striking correspondences appear. In 6.9 Paul alludes to Psalm 117 (virtually the next Psalm, since 116 is only four lines long). Paul writes:

> as dead yet – look! – we live,
> as punished (*paideuomenoi*–disciplined) yet not put to death...

The Psalm says:

> I shall not die but live
> and tell the works of the Lord.
> With discipline the Lord disciplined me (*epaideusen*),
> and he did not hand me over to death.

Now if we look back over this, the second Psalm to which Paul has clearly alluded, we find the following points:

1. In affliction (*thlipsis*), I called on the Lord (v. 5).
2. The Lord is my help (v. 6).
3. It is good to hope in the Lord (v. 9).
4. The voice of rejoicing and salvation in the tents of the righteous: the right hand of the Lord has worked power (*dynamis*).

Now Paul has just spoken (6.4; 7) of recommending himself as God's minister, in the power (*dynamis*) of God, and the themes of God's power and his empowering of Paul will appear again in important contexts: 9.8; 10.4; 12.9–10; 13.3–4. Needless to say, the other points are all relevant to material in this epistle.

A few verses after alluding to Psalm 117, Paul alludes to Psalm 118. 'Our heart is wide open', he says, using the same words as the Psalm (v. 32): 'whenever you make my heart wide open'. Immediately before Paul has spoken of his mouth being open, a phrase found all over the Psalter. Frequently in this Psalm, the Psalmist speaks of himself as God's *doulos*, slave, and of living through keeping God's word. What encouraged (*parekalesen*) the Psalmist in his humiliation (*tapeinōsis*) was the fact that God's word gave him life (v. 50). The Psalmist prays that God will teach him goodness, discipline and knowledge (*gnōsis*) (v. 66). And in verses 130–1 we find:

> The revelation of your words sheds light
> and gives understanding to infants (*nēpioi*).
> I have opened my mouth and drawn breath (*pneuma*)
> because I desire your commandments.

It is difficult to avoid relating these words to what Paul was saying previously about knowledge and enlightenment (4.6); and the Corinthians he treats as 'infants' (*nēpioi*) in 1 Corinthians (3.1). There too he stresses the prime importance of keeping the commandments of God (1 Cor. 7.19); and, as we shall see, it is the obedience produced by the spirit (*pneuma*) which makes the new covenant effective where the old simply led to condemnation.

Many other allusions keep appearing, which seem to confirm the impression that this group of Psalms is far more deeply embedded in Paul's thought than the obvious allusions might suggest. It is interesting to note that Paul's warnings about association with the unfaithful which immediately follow (6.14—7.1) are not dissimilar to the distance the Psalmist puts between himself and those who act with iniquity (*anomia*; cf. 2 Cor. 6.14), and if we turn back a bit in the Psalter, we find expostulations against idolatry (Ps. 113; cf. 2 Cor. 6.16).

Indeed in that Psalm too we find material which now appears fascinatingly relevant:

> Not to us, O Lord, not to us
> but to your name, give glory
> for your mercy and your truth's sake.

We have already suggested that Paul is concerned with the question of true glory, the glory given to and received from God, rather than reputation among men. Paul is also conscious that his entire ministry depends upon the mercy of God (4.1).

In other words, links with the Psalms do not begin with the explicit quotation of Psalm 115 in 4.13: Psalm 113 lies behind the previous section. Besides, in Psalm 111.3, *doxa* and *ploutos* (glory and riches) are said to be in his house and v. 4 speaks of light springing up in the darkness for the upright: although a different text is actually quoted, the reference to light can be paralleled in 4.6, while true *doxa* has already been discussed and true riches will be the subject later. Moving back in the Psalter again, we find several references to the eternity of the covenant in Psalm 110 (*diathēkē*), as well as other relevant points:

> He announced the strength of his works to his people
> to give them the inheritance of the nations (*ethnōn*).
> The works of his hands are truth and judgement,
> all his commands are faithful (*pistai*).

Naturally enough Paul would read this in terms of the Gentiles (*ethnōn*) inheriting the eternal covenant of the Spirit (2 Cor. 3), along with God's faithful keeping of his words of promise (1.18ff.), his truth and his judgement (cf. 2 Cor. 5.10 etc.).

So far then we have found that Psalms 110—118 have a particular bearing on what Paul is saying in this epistle; it is perhaps not irrelevant to note that 112—117 (= 113—118 Hebrew) are the Hallel Psalms traditionally used in the synagogue on the occasion of great festivals. Paul almost seems to follow themes in progression from a group of Psalms of which the core might well be particularly familiar and significant to him. The correspondence is not close enough to suggest a deliberate modelling of his argument on these Psalms, especially since he explicitly alludes to many other scriptural passages and rarely the Psalms themselves. But there is enough to provide a clue to Paul's profound dependence on the Psalter in his life of faith, worship and mission.

If we were to range more widely over the Psalter, we would find more hints that this gives a quite fundamental insight into the basis of Paul's assurance. Throughout the Psalter we find the language of hope, trust and confidence in the midst of affliction. The *doxa, gnōsis* and *dynamis* of God (his glory, knowledge and power) is a principal concern of the Psalmist. Even more suggestive is the description of those who are wicked and cause oppression: they use trickery and speak with tricking lips (*doliousin*, Paul's word in 2 Cor. 4.2). By contrast the Psalmist speaks with boldness/freedom (*parrhēsiasomai*: Ps. 11; 2 Cor. 3.12). Exulting (*kauchesthai*) in the praise of the Lord appears in contrast to exulting/boasting in the wrong things (idols, riches, one's own strength, etc.). There seems to be a deep correlation between the wicked in the Psalms and Paul's opponents. Finally the Psalmist prays to be led in God's way, anticipating Paul's insistence that he follows where God leads. If, as is very probable, the Psalms were his lifelong prayerbook and hymnbook, it is scarcely surprising that they almost unconsciously moulded his spirituality, and as his focus shifted from Pharisaic ideology to apostolic vocation, so the words of the Psalms came to carry new meaning and significance for his life of faith.

2 THE IMPORTANCE OF THE PROPHETS

> O God, I hoped in you, lest I should be for ever ashamed.
> In your righteousness, rescue and deliver me,
> Incline your ear to me and save me.
> My God, rescue me from the hand of the sinner,
> from the hand of the law-breaker and unrighteous.
> For you are my endurance, Lord;
> my hope is in the Lord from my youth (Ps. 70.1,2,4,5).

A typical lament Psalm it seems, with all the resonances with 2 Corinthians we have been noticing. But the significant point is that it goes on:

> On you I have been fixed from the belly,
> From my mother's womb you are my protector (LXX)
> (Heb: you are the one who took me from the womb).

Psalm 21.10–11 makes a similar point:

> You are the one who took me from the belly,
> My hope from the breasts of my mother.
> On you I was cast from the womb,
> From my mother's womb you are my God.

This sense of destiny from birth is found also in the prophets. Probably the most well-known example is that of Jeremiah. At his call-vision he hears the words:

> Before you were formed, I knew you in the womb, and before you came out of the womb, I sanctified you, I appointed you a prophet for the nations (Gentiles).

A similar thought is found in Isaiah 49.1,5, but for the moment let us reflect on the extraordinary number of correlations between Jeremiah and Paul's own sense of call. It is in Galatians that Paul uses a phrase that picks up this sense of destiny from birth:

> …he who set me apart from my mother's womb and called me through his grace (Gal. 1.15).

Is it not likely, then, that Jeremiah's call to be a prophet to the nations affected Paul's sense of call to be apostle to the Gentiles? In 2 Corinthians we find some confirmation that Jeremiah's call-vision was significant for Paul. Jeremiah was set over nations and kingdoms to uproot and raze to the ground and destroy, and to build up and plant (LXX). Twice in 2 Corinthians Paul speaks of the authority he has been given 'to build you up not tear you down' (10.8; 13.10) and he refers again to building up in 12.19. In 1 Corinthians he had spoken of himself planting and Apollos watering. The resonances and contrasts with Jeremiah are surely significant.

In the book of Jeremiah, there are references back to this task of tearing down and building up in a number of highly significant places. Immediately before the well-known passage about the new covenant, which is indisputably significant for Paul in 2 Cor. 3, we find a passage that reads as follows:

> Therefore, behold days are coming, says the Lord, and I will sow Israel and Judah, seed of men and seed of cattle. And it shall come to pass, as I have farmed them to destroy and bring evil, so I will farm them to build up and to plant, says the Lord (LXX 38.27–8).

Similarly in 24.6, the promise is given:

> ...and I will build up and I will surely not destroy and I will plant them and surely not pull them up.

This passage goes on to speak of giving them 'a heart so that they will know me, that I am the Lord, and they will be a people for me and I will be God for them, because they have turned to me with the whole of their heart'. This is an anticipation of the language in which the new covenant is described in Jeremiah 31. 31ff. (LXX 38.31, following the words quoted above). The new covenant will not be like the old one which they broke, but 'I will put my laws in their mind and I will write them on their hearts; and I will be God for them and they will be a people for me'. One citizen will not have to teach another to know the Lord. For 'they will all know me...'.

Now the significance of these passages for Paul is without question. He is claiming to be the apostle of this very new covenant which Jeremiah heralded. The reason he needs no letters of introduction is that he is the ambassador entrusted with the new treaty document, and the new treaty is not written on paper or stone, but on the heart. He has already delivered it in Corinth, and what is written on their hearts is the guarantee of his apostleship (3.1–6). The new covenant means that with the gift of the Spirit they have knowledge of God and of his will; his laws are written on their hearts. Hence they are responsible for obeying God and Paul is not lord over their faith (1.24). On the other hand, their very doubts about Paul threaten their relationship with God. Since he is God's spokesman, commissioned to deliver the message of reconciliation – 'I will remember their sins no more' (LXX Jer. 38.34) – if they turn their backs on him, they will find themselves faced with his authority to tear down:

> Behold, those whom I built up, I will tear down, and those whom I planted, I will pluck up (LXX Jer. 51.34).

It is the last thing Paul wants to do, but he will do it if he has to, and they should not be too complacent because he did not manage to bring himself to it last time he came (13.1–10). Yet Jeremiah affirmed that the new covenant would be an eternal covenant which would not be taken away – that the fear of God would be given in their hearts so that they would not turn away from God (LXX Jer. 39.40). Paul's plea is urgent, and yet his confidence that in the end it will all come right, that God is the one who brings life out of death, encouragement in affliction and peace out of conflict, is rooted in his sense of the fulfilment of Jeremiah's prophecy. In the end they will fully understand one another, and be proud of one another before the judgement seat of God. For they depend on Paul, the ambassador of God, and he depends on them, the fruit of his obedience to his call (1.13–14; 5.6–12).

But the end is not yet, and meanwhile Paul faces false apostles just as Jeremiah faced false prophets. One cannot help feeling that it is no accident that just as the lament-psalms were significant for Paul, so there are many connections between those Psalms and Jeremiah. Some connections we noted at the beginning of this section, and others may be traced, especially in the passages known as Jeremiah's confessions. He feels the whole world against him, and even doubts his vocation, cursing the day he was born. Did Paul ever have doubts? Sometimes it seems not, but suddenly at the beginning of chapter 4, he mentions the mercy of God, and he seems aware of the terrible nature of a ministry which may bring death to the perishing – who is adequate for these things? Paul is perhaps not as insensitive as appears at first sight. And might it not be true that his anxiety about Corinth is an expression of his own self-doubt? If they do not respond, if they are not reconciled, if they do allow themselves to be led astray by the others, whoever they are, does this not mean Paul loses one 'sign' of his apostleship? Perhaps, like Jeremiah, he cries out somewhat like the Psalmist, 'Every man is false'. Yet ultimately, the doubt is not there, because of the certainty that fulfilment is taking place, and above all this is guaranteed by the resurrection of Christ.

So Paul does not explicitly pick up Jeremiah's laments. Yet there is one more significant link with Jeremiah: Paul's key text on the subject of 'boasting' comes from Jeremiah rather than the Psalms. The full text in the LXX of the passage Paul quotes in 2 Cor. 10.17 is as follows:

> Let not the wise boast in wisdom,
> Let not the strong boast in strength,
> Let not the rich boast in riches,

But let the one who boasts boast in this –
To know and understand that I am the Lord
Doing mercy and judgement and righteousness on the earth
because in these things is my will, says the Lord

(LXX Jer. 9.23ff.).

It seems particularly significant that Paul first referred to this passage in 1 Cor. 1.31. There he sets up against the wisdom of the world the foolishness of God, and in fact later in the discussion accuses the Corinthians of being wise, rich, and strong, by contrast with himself: 'Already you are replete; already you are rich... We are fools because of Christ, but you are wise in Christ; we are weak, but you are strong; you are honoured (*endoxoi*, glorified), we are dishonoured' (1 Cor. 4.8,10). Paul is here attacking their arrogance, and using irony to do so. Surely his picking on wisdom, riches and strength is a deliberate allusion to the Jeremiah passage, and we look in vain for precise information about the things the Corinthians took a pride in. And surely the passage as a whole gives us useful insight into 2 Corinthians, where proper pride in the glory given by God, the wisdom given by God, the riches overflowing from God, the power of God made manifest in weakness is so persistently contrasted with improper pride, the wrong kind of 'boasting', the desire for worldly glory and success, watering the gospel down for the sake of cash, and claims to power and wisdom. Paul is determined to cut down the very basis of such false pride – this surely is the implication of 11.12, though few translations make it clear (see further Chapter 4).

Paul's boast is in the Lord, in that single-minded concentration upon God which is the very basis of his ministry. It is almost as though he quotes Jeremiah's words (LXX 10.23):

I know, Lord, that a man's word is not his own;
Nor does a man journey and plan his own way.

In fact, as Jeremiah pointed out (LXX 17.5,7), a man is cursed who has hope in man and relies on the flesh of his arm while his heart is turned away from God; whereas the man who trusts in the Lord is blessed, and the Lord will be his hope. He expects to be saved because God is his 'boast' (*kauchēma*, v.14). Surely the words of Jeremiah are deeply written into Paul's self-understanding. In fact in the ensuing verses the prophet is asked, 'Where is the word of the Lord'; and says in the LXX version, which is rather different from the Hebrew, 'I did not tire from following after you and I did not desire the day of man. You stand by. What passes my lips is before your face.' This seems to be precisely what Paul is claiming about himself. Others demand proof that Christ speaks in him, but he knows that God is his 'boast', and his conscience is 'open' to God to whom ultimately he is answerable.

And still there are more connections. For in Jeremiah 21.8 we find: 'Behold I set before you the way of life and the way of death.' As for Jeremiah, so for Paul, the demand made on the hearer is a life and death decision. For some he is a stench from death to death, for others a scent from life to life (2.16). The prophet Hananiah died after Jeremiah had prophesied against him – is Paul terrified of using the power to destroy because of that precedent? Is that one reason why the plea to his children in Corinth is so desperate? Is that why he did not dare to exercise that power on his first visit, and ends his letter with warnings about the power of Christ speaking in him? He would rather exercise the ministry of building up than tearing down, but like Jeremiah he is up against it. There are rivals who are false and whom God did not send (Jer. 14.14ff.). They have false visions and are full of deceit. Who among them has stood in the council of the Lord to perceive and hear his word? Let him who has the word of the Lord tell it faithfully (Jer. 23.18,28). The people of God have become adulterers, and even brothers are deceivers and slanderers (Jer. 9.1–6). They refuse to know me, says the Lord.

Now Jeremiah was not the first or last prophet to speak in those terms, and it is perhaps significant that Hosea and Ezekiel, like Jeremiah, are explicitly quoted in 2 Corinthians. For both, the adultery of Israel was a major theme: they are a rebellious people: they have eyes to see and do not see, ears to hear and do not hear (Ezek. 12.2). Paul's conviction that the eyes of the unfaithful have been blinded and that people will be condemned for not responding, is not unlike such material, and just as Jeremiah had the power of life and death, so did Ezekiel (3.16ff.; 11.13).

In fact, Ezekiel is clearly important for Paul. A constant

refrain in the book concerns the vision of the glory of God (1.28; 3.23; 8.24; 39.21,29; 43.1-5). Of course Paul's claim to have been caught up to the third heaven and to have heard 'unutterable utterances, things that a human being may not speak' has apocalyptic parallels, but behind them are the visions of Ezekiel and the belief that the true prophet is admitted to the counsels of God (1 Kings 22). The Spirit is important to Ezekiel more than any other prophet: the Spirit tells the prophet to stand on his feet and not be afraid of hostile people to whom he has to proclaim his message (2.1ff.). The urgency of Ezekiel's message of doom in chapters 6 and 7 matches the urgency of Paul's plea to the Corinthians. In 18.30, the call to repentance is associated with the need for a new heart and spirit, and 11.19 is about giving a new heart and spirit, tearing out the stony heart and giving a fleshy heart – a text clearly alluded to in 2 Cor. 3.3. Ezekiel 37 contains the famous vision of resurrection in the valley of the dry bones, but also a passage about the covenant and holiness, one verse of which is quoted by Paul in 2 Cor. 6.16:

> And I will give them a covenant of peace, an eternal covenant will be with them, and I will put my holy things in their midst for ever. And my dwelling-place will be with them, and I will be their God and they shall be my people. And the Gentiles shall know that I am the Lord who sanctifies them inasmuch as my holy things are in the midst of them for ever (Ezek. 37.26-8).

Clearly reference to Ezekiel lies on the surface of Paul's text, and this makes it the more likely that his warnings about the Day of the Lord, about false visions and false prophets, and his condemnation of God's rebellious people may have affected Paul. Does not the background in Jeremiah and Ezekiel explain why Paul could regard the Mosaic covenant as a covenant of death and condemnation? For that is in fact what it had led to – the destruction of the exile. Now the new covenant of the Spirit had been delivered. It was to bring about life and new creation; yet somehow in the 'between-times' before the End was consummated, destruction was still at work for those who proved unfaithful.

And given the clear allusions to Ezekiel, as well as these dynamic parallels, perhaps we find here the clue to the mysterious 'thorn in the flesh' (our 'splinter under the skin'),

the irritant about which Paul says he prayed three times, and got
the reply, 'My grace is sufficient for you' (2 Cor. 12.7–9).[4] The
word is found in Ezekiel 28.24:

> And there will no longer be a bitter splinter (*skolops*) and sharp thorn for
> the house of Israel among all the people dwelling around them who have
> treated them with contempt.

Behind this lies the text of Numbers 33.55:

> But if you do not destroy the inhabitants of the land from before your
> face, then those of them you let remain shall be as splinters in your eyes
> and javelins in your sides, and they will be enemies in the land where you
> dwell.

It is surely more than plausible to suggest that Paul's thorn in
the flesh was the irritation caused by the interlopers and unfaithful in his churches, who like the Canaanites of old tempted
Israel to apostasy. It is after all a messenger of Satan, and Satan
is all too capable of getting a toe-hold in the church (2.11), and
of disguising himself as an angel of light (11.14).

The other prophet Paul quotes in 2 Corinthians is Isaiah, and
as in the case of the Psalms, we soon discover that the passages
from which he quotes are of particular significance for the epistle
as a whole. The words he uses in 2 Cor. 6.2 come from a passage
addressed to the Gentiles. The prophet claims to have been
called from his mother's womb, as Paul did (see above). God
says: You are my slave (*doulos*), and I will be glorified in you.
The prophet says: I will be gathered and glorified before the
Lord, and God is my strength. God says: Behold I have appointed you as a light to the Gentiles. God is described as 'the
one who has rescued you' (*rhysamenos*, as in 2 Cor. 1.10). The
Holy One of Israel is faithful (*pistos*), and 'chose you'. Then
come the words quoted in 2 Cor. 6.2: 'At the acceptable time I
heard you and on the day of salvation I helped you'; followed
by 'I gave you for a covenant for the Gentiles to restore the
earth and inherit the inheritance of the desert, saying to those in
chains. Come out, and to those in darkness to be unveiled.' The
LXX could be interpreted by Paul not in terms of the restoration
of Israel after the exile, but of the inheritance of the Gentiles,
and the unveiling that occurs when one turns to the Lord. A few
phrases later the LXX text says that 'the one who has mercy'
will 'comfort' them (*parakalesai*), that they will come from afar,

and God will have mercy on his people and 'comfort' the
downcast (*tapeinous*) of his people.

In other words, we find yet another concentration of words
and themes that are particularly significant for this epistle. The
passage is among those we would call the Servant Songs, and it is
interesting how many of these passages contain such significant
material: the sense of election and destiny, the reliance upon
God, the presence of the Spirit, the focus on the Gentiles. In
6.17, Paul apparently alludes to Isaiah 43.6: 'Bring my sons
from afar and my daughters from the corners of the earth, all
who are called by my name.' The previous verse says: 'Be not
afraid – for I am with you'; and the succeeding verses speak of
the moulding of God's servant and the gathering of the Gentiles.
A bit further on God speaks of making all things new, a theme
that returns in 48.6 and 65.17, and may lie behind the 'new
creation' of 2 Cor. 5.17.

In fact what we know as Deutero- and Trito-Isaiah is full of
suggestive material. The great opening cry, 'Comfort ye, comfort ye, my people', uses *parakaleite*, of course; for the humiliation (*tapeinōsis*) is over, and sin forgiven. The glory of the Lord
is to be revealed; the glory of man is as the flower of the field.
Salvation and proclamation of the good news is the theme of this
passage. Isaiah 55 is another passage alluded to when Paul says,
'the one who provides seed for the sower, will also provide
bread for eating' (9.10), and again we find it is a significant
passage: 'Bend your ears and follow my paths. Hear me and
your soul will live in good things, and I will make an eternal
covenant with you. Behold I will give you as a witness to the
Gentiles... My plans are not your plans, and my ways are not
your ways.' There is simply too much material to survey in
detail.

And moving back into the earlier chapters of the book, we
find the same expressions about Israel's harlotry, wickedness,
faithlessness and rebellion as already noted in other prophets,
(e.g. Isa. chapter 1), alongside frequent reference to the glory
and enlightenment of God, the need for knowledge of him (e.g.
4.2–16; 6; 9; 12; 25, etc.). Those who make plans without God
are condemned (30). The wisdom of the wise is to be destroyed
(29.14). The pride of the high and mighty is to be brought low,
and God alone is to be exalted (2.10–17). 'My people will see the

glory of the Lord... Be strong... Comfort those who are dispirited' (35.2-4). Is it not significant for 2 Corinthians that the Spirit of God that will rest on the stem of Jesse is the Spirit of wisdom and understanding, of counsel and might, and of knowledge (*gnōsis*)?

So we may conclude, surely, that Paul had assimilated much of the prophets, and his dependence upon them goes far beyond the specific quotations and allusions that he makes. From them he found the terms and ideas in which to interpret his own vocation and role. From them he learned to discern what was going on in the disturbed church at Corinth. From them he learned what his message had to be, a message of encouragement, and yet also coming with the tones of warning and appeal. As far as Paul was concerned, what was going on was a living out of the vision of the prophets as he became ambassador of the new covenant and preached good news to the Gentiles.

3 THE IMPORTANCE OF THE WISDOM LITERATURE

If one looks up a key word like 'boast' (*kauchasthai* and related words) in the LXX concordance, it is interesting to discover that the bulk of significant references outside the Psalms and the key Jeremiah text occur in the wisdom literature.

> Who will boast of having a pure heart?
> Or who is bold enough to claim purity from sin?

asks Proverbs 20.9. Sirach warns about boasting in clothes or being proud on the day of glory (worldly success, presumably) (Ecclus. 11.1-4). But wisdom is her own recommendation, and 'exults' in the midst of her people. She opens her mouth in the *ecclēsia* of the Most High and 'boasts' in the presence of his might (24.1-2). The person who applies himself to God's Torah and searches out the wisdom of the ancients will be filled with a spirit of understanding, will give thanks to God in prayer, and will glory (boast) in the law of the Lord's covenant (39.1-8). These are virtually the things Paul requires of the church. In celebrating Elijah's feat, the author asks, 'Who can "boast" like you?'; and Simon son of Onias, worshipping in the midst of the

people, lifts his hands over the whole assembly of the sons of
Israel to give the blessing of the Lord, and to 'exult' in his name
(50.20). There is an appropriate 'boasting', namely boasting in
the Lord and not in one's own wisdom.

On the other hand, the wicked are tricksters and there is
deceit in their lips – the Wisdom literature has much the same
refrain as the Psalms. Those who do not think straight, lie in
wait for the upright man, on the grounds that he opposes their
doings, charges them with sin, considers them counterfeit, pro-
fesses to have knowledge of God and be his child, boasting that
God is his father; they test him with insults and torture, for
their wickedness blinded them and they did not know God's
secrets. But the souls of the upright are in God's hands
(Wisd. 2.12ff.). All wisdom comes from the Lord, and to fear
the Lord is glory (*doxa*) and exultation (*kauchēma*) (Ecclus. 1.1,
11). So

> Do not exalt yourself, that you may not fall
> and bring disgrace upon yourself,
> And the Lord will reveal your hidden deeds
> and throw you down in the midst of the congregation,
> Because you did not come to the fear of the Lord,
> but your heart was full of deceit (1.30).

Almost the first instruction in the Book of Wisdom is to
'think on the Lord in goodness, and seek him in singleness
(*haplotēs*) of heart'. Once again we find Paul's purposes, and his
characterization of his opponents illuminated by writings that
he probably regarded as Scriptures.

This is in fact another rich vein of material which it is impossible to exploit to the full here. Both the wisdom of Sirach and
the Book of Wisdom illuminate Paul's perceptions over and over
again. Chapter 2 of Ecclesiasticus is about trusting God in the
midst of testing and affliction: if you are to serve the Lord, this
is what you are to expect. Other passages speak of humiliation
suffered for the sake of glory (20.11) and of the blessings that
will come upon those who fear the Lord: he lifts up the soul and
gives light to the eyes, and bestows healing and life – he is a
mighty support, and the one who fears him will have no dread
or fear, even though often in danger of death, since the Lord is
his hope (34.12ff.). A passage in the Book of Wisdom about the

need for God's Spirit to understand his counsels, and about the body's earthly tent burdening the thoughtful mind (9.13ff.) illuminates several passages in the Corinthian correspondence (e.g. 1 Cor. 2.11ff.; 2 Cor. 4.16ff.). Ecclus. 24.15 speaks of wisdom giving off a perfume (*osmē*) and a sweet smell (*euōdias*), language used in 2 Cor. 2.14–15 of God's use of Paul to spread knowledge of Christ. That Paul identified Christ with wisdom, and wisdom is described as a mirror in the important passage in Wisdom 7, may well be significant for 2 Cor. 3.18. These are just hints of how potentially significant these books are for understanding Paul.

And 2 Corinthians itself provides the clues to the significance of the older wisdom book, Proverbs; for as every Greek Testament or Bible with references indicates, there are several quotations from the Book of Proverbs, notably in 2 Cor. 8 and 9, and possible allusions elsewhere. Even without further examples or discussion, the influence of this literature on Paul can hardly be doubted.

4 PAUL AND THE SCRIPTURES

Our survey of connections between Paul's writings and the Scriptures has been by no means exhaustive. But enough has been shown to document our case: Paul had 'lived' in his Bible, used it in study, devotion and prayer, to the point where certain features of the scriptural material had come to mould his self-understanding and his discernment of what was going on in the conflict between himself and the church at Corinth.

But the most important part of the Scriptures for a Jew, namely the Torah, we have not so far explored. One reason for this is that Paul and the law is such well-trodden ground and much has been written that need not be repeated. But scholars' treatment of what Paul says about the law in 2 Corinthians is usually affected by conclusions reached through study of Romans. This, we believe, is unfortunate. In fact we think that careful study of 2 Corinthians might illuminate the argument of Romans in significant ways. Be that as it may, clearly some discussion of Paul's perception of the law, and of his use of it as 'Scripture', must be undertaken. Besides, it is passages in

Torah, as well as the prophets, which provide the basis of his 'midrash' in 2 Cor. 3.

2 Cor. 3 is a notoriously difficult passage to interpret, and apart from the commentaries, there have been a number of attempts to sort out the sequence of thought in this passage.[5] To these discussions we refer any serious student of the text. We also refer readers to other studies of Paul's use of Scripture for technical discussions of method. But there are a number of observations that can be made which bear upon the concerns of this chapter. Paul was deeply engrained in the scriptural material, and regarded it as Torah (revelation, teaching), even as he rejected the understanding of it with which he had grown up. This is clear from 2 Cor. 3.

For Paul the clue was provided by the prophets. The fact of the matter was that the covenant mediated by Moses had brought about destruction, death and the exile. This rather than 'legalism' and its consequences, is surely the implication of his phrases 'the ministry of death' and 'the ministry of condemnation'. The outworking of the old covenant was written in the pages of history, and the effects of its curses ran on into the present. The only solution to the problem of disobedience was a new covenant, a covenant written not on stone or in any other kind of document (a covenant was after all a legal instrument which might be recorded by inscription or in a sealed roll, and the latter could be carried like a letter and delivered by a servant or ambassador (*diakonos*, minister) – it is not surprising Paul gets tied up over stone tablets and ink when he has got in mind both letters of recommendation and the tablets given to Moses!). This new covenant would be written on the heart, which implies a fundamental re-creation of sinful humanity in the image of God, to be as it was intended to be, to be obedient to God's will without conflict or distraction.

But the fact that condemnation and death was the result of Moses' covenant did not mean that it was not God's covenant, or that it lacked God's glory. For Paul, Moses' covenant has been superseded, and yet in a real sense it has also found its true fulfilment. The covenant of the Spirit ensures that the will of God expressed in Moses' covenant is actually carried out. Hearts have been remoulded. People do not need to teach each other any more what God's will is, because they all know him

(Jeremiah and Ezekiel). Rules and regulations are superseded by direct perception of the Spirit leading and guiding in the paths of righteousness. They do not need any *halakah* nor does Paul lord it over their faith. The mere fact that this covenant is written on their hearts is his authentication as apostle, as the one sent as ambassador to deliver the all important 'document'.

But this means that even more than Jeremiah, Moses is the figure on which Paul's ministry is modelled; for like Moses he is God's delegate, the spokesman sent with a covenant. Moses' glory was true glory, but it was veiled. Skilfully Paul picks up and develops in midrashic fashion the story of Exodus 34. The people could not stand the reflected glory of God – that was why Moses' face was veiled. But for Paul the veil is to conceal the fact that the glory was fading – the Mosaic covenant was on the way out – it has its 'end', which implies both that it is obsolete and that it has found its fulfilment (we translate 'outcome'). By contrast the glory of the apostles is constantly on the increase, as they reflect (or perhaps behold) the glory of the Lord and are more and more conformed to the image God intended – but I guess Paul means 3.18 to refer also to all those with the new covenant inscribed on their hearts; for the knowledge of God they have all received with that covenant has come to all because God 'has shone on our hearts to (bring) the enlightenment (which is) the knowledge of God's glory in the face of Christ' (4.6).

Clearly Moses is the 'type' or 'model' of Paul's role. Now Moses faced grumblers and doubters in the wilderness, as Paul did in Corinth, and Moses dismissed people from the camp to avoid pollution. Perhaps this is illuminating for understanding Paul. Certainly other details about Moses seem to be: with Moses God spoke 'mouth to mouth, clearly and not in riddles; and he beheld the glory of the Lord' (Num. 12.8). And 'the Lord used to speak to Moses face to face, as a man speaks to his friend' (Exod. 33.11). That is *parrhēsia*, free speech, boldness in the very presence of God, something that current exaltation of Moses made much of (Philo, etc.). Yet Paul emphasizes the veil, rather as the author of John's Gospel emphasizes the fact that 'no one has ever seen God' – Moses only saw his backparts (John 1.18; Exod. 33.18ff.). The glory and *parrhēsia* of the old covenant were real, and that is the kind of glory and boldness we

also claim, says Paul; but it has been overwhelmingly superseded. So we boldly exercise the power of free speech without
any veil. We have been open and straightforward in every particular. We have nothing to hide. With unveiled face we behold/
reflect the glory of the Lord (the Moses parallels could support
either interpretation; for fuller discussion see the following
chapter). When Moses turned to the Lord, he removed the veil;
so now turning to the Lord takes the veil off the old covenant.
It is seen to be superseded by the covenant of the Spirit.

It seems to us unlikely that in 2 Cor. 3 Paul is answering
claims or arguments of his opponents. It seems that here again
we touch the roots of Paul's self-understanding in his deep
assimilation of the Scriptures. The sense that the Word of God
had begun to be fulfilled in Christ set loose a flood of creative
insight, as Paul saw himself caught up in the fulfilment process.
The Scriptures were about what was going on, they were his
guide and they gave him his prayers.

Now it is true that Paul's conscious use of Scripture in argument, and his methods of interpretation, are often illuminated
by rabbinic parallels, and by study of the methods of midrash,
typology and allegory. But the consequence of that kind of
technical study is often to distance Paul's use of Scripture from
ours, and to raise serious questions abut the legitimacy of Paul's
hermeneutic. In the face of this, 'liberal' critics are likely to
conclude that we should not feel tied to Paul's use of Scripture;
we are free to criticize it, and to observe its cultural conditioning.
Conservative interpreters, who wish to take Scripture more
literally than Paul, tend to say that Paul's 'free' use of Scripture
according to the 'spirit' not the 'letter' was justified then, when
the implications of the radical newness of Christ had to be
worked out, but cannot be justified for us. It seems to us that
neither conclusion is very satisfactory.

What we have been observing in this chapter seems to us to
provide a possible dynamic hermeneutic. Just as Paul's sense of
vocation led him to identify with figures in the Scriptures, and
to assimilate the words of Scripture devotionally, to the point
where they gave him discernment into his own situation, so
we suggest it is possible for Scripture to have such a creative
bearing on the lives of believers in different ages, cultures and
situations, not through some kind of search for mechanical

correspondences, but by a two-way process of bringing a situation to bear on reading the Bible, and letting the language of the Bible provide a language for expressing and even discerning what is going on in the present. For Paul everything was to be made captive to Christ. In a similar way, text needs to be tested against text, and all needs to be subject to the Spirit of Christ. But the Spirit means freedom. The use of critical method, liberation from literalism, can make possible a more dynamic 'living in the Bible'; for the new covenant is not based on the letter but on the Spirit.

NOTES

1   Bruce Malina, *The New Testament World*, Insights from cultural anthropology (London 1981).
2   P. T. O'Brien, *Introductory Thanksgivings in the Letters of Paul*, Novum Testamentum Supplements 49 (Leiden 1977).
3   E. P. Sanders, *Paul and Palestinian Judaism* (London 1977).
4   The traditional view is that the 'thorn in the flesh' was some kind of ill-health, and there has been much speculation as to what it might have been. Already some have questioned this approach: see H. Clavier, 'La santé de l'apôtre Paul', and Ph. H. Menoud, 'L'écharde et l'ange satanique (2 Cor. 12.7)' in Sevenster and van Unnik, ed., *Studia Paulina* Festschrift for J. de Zwaan (Haarlem 1953).
5   See Colin Hickling, 'The Sequence of Thought in II Corinthians Chapter Three', *NTS* 21 (1975), 380–95; Morna Hooker, 'Beyond the things that are written? St. Paul's Use of Scripture', *NTS* 27 (1981), 295–309; and A. T. Hanson, 'The Midrash in II Corinthians 3: A Reconsideration', *JSNT* 9 (1980), 2–28.

4

Determining the Meaning of the Text

There are some who would argue that meaning cannot be
determined. The interpreter brings so much to the task that the
results depend upon the standpoint from which interpretation is
undertaken. Now clearly there is some truth in the observation
that the questions asked of the text, and the presuppositions of
the interpreter, inevitably affect the outcome. But the reaction
against claims to 'objectivity' in exegesis can easily go too far.
It is simply not true that all is relative, or that interpretation
always involves both circularity and subjectivity.

This chapter will approach the question of determining meaning in an entirely pragmatic way. Clearly it would be easy to get
involved in complex philosophical questions, and such a discussion would not be irrelevant. But what we are interested in
doing is observing what happens when one is actually trying to
understand a particular text, and so reaching conclusions of
both a theoretical and practical kind about the process involved.

Let us begin with some commensense observations on debates
about meaning in everyday life. This serves to remind us that no
one can make statements mean whatever they like – that to some
extent meaning inheres in the language used, is 'objective' and
therefore discussable. Suppose someone says something. The
following reactions are possible:

(1) 'You said so-and-so.' 'No I did not. I said so-and-so.' The
original statement has been rephrased, and the originator of the
statement objects to the rephrasing because it does not convey
what was intended. The hearer has to admit to having misunderstood. We normally grant that the originator of a statement has
the right to adjudicate about its meaning.

(2) 'You said so-and-so.' 'Oh, did I? That's not what I meant. What I meant to say was so-and-so.' The original statement has been repeated. The originator of the statement agrees that the repetition is accurate, but suddenly recognizes that it was inadequate as a statement of what was intended. Another attempt to convey the meaning is made. We normally recognize that linguistic use and meaning are not necessarily identical, though clearly we always try to get as near as possible to articulating what is really meant. We normally admit also that there are variant ways of expressing meaning, that not all are as adequate as each other, and once more that the author of the statement has the right to adjudicate between more and less adequate attempts to express the meaning intended.

But the discussion might take a different course:

(3) 'You said so-and-so.' 'Oh, yes. I did not have that in mind when I spoke. But of course what I said could mean that.' Here the hearer has had insight into potential meaning of which the originator of the statement had been entirely unconscious. In a case like this further discussion about whether the proposed meaning is possible or not does not depend on the intention of the author, but on the potential of the linguistic statement made. The author could conceivably express reservations about the proposed meaning, and give reasons why it does not seem possible to interpret it that way. But in the end the originator of the statement does not have the last word. A third party might be involved in the adjudication, and the outcome of the adjudication would depend upon the fact that language belongs to the public domain, and is not private or esoteric. It is a matter of discussion whether the statement could objectively carry one meaning or the other, and the argument can only be settled if good reasons are advanced for one or other view. If language were private or esoteric no communication would be possible, and no debate about meaning could occur.

On the other hand, an individual may use language in an idiosyncratic way, so that the course of discussion might go:

(4) 'You said so-and-so.' 'Well not exactly. You see when I use such-and-such a word, it has such-and-such associations for me. So for me, the statement I made has a lot more overtones than you suggest.' Now there are factors involved which only the author of the statement knows. The audience is at a dis-

advantage until informed of these factors, and communication will only be half successful until this extra information is conveyed.

On the other hand, the originator of the statement may not have used the ways of expression that come most naturally, but with an eye to the audience has 'translated' into the hearer's 'language'. The conversation might then go:

(5) 'You said so-and-so.' 'Yes. But I would not choose to put it that way. I was trying to express it in a way that you would find easier to grasp.' The ensuing discussion would clearly involve dialogue about one another's 'language'. All cross-cultural communication will involve something along these lines, even if a common language is being used. The same phrases may mean utterly different things to different people depending upon the total context in which they are used, the way they have been used in past communication with another group, and so on.

Now clearly debates about what a text means cannot follow precisely the same course. The author is not present, and in a sense, the text is independent of the author who no longer has control over it. That much we must concede to those who assert that the writing–reading relation is not a particular case of the speaking–hearing relation.[1] Dialogue is not possible. On the other hand, the complex nature of language communication is unchanged. The author did consciously mean something, and the original intention of the author bears upon the question of meaning. Some meanings the author would probably rule out of court, and careful study of the whole of a particular author's writings might provide good reasons for stating without fear of contradiction that the author did not mean so-and-so. If that can be shown, then the suggestion that a particular sentence does mean what the author clearly did not intend can surely be dismissed. You cannot make a text mean anything you like, and the author's intention has some primacy in determining meaning.

But meaning is not limited to the author's intention, and how the reader reads it also bears on the question of meaning. The text has the potential to transcend the intention of the author. But it is equally possible that the reader's limitations will reduce perception of meaning. The author knew things the reader does not. The author had his own history of language communication, and presupposed all kinds of associations and resonances to which the reader has no access. The author may have adopted the 'language' of his addressees, or developed idiosyncratic usages. Discussion of meaning must involve the search for that kind of information. Determining meaning is not an esoteric or private activity, but something that involves research and discovery, providing reasons for deciding one way or another. Language is in the public domain, and whether authorial intention is given primacy or not, meaning is not simply a matter of subjective response.

Debates about meaning proceed by a process of paraphrase or 'translation': does an alternative way of putting it express the meaning adequately, inadequately or even improve on the original statement? The same is true in interpreting a text. Of course, given the absence of the author, it is a bit dangerous to try and improve on the statement, or to say that he did not mean what he said but something else. But it may be necessary to ask how he came apparently to contradict himself, and to discover that such contradictions appear only on the surface of the text. Discerning meaning depends upon insight into the overall thrust, as we have already indicated. But it works by means of providing alternative ways of expression. Précis to bring out the drive of the meaning, paraphrase to try and capture the sense, the provision of alternative words or phrases to explain less familiar terms, explanation of resonances by indicating parallels – such are the techniques of 'commentary'.

Where a statement is clear, there is no need of commentary. But in the case of a text from the remote past, written in an ancient language no longer in use, or if in use much changed over the centuries, a good deal of explanation will be required. The explanation will begin, as already noted (Chapter 1), as an extension of translation, justifying the choice of particular ways of rendering the text compared with other possibilities. But inevitably the more significant the statement, the greater the need to try and unpack its potential levels of meaning, and the less easy to determine that one way of taking it is superior to another. That does not mean, however, that anything goes, or that the endeavour to determine meaning is fruitless or lacking in objectivity. Meaning is debatable. The intention of the author, the way the audience would have responded or heard the text, the meaning inherent in the language used – all these are 'objective' realities which may be discussed by 'third parties' in the endeavour to ascertain meaning.

The traditional commentary undertakes this explanatory task in sequence. The interpreter deals with each point of interest or difficulty as it turns up, and all kinds of different sorts of comment are inevitably mixed up together. As we have already indicated, we do not propose to produce our commentary in this book, or even a specimen of it. There are plenty of traditional commentaries (listed on p. 277 below). What we are trying to do is to reflect on the interpretative process, and so in this chapter we will take some examples of debates about meaning. We will note the different kinds of debates that arise, and observe the kinds of arguments used to try and settle those debates.

In the process it is inevitable that our approach to interpreting Paul will emerge, and in conclusion we will reflect again on the question how far interpretation is an objective activity, and how far the insight, judgement and perspective of the interpreter make all the difference. Debates may be about 'objective' realities but they are not all settlable, and commentators do not all reach the same conclusions. Besides, interpreters notice different things, and regard different things as important for understanding the text. The stance of the interpreter is important. But there is a difference between exegesis and eisegesis, between insight and imposition. It may not be easy to set up criteria for deciding exactly where to draw the line between them, but there is a line, and it is that which we hope to illuminate in this chapter.

1 DETERMINING THE MEANING OF WORDS

Words in one language are not usually precisely equivalent to words in another. Of course if they refer to concrete objects like chairs or tables, their equivalence will be considerably higher than if they refer to abstract ideas, as long as we make allowance for differences in style characteristic of different cultures. But there is bound to be a wide range of vocabulary where different approximate equivalents have to be given to get some sense of different possible meanings and usages. Translation involves making judgements about the best possible choice. But when we are dealing with an ancient text written in a form of language different from any currently in use, there are additional constrictions to overcome. Sometimes we simply do not know exactly what a word did mean, and therefore how to translate it appropriately. It is problems of this kind which we will attempt to illustrate and discuss in this section.

(i) HOW DO WE DISCUSS MEANING WHEN THE ORIGINAL SENSE OF A WORD IS UNKNOWN OR DISPUTABLE?

As an example of this problem we will take a case to which reference has already been made: does *katoptrizomenoi* in 2 Cor. 3.18 mean 'reflecting' or 'beholding'? It hardly needs to be pointed out that that kind of decision is one which requires careful examination of the evidence. It is an 'objective' question, not something that depends on the perspective of the interpreter.

The word basically means 'to produce an image in a mirror', or 'to cause a reflection'; in the middle voice it seems to mean 'to use a mirror' or 'to look at oneself in a mirror'. This appears to leave open the question whether it means 'behold' or 'reflect' in 2 Cor. 3.18. One way of settling the question is to examine usage in all available texts of the right period. This is done in an article by J. Dupont.[2] He finds that the parallels suggest the word should mean 'behold'. But the conclusion of his survey is that Paul uses it in an idiosyncratic way. The context becomes the all important evidence for determining what is meant by the word. The dative 'with unveiled face' does not make sense with using a mirror to behold something, argues Dupont, and he concludes that Paul means 'reflect' even though there is no parallel for this meaning in the comparative literature. Most recent commentators, however, regard the research into usage as most important, and choose to render 'behold'.[3]

The discussion shows that two objective tests may be used to try and determine meaning. The first is evidence elsewhere of common linguistic usage, the appeal to the fact that language is in the 'public domain'. In this case the force of this is heightened by the observation that other texts suggest that transformation takes place by 'beholding' God, and that seems to be what Paul is talking about here (see Bultmann for examples). Philo uses the middle form of the word when speaking of looking for the manifestation of God in created things and only beholding the reflection of God's being in God himself.[4] So not only usage elsewhere, but usage in similar kinds of contexts points to 'behold' as the appropriate translation, and the ancient versions of this passage (translations into other ancient languages, like Syriac, Coptic, Latin, etc.) show that they understood the word to mean 'behold'. The test of usage points very clearly in the direction of 'behold', and it is an objective test.

The second test is context. It is not impossible that the author has 'bent' the language to express something a bit different from common usage, and our evidence of usage is somewhat limited anyhow. What sense fits the context best? Dupont takes it that Moses is the explicit parallel in 2 Cor. 3.18. The shining of Moses' face is presumed to be a reflection of God's glory. Like Moses before God, 'we all' with unveiled face reflect God's glory. But others (e.g. Bultmann) take the context to imply the other meaning. There is a contrast drawn between 'we all' and the Jews whose hearts are veiled, according to v.15. They could not gaze on (*atenisai*, vv. 7, 13) God's glory in Moses' face, but 'we all' can behold the glory of God. Clearly the argument from context can go either way. But it is a case of observing and weighing up what is there in the text, not simply choosing arbitrarily what happens to suit the interpreter.

A third test in a case like this, where other texts clearly lie behind what is being said, would be to explore the background. To some extent we have already done so in the previous chapter. The Exodus text which lies behind Paul's midrash does not actually say that Moses reflected God's glory, and Numbers 12.8, speaking of God's open communication with Moses, states that 'he saw the glory of the Lord'. Is Paul conflating Numbers with Exodus? Hanson[5] has suggested that Paul is referring to the tradition that Moses saw the visible aspect of the invisible God, namely his image or glory, and that Paul identified this with the pre-existent Christ. On the other hand, if Paul had only the Exodus material in mind, it may be relevant that in the previous chapter God refuses to grant Moses' request that he might see his glory, on the grounds that no one can see God and live, a point exploited by the author of John's Gospel (1.18).

If we take one possible set of background texts, we will reach the conclusion Paul meant 'behold'; if we take another, we will reach the conclusion he cannot have meant that, and 'reflect' is more likely. So it does not seem possible to settle the question that way.

But it does raise the question why, if he simply meant 'behold', Paul chose to use this ambiguous word rather than a straightforward word for 'see' (cf. *eiden* in Numb. 12.8; and *atenisai* in 2 Cor. 3.7, 13). The answer must surely be that the metaphor of 'mirror' is not to be regarded as attenuated, especially given the fact that in the same sentence the 'image' (*eikōn*) is also referred to. Perhaps the demand for a decision between 'behold' and 'reflect' is distorting our apprehension of the meaning of the text. If we look in a mirror we see ourselves, and in some Greek texts this image is used to express the same sentiment as the old tag: *gnōthi seauton*, know yourself. But the light reflected in the mirror catches our own face. We both behold and reflect. We see ourselves as the glory of God; for man is the image and glory of God, according to Paul (1 Cor. 11.7). We see ourselves in the light of Christ, in the process of transformation 'from glory to glory' into the very image of God which we were created to be. This is a transfiguration reflecting the glory, the splendour, of God himself, mirrored in the face of Jesus Christ (4.6). As we use that mirror, we both 'behold' and 'reflect' God's glory. Something like this is anticipated in the homilies of John Chrysostom, who insists upon the reception of a ray of the glory of the Spirit; 'not only do we behold the glory of God, but from it receive also a sort of splendour' (*Hom.* VII). Many of the parallels Bultmann cites would seem to bear a similar double meaning.

Maybe the best we can do is to translate 'mirror', though if we do English usage means it will suggest 'reflect'. But I wonder if that matters when the total context seems to point to affirmation that a glorious transfiguration is taking place through receiving the glory of God. The same Greek verb (*metamorphoumai*) is used in Mark's narrative of the transfiguration of Jesus, and the splendour and light he describes is surely an expression of the same idea: that true glory is the glory given by God, a reflection of God's own glory. The illumination of the face by God so that the illuminated one becomes a light to bring knowledge to the world for the sake of God's glory is an idea which emerges from several passages in the Dead Sea Scrolls.[6] Despite the weight of evidence about Greek usage, there are good reasons for thinking that Paul intended to suggest not merely beholding, but reflecting.

Furthermore, it seems to me that the context does suggest that the parallel with Moses is uppermost, rather than the contrast with the Jews – indeed, I think the primary reference of 'we' is the apostles, the ministers of the new covenant whose gospel is not veiled (4.3). This is part of Paul's 'apologetic', not a contrast between Judaism and Christianity, a thoroughly anachronistic way of putting it anyway! But as recipients of the new covenant, all believers have 'turned to the Lord' and had the veil removed. So what is true for the apostles is also true for those who respond to their gospel. All alike have the gift of the Spirit and 'know God'. All alike mirror God's glory and are being transformed into his image through Christ – except for those whose minds have been blinded (4.4).

Now let us observe what has happened in the last stage of the discussion. The interpreter has taken up a position in the dispute, partly by weighing the evidence advanced on either side, partly by attempting to transcend the established terms of the debate, partly by drawing on other external evidence not so far exploited, partly by appeal to the importance of the wider rather than the immediate context. The thrust of the whole passage 2.17—4.6 concerns the appropriate glory of the minister of the new covenant, a glory received from God, not sought from men. The word chosen suggests a living metaphor which enhances that overall theme, and seems more appropriately rendered 'reflect' than 'behold', though certainly implying the latter also. A conclusion has been reached. Following through the discussion has contributed to a process of determining the meaning, and it has been assumed throughout, though not explicitly noted, that what we mean by 'meaning' is 'what Paul intended to convey'.

Now clearly, in this process of determining meaning, the judgement of the interpreter has been exercised, but it is judgement in assessing 'objective' evidence and arguments, not a merely 'subjective' response. The insight of the interpreter has contributed, but the validity of the insight depends upon its response to the maximum number of relevant features in the text, not on some esoteric or mystical intuition. There can be no absolute certainty that the right conclusion has been reached, but that lack of certainty is no reason to despair concerning the objectivity of the enterprise. It does highlight the problem that translation is inadequate, however; for if we choose 'reflect' the word does not in English also convey the sense of looking. Only exegesis can unpack all the meaning inherent in the text.

(ii) HOW DO WE DEAL WITH WORDS WHERE GREEK AND ENGLISH LACK PRECISE EQUIVALENTS?

There are a number of key words in 2 Corinthians which are difficult to translate because precise equivalents do not exist in English, and decisions have to be made as to how best to render them. Can we find one word sufficiently close to bring out the possible connections, or are words simply used in more than one sense and therefore must be given different equivalents in different contexts? Do we have to resort to paraphrase to bring out the sense? Must we add comments before the English reader has any hope of grasping what is involved in the text? Could words be taken in different ways so that the Corinthians might have read them in a way Paul never intended? We will illustrate the problems with several examples:

(a) A word with complex cultural associations – *parrhēsia*.
This example relates closely to the passage we have already been discussing. In 2 Cor. 3.12, Paul writes: ...we act with much *parrhēsia*. The RSV simply translates 'we are very bold', but Barrett translates 'we exercise great freedom'. We have chosen to overtranslate if anything, with the phrase 'we boldly exercise the power of free speech'. What is it that lies behind this struggle to find a suitable expression?

Parrhēsia means 'free speech'. In the democratic assembly of classical Athens, the citizen had the freedom to speak out. The person with *parrhēsia* was therefore a person with power and influence, someone with *exousia*, substance (compare our expression a 'man of substance', i.e. with property, authority, weight in public). To be highly thought of, able to influence decisions and attract a following was to have *doxa*, reputation.

So, as in 2 Cor. 3, *doxa* and *parrhēsia* were closely associated. But with the decline of democracy, *parrhēsia* meant the courage to speak out when social pressures were against it. It was associated with speaking the truth, with frankness and openness. Only the trusted friends of the mighty were able to exercise this virtue. The fact that God spoke face to face with Moses as a man speaks with his friend, meant that Moses had *parrhēsia* with God (Exod. 33.11). The fact that God spoke 'mouth to mouth' with Moses and not in riddles (Num. 12.8) expresses another aspect of *parrhēsia* increasingly found in revelatory literature – it was direct expression of the truth, rather than veiled or symbolic circumlocutions. In the LXX God acts and speaks with *parrhēsia*, wisdom speaks with *parrhēsia*, and the righteous possess *parrhēsia* – they can address God in prayer with joyous *parrhēsia* (Job 22.26).[7]

Now in 2 Cor. 3, Paul clearly contrasts this *parrhēsia* with the veiling of Moses. Eventually he has to concede a certain veiling of the gospel (4.3), but until that point the fundamental contrast is between his own bold freedom of speech, his frankness and openness, presumably in proclaiming the new covenant, compared with the lack of *parrhēsia* in Moses' case. But this *parrhēsia* towards others is grounded in *parrhēsia* before God, a *parrhēsia* Moses himself had, since when he turned to the Lord the veil was removed, his face reflected God's glory, and he spoke with God face to face, as a man speaks with his friend. Paul does not deny the qualities people like Philo were claiming for Moses. He simply 'outpaces' them with a greater glory and a greater *parrhēsia*. And Paul's claim to *parrhēsia* also bears upon the charge that he has not been candid or straightforward with the Corinthians: it contrasts with the 'shameful secrets' and trickery which he has forsworn (4.2).[8]

For Paul *parrhēsia* has these positive overtones. But in Greek literature we find *parrhēsia* can also have negative associations. *Parrhēsia* may be induced by drinking too much wine! Cynics who claimed freedom and *parrhēsia*, invited criticism for their insolence, and were sometimes banished for frankness and excessive freedom. Plutarch is careful to describe *parrhēsia* as the correlate of friendship, free from arrogance and ridicule, yet not flattery. It is an art, the ability to say the right thing at the right moment. Clearly *parrhēsia* could be misused.[9] How did the

Corinthians hear Paul's claim to *parrhēsia*? Did they feel that his powerful letters of condemnation and warning were going a bit far? Was it just another dubious bit of self-commendation? What Paul saw as confidence in God, was perhaps from their point of view unjustifiable self-assertion with no proper guarantees, the insolent arrogance of *parrhēsia*.

Certainly they could never have spotted the possible association between *parrhēsia* and removing the veil to which van Unnik[10] has drawn attention. Apparently the Aramaic expression for 'confidence' means literally 'to uncover the face'. Maybe Paul knew that, and it facilitated the complex movement of his thought in this passage, but his audience can hardly have been expected to pick it up. However, quite clearly, the dynamics of the language need not be confined to what the author consciously had in mind, or what his original readers might have managed to discern. It is quite justifiable to uncover potential subleties of use and response which may or may not have been in play. And if that is so, then obviously a simple translation cannot possibly convey all the potential overtones, consciously or unconsciously in play when this word was used. On the other hand, spelling it all out seems to invest it with greater significance than may be justified.

So examination of the original meaning of individual words is relevant and illuminating, but in the end their importance is relative to the meaning of the whole. Once again the judgement of translator or interpreter is bound to play a large part in determining the choice of equivalents, and the amount and character of the information passed on. But it is knowledge of the relevant cultural context that is required, and clearly some interpreters will speak with greater authority than others because they have the relevant information. There is a difference between informed interpretation and amateur instinct.

(b) A word with a complex range of meaning – *charis*.
An obvious example of a highly significant word with a range of meanings which cannot always be translated in the same way is *charis*. Our equivalent word 'grace' has a considerable range, which largely corresponds with Greek usage: the 'grace' of a dancer is different from 'grace and favour', yet there is something similarly 'gracious' about the manner in which each is

done. For Paul the word very often refers to acts of God's grace
or his gracious character, and the sense of 'grace and favour' is
therefore uppermost, intensified by its theological context. But
this grace of God somehow spills over into the lives of believers,
so that Paul 'conducts himself...not in human wisdom but in
God's grace' (1.12). English can express the thought using the
same words, even if we might want to go on at some length to
try and unpack all that is meant.

But when we read *charis tōi theōi...* in 2.14 we know that the
word is being used in a different way because of the associated
words, and that it is appropriate to translate it 'Thanks be to
God...'. In Greek giving and receiving, grace and thanksgiving
are intimately connected in a way that is not true in English.[11]
Paul almost spells this out in 4.15, where we read, '...so that
grace abounding through more and more (of you) may cause
thanksgiving to overflow to the glory of God'. This becomes
abundantly clear in the thought of chapters 8—9: the generosity
of the Macedonian churches is a result of God's grace; they beg
for the grace of partnership in ministering to the saints; Titus
is encouraged to perfect the same grace in the Corinthians, for
they are to overflow with this grace too; the example is the grace
of our Lord Jesus Christ. But *charis* means 'thanks' in 8.16 and
9.15: 'Thanks be to God...'. In 9.15 it is thanks for his
'inexpressible gift', which appears to be the 'extraordinary
grace of God upon you' mentioned in the previous verse, and
anticipated in 9.8 where it is stated that 'God enables every
grace to overflow into you'. And the result is to be their
generosity, their participation in what might more appropriately
be described as a 'gracious task', the translation we use in
8.19.

But the Greek word *charis* is connected with the verb of
greeting, *chairein*, which may also mean 'rejoice'; so it can
almost mean the same as *chara*, joy. Indeed, that is what it
seems to mean in 1.15, though it is a debatable point. Fee[12]
argues that it is another example of the word meaning 'gracious
task', and the Corinthians were the ones who would have had
the opportunity to render support (grace) to Paul if he had
come. Furnish prefers 'benefit' as being somewhat ambiguous
and implying 'blessing' or 'grace', assuming that Paul is the
donor. But Chrysostom comments that by *charin* Paul means

charan, and some manuscripts have *charan* instead of *charin*, which may imply that that was the sense in the mind of at least some copyists. It is true that this sense is unparalleled in Paul; but joy and rejoicing are seemingly associated in Paul's mind with grace and thanksgiving, with gifts of grace (*charismata*) and forgiveness (*charisasthai*). Probably the association was quite unconscious, but all these Greek words have the same root, and there are places in the epistle (e.g. ch. 2) where these ideas are clustered together. It seems that there are meaningful connections in one language which simply cannot be expressed in another. To catch the echoes requires explanation, or knowledge of Greek. The interpreter needs to be able to pick up the resonances, and to that extent, the associations are dependent upon the sensitive receptivity of the reader. But the resonances are there in the language, and picking them up depends on linguistic information. The interpreter without that information is at a disadvantage. Translation exaggerates the different meanings.

(c) A word which is simply untranslatable – *dokimē*.[13]
We take the word *dokimē*, and its associated verb and adjective, as an example to illustrate the problems that arise where there is no real equivalent. It is extremely difficult to render sentences where it occurs. The sense of the verb is something like 'test' or 'put to the proof'. In 2 Corinthians, the idea of being tested, or proof being demanded, occurs in a number of different contexts. In 2 Cor. 2, Paul claims to have written the stern letter in order to know their 'proof', whether they are obedient in everything. But that way of putting it is simply not English, except in very specialized contexts such as the 'proof' of a gun. It means he has set them a test to find out their true character. We have paraphrased: to know how you would respond to being put to the proof.

In 2 Cor. 8 and 9, we find the Macedonians have been put to the proof by affliction (8.2), and that Paul is again putting the love of the Corinthians to the proof in requesting their participation in the collection (8.8; 9.13). The brother he sends has already been put to the proof and been shown to be enthusiastic or zealous in the cause many times over many matters (8.22).

But the person ' approved ', in the sense of having been put to the proof and not found wanting, is not the one who recommends himself, but the one the Lord recommends (10.18). The 'test' or standard of judgement, corresponds with Paul's contrast between appropriate and inappropriate boasting. In 2 Cor. 13, it becomes apparent that the Corinthians want 'proof' that Christ is speaking in Paul. But Paul tells them to 'prove' themselves, in the sense of demanding proof of themselves, or putting themselves to the proof. To be 'unproven' or 'untested' is not a good thing. Paul is 'approved', but will behave as if he is 'unproven' if only that will help them do what is right. It is easy to see the association of ideas in this passage in the original Greek, but to produce a translation is virtually impossible. It seems that the Corinthians think they have put Paul on trial, but he claims to have been 'tried' already, presumably implying that he has been tried by a higher court, and suggests that they need to examine themselves, because in the end there is no advantage in escaping the 'trial'. When Paul says in Romans 6.4 that endurance produces *dokimē*, it is often translated 'character'; but behind lies this notion of 'proof'. It is through this 'proving' that hope is made possible, and that hope is the hope of ultimate salvation from condemnation at the final trial.

As Betz saw, the issue of *dokimē*, who needs to be 'proved', and the criteria by which this 'proving' is to be carried out, is at the heart of the argument of this epistle. Whether the Corinthians are *dokimoi* or not depends on whether they concede *dokimē* to Paul or to his opponents. So this untranslatable word lies at the heart of Paul's apology, while also enabling him to turn the tables on his critics; because in the end, they cannot put him on trial; the final judgement in the heavenly court hovers over them all. Their mutual dependence when that final judgement comes, because they depend on the ambassador for their membership of the new covenant community, and he depends on them for proof of his faithful service in response to the vocation of God, means that the issue of their relationship is the real *dokimē* – the testing and the proof – by which they will all be judged.

No English translation can possibly bring all this out, still less the way Paul's demands in 2 Cor. 13 are related to his warnings that the *dokimē* he will bring if he comes and finds them not as they should be, will be the *dokimē* that the power and word of

Christ is in him. Should we translate *dokimoi* in 13.7 as 'approved' or as 'proved right'? Should we translate *adokimoi* as 'unproved' or 'proved wrong' or 'unapproved'? The choice is impossible. But the one thing this discussion does show is this: to pretend that interpreters without knowledge of Greek are in as privileged a position to understand the text as interpreters with that linguistic knowledge is clearly unacceptable. It is possible to acquire tools which enable understanding to increase. However distorting an interpreter's presuppositions may be, there are facts which affect the interpretative process which can be learned, and which can reduce the effect of false presuppositions by reducing ignorance. There is an objective element in interpretation.

2 CONSTRUING SENTENCES

Different languages have different structures, and understanding how the structures work is essential for discerning meaning correctly. To translate literally word for word may be to misrepresent, because word order provides signals about sentence structure, and conventions differ in different languages. There are a number of places in 2 Corinthians where the way in which sentences are construed is crucial. In the case of 2 Cor. 1.17b we have come to the conclusion that all English translations and standard commentaries have construed the Greek incorrectly. As a result people have failed to understand Paul's sequence of thought, indeed his meaning. The full argument has been presented in a necessarily technical paper published in the *Journal of Theological Studies*,[14] to which interested readers are referred. Here let us explain what is involved, and the kinds of reasons advanced for the alternative way of reading the text.

Conventions for expressing 'X is Y' are quite different in Greek and English. English depends entirely on word order to indicate which is the subject and which is the complement. Word order in Greek is not such a strong signal; because words are inflected and their changes in form signal their function in the structure of the sentence, it is usually possible to change order around and still have essentially the same meaning, though with a changed emphasis. Not so, however, in a sentence of the form 'X is Y', because both will have the same form. In order to signal the subject, Greek would use the article (roughly equivalent to 'the' in English), and omit it with the complement: e.g. both *ho logos ēn theos*, and *theos ēn ho logos* mean 'the Word was God', not 'God was the Word'. Greek can also quite happily omit the equivalent of 'was' or 'is' and still mean the same thing. The crucial signal is the article.

If you read 2 Cor. 1.17 in Greek, you will find in the majority text what is usually referred to as a double *Nai* (= Yes) and a double *Ou* (= No). There is some manuscript evidence for a single *Nai* and *Ou*. Now English translations and most commentators have assumed that whether it is single or double is irrelevant: if it is doubled it merely doubles the effect, as it would in English. But if we approach the longer form of the text remembering the point made in the last paragraph it looks very different. The first *Nai* with the article should be the subject, and the second *Nai* without the article should be the complement. So it would mean 'Yes is yes' and 'No is no'. An exactly parallel phrase is found in James 5.12, and the context there indicates that it must be construed that way; it means 'Let your Yes be yes and your No be no'.

But can the doubled *Nai* and *Ou* be taken that way in this context? There are two apparent difficulties. The first is that this subordinate sentence appears to be explaining what it means to make plans 'according to the flesh'. The natural expectation is that that implies inconsistency and unreliability rather than yes being yes and no being no! For most commentators this is an insuperable objection to taking the text in the way proposed. But we believe they have misconstrued the sequence of thought in the passage. Furthermore, they have ignored the fact that there is also an insuperable objection to taking it the way generally proposed, namely that it means inserting a phrase which is simply not in the Greek text (as Barrett does not hesitate to acknowledge in his commentary): the text is usually taken to refer to the inconsistency of saying 'yes yes' and 'no no' at once, but there is nothing in the original Greek sentence to represent 'at once'. Furthermore, Paul in fact admits a few verses later that he did not come as expected, which is hardly consistent with an unqualified assertion of consistency here. We suggest that 'to make plans according to the flesh' is to behave according to 'fleshly wisdom', and so stick to your diary. Paul has already said he has not conducted himself 'in human (fleshly) wisdom but in God's grace' (1.12), and we wish to suggest that that implies that he rejects the wisdom of behaving as expected for the unpredictability of one entirely subject to guidance of the Spirit. To make plans according to the flesh means according to human wisdom, and is the opposite of what commentators have assumed.

The second difficulty is the presence of *par' emoi*, which means 'with me'. Many commentators have assumed that this is unemphatic, and the more paraphrastic modern translations generally omit it. The NEB, however, gave it weight:

> Or do I, when I frame my plans, frame them as a worldly man might, so that it should rest with me to say 'yes' and 'yes' and 'no' and 'no'.

We believe that this is right. The point is that Paul is claiming that his travel plans do not 'rest with me', but with God, since he is entirely under God's direction. Now to have that kind of weight, it is necessary to take *par' emoi* as the predicate or complement after the verb *ei*, which might seem to invalidate our earlier point. If the short text is read, it is easy to construe the clause as meaning: 'so that "yes" and "no" rest with me'. But in the case of the long text, it does not seem so easy to combine both observations at once.

However we do not believe that this is a fatal objection, not least because it is evident that this is how the longer text was read and interpreted by John Chrysostom, whose own language was Greek. Greek, as we have observed above, often omitted the verb copula 'is', and it is still possible to take the second *Nai* and *Ou* as predicative, understanding the necessary infinitive. We would therefore propose the following translation:

> 'Or do I make plans at the human level so that it's in my hands that yes be yes and no be no?'

So either text may bear the sense we propose, and the correct reading must be established on other grounds.

We would urge this unconventional interpretation for two reasons. The first is linguistic, and the grounds for this have already been spelled out. The second is that it makes far better sense of the overall context. Not only does the usual way of taking it necessitate adding phrases which simply are not in the text, but it also makes commentators observe that Paul makes a theological digression in verse 18, for no apparent reason except that he always tends to do such things. If our interpretation, which was also that of John Chrysostom, is correct, then there is every reason for Paul's so-called digression. He has excused his failure to come to Corinth in spite of his promise by referring his movements to God. So is God unreliable? Paul has to assert the faithfulness of God to his promises, and the reliability of his gospel, because what he has said could well induce doubt about both. This also leads me to believe that when we come to the climactic sentence in verses 21–2, there is a different group meant by 'us' in the two halves of the sentence. 'God is the one who gives us our guarantee with you in Christ and has anointed us', is about God guaranteeing the apostleship of Paul and his fellow-workers; but the second statement about the God who sealed those who belong to the new covenant and gave them all the downpayment of the Spirit, applies to all believers. This God whom the Corinthians know and have experienced, is the one who is faithful and the one who guarantees Paul's apostleship, whatever his apparent inconsistency.

As noted above, 1.12 made a suggestive contribution to this insight into what constitutes the nub of Paul's account of his failure to turn up as promised. But the conclusions reached also affect the way we understand the statement in 1.12:

> For our pride lies in the witness of our conscience that we have conducted ourselves in the world with the single-minded commitment (lit. 'single-ness' or 'purity', depending upon which reading is adopted) and straight-forwardness of God, not in human wisdom but in God's grace, most of all in our dealings with you.

We have argued that Paul is claiming that he is entirely under the guidance of God, a point reiterated in various ways through-out the epistle (cf. 4.7ff.; 6.4ff.; 12.9–10; 13.4). He is not self-sufficient – his sufficiency is of God (3.5–6). So 1.12 is not just about 'purity', or 'simplicity' and 'straightforwardness' in relation to the Corinthians, qualities contrasting with implied duplicity, qualities which are 'of God' in the sense of being 'divine'. It is about the single-mindedness of one concentrating solely upon God and his purposes.[15] If we read *haplotēs* (singleness) and take into account those other texts in the epistle where this word occurs, we will find that in those other cases, it does not naturally refer to the opposite of duplicity, but rather to single-minded commitment: it appears in 2 Cor. 8 and 9 concerning commitment to the collection, and in 11.3 concerning the Corinthians' 'betrothal' or commitment to Christ. If we read *hagiotēs* (purity), the meaning must surely be purity of intention. Which word to read is a difficult textual question, and the arguments for each are about equally balanced.[16] But again the fundamental sense seems unaffected, and the overall context provides a deeper dimension of understanding than is reached simply by attending to individual words.

As we reflect on method, it is important to notice several points about this discussion. Firstly what began as a question concerning the proper way to construe a sentence has moved to observations about an important aspect of the text as a whole, illustrating yet again the complex interrelationship between understanding the whole and understanding detailed points. Secondly, establishing a case that a text should be understood one way not another, depends on being able to show why one way is unsatisfactory by pointing out its inherent difficulties and giving good reasons for adopting another approach. This involves arguments based on linguistic usage and overall context and sequence of thought. Once again these are matters of objective fact about the text, and neither depends on 'instinct', or at least not an instinct uninformed by knowledge and experience. The process is not simply subjective.

Still less is the question of the wording of the text a subjective matter. We have noted in our discussion two points at which the wording of the text is uncertain. The reason for this is that there are different wordings in different manuscripts. However difficult it may be to determine what the original wording was, it is a matter of fact that the original wording was either one thing or another, and where there is uncertainty it will mean the precise meaning is inaccessible. We have suggested that the overall meaning is clear whichever reading is adopted in the two cases mentioned, but this is not always the case. Even so there can be no grounds for rejecting the discipline of trying to ascertain what the original was by known methods and arguments. It is simply unreasonable to say that because there is disagreement and uncertainty, therefore the questions are not objective, but relative. That is effectively to suggest that anyone can rewrite the text how they like.

3 TRACING THE SEQUENCE OF THOUGHT

As we move to bigger units, the relationship between exegesis and translation ceases to be so intimate, and the need for technical competence is less obvious at first sight. Given a reasonably good translation, is it not possible for anyone to read it and follow the argument? Does this not depend on 'insight' rather than knowledge? Of course, there is something in this suggestion, though it is to be noticed that we are talking about insight into the sequence of thought that objectively inheres in the text, not something read into the text by the interpreter.

In fact, however, thought patterns are to some extent culture-bound, and an uninformed 'visitor' to foreign territory will not necessarily follow the argument. The fact that Paul thinks like a Jewish Rabbi has been illustrated over and over again by specialists, and to realize this makes an enormous difference to our understanding of how his thought develops. For example, he often argues *qal wahomer*, from light to heavy. Thus in 2 Cor. 3, he moves from what is glory to what is yet more glorious, and produces not so much a contrast as a 'capping'. Any exegesis which attempts to suggest that Paul is simply doing Moses down, is not true to his form of argument. In the light of this, the debate about whether *telos* (end) means the fulfilment or the finish surely misses the point. It means both.

Yet even with this information, the sequence of thought in 2 Cor. 3 is still exceedingly complex, and has given rise to many discussions.[17] Paul is constantly suspected of digressing, or changing his line of argument in mid-stream. If this is so, it seriously weakens arguments for dislocation and dissection based on incoherence, since it suggests that Paul's thought tends to be disjunctive. But perhaps lines of argument that seem opaque to us, were not so for him. Sometimes his changes of direction can be explained in the light of features of the scriptural text that lies behind his argument, sometimes by the fact that he clearly worked with different presuppositions. Sometimes, as we saw in the discussion of *dokimē*, knowledge of Greek can indicate connections we would never have realized were there. Sometimes, as van Unnik has shown, knowledge of Aramaic can explain how associations may have formed in

Paul's mind which are not obvious to us. Apart from the example mentioned earlier of 'unveiling' being associated with *parrhēsia*, there is the association of 'Amen' with faithfulness (*ne'emān*), and its use as the Aramaic equivalent of the Greek *nai* (Yes): this may help to explain the sequence of thought in 1.17–20.

To some extent, then, following the 'logic' of a text like this depends upon background information, and on cross-cultural awareness. It may also involve insight into the workings of Paul's particular mind, and that too develops through constant endeavour to understand what he has written, and so is based on knowledge of objective texts, not on uninformed instinct. Hickling notes how often Paul exhibits a 'sudden change in the level of what is being discussed', an 'abrupt transition to the intensely theological from a relatively trivial starting-point', and documents this with examples. So while there is clearly a large element of judgement involved, and interpreters clearly do come to quite different conclusions, at this level also, interpretation involves knowledge, testable evidence, and argument. It is not simply relative or subjective.

The extent to which interpreters differ, however, is significant, and two fundamental reasons for this can be detected. In the first place, interpreters are bound to notice different things in the text and to regard different aspects of the argument as the clue to understanding the movement of thought. Each consequently points up what seems most important and plays down other elements. Inevitably interpretation then appears to descend to the dogmatic presentation of incompatible and apparently subjective readings of the same text: commentaries simply contradict each other, and commentators simply dismiss other people's ideas as unpersuasive. In the second place, prior assumptions about overall coherence or lack of it affect the way any given passage is read. One commentator will be sceptical and exaggerate the difficulties, another will be sympathetic and discount the problems. Once we had come to suspect the unity of the epistle, we could not help endeavouring to trace a reasonable sequence wherever others had challenged its possibility.

But even so this does not mean all is relative. Only ongoing debate and critical testing can settle the question whether we are right or not. How many passages make better sense on this hypothesis? How much have we 'forced' the text to conform to our view of it? Are the sceptics persuaded by the cumulative force of our observations? Whether we are right or not is a matter of fact, and arguments one way or the other are concerned with evidence to demonstrate that one position or the other is right. Different interpretations can be checked against the text, and sometimes it becomes transparently clear when that is done that one interpretation is superior to another. It is simply not true that anything goes.

In the chapter on the thrust of the text, we have tried to demonstrate the overall sequence of thought. In the chapter arguing for the unity of the epistle, we have tried to outline reasons for seeing the supposed 'seams' between different bits in a more constructive light. It is impossible to engage in an exhaustive treatment of all the passages in 2 Corinthians where questions about sequence arise. So here let us just observe the treatment of one final example of what might be perceived as a difficult thought-progression.

The problem may be put thus: If we are right in thinking that Paul's first defence against criticism for not coming as promised, is a claim that he is under God's guidance and is not his own master (1.17ff.), then why does he go on to suggest that he had his own reasons for not putting in an appearance in the following paragraph (1.23ff.)? Chrysostom, whose exegesis we have followed for the first point, was quick to suggest that Paul presents us with something of a contradiction when he says, 'To spare you I did not come.' He resorts in the end to the exceedingly improbable suggestion that Paul is referring to a different occasion.

But first he posits the idea that the Spirit suggested to Paul that however much he wanted to go, it would be inadvisable, and he should spare them. I suspect that Chrysostom was feeling after an important insight here, namely that decisions taken *kata pneuma* (according to the spirit), could involve human sensitivity and tact, as well as divine direction – indeed, either or both could have suggested that time was needed for repentance. After all, Paul is warning them yet again by the end of the letter, that his arrival may not be the happy occasion either side might hope for. Here he affirms their independence in the Spirit: he does not lord it over their faith. The new covenant in the Spirit means they have direct access to knowledge of God's will, and his prophetic condemnation should not be necessary. So under God's direction he gave them time to recollect themselves, and it was to spare them that he did not come.

This leads Paul to develop the theme of their mutual love and dependence upon one another, already summarized in the opening statement of his defence, 1.12–14. As indicated in an earlier chapter, the reference to his anxious wait for Titus is not part of a broken-off narrative, but part of his expression of concern for the church. But God's direction of his mission is never far from his mind, as the outburst in 2.14 proves. Thus the whole hangs together, and leads into the complex midrashic argument of 2 Cor. 3, which explains both Paul's vocation and their mutual dependence.

The features of that complex argument also hold together if one looks not for linear 'logic', but explanatory progression. From our standpoint, *non sequiturs* seem to multiply as one works through the passage.[18] If the glory Paul claims is so much greater than that of Moses, you would think he would need a thicker veil to avoid dazzling his audience. But in fact Paul suddenly turns to the *parrhēsia* and openness of his gospel. The logical connection between the veil over Moses' face and the hardness of Israel's heart is far from obvious. Yet if we take together the whole passage 2.14—4.6, we can see that negative response to Moses foreshadows negative response to Paul, just as Moses' glory is the type of the greater glory Paul receives. Several things are in play at once, and the shifts are not so abrupt as is sometimes thought. Similarity and contrast run through the whole midrash, and sensitivity to its winding exegetical argument can produce understanding, if it is properly informed both about the scriptural passages on which it is based and the methods of exegesis current among Paul's rabbinic educators. It is also important to observe how the passage subtly moves from characterizing Paul's apostleship and indicating its credentials, to involving those who respond to his mission, those to whom he has delivered the new treaty-document which is not a document, but the gift of the Spirit. Their response is his letter of recommendation, and they all behold the glory of God in the face of Jesus Christ, and reflect it in their own transformation. The midrash is about Paul's ministry, but it is also about the mutual dependence of the apostle and the community he addresses, and the dangers of not responding to his appeal.

Looking back over this exposition, we may wish to observe its apparently dogmatic stance and persuasive style: surely this is what Paul is on about. It is an appeal to read the text this way rather than an argument or proof. Yet it illustrates the fundamental point: on the one hand determining meaning involves pointing out significant connections that exist in the text. It is not a purely subjective matter. On the other hand, what catches the interpreter's interest, and whether the interpreter reads the text with the presumption of unity, or the presumption of disjunction, inevitably makes an enormous difference to what is found in the text. The 'subjective' element has to be admitted. But the validity of the conclusions reached depends upon evidence in the text, and that is objective.

4 DISCERNING THE REFERENCE OF THE TEXT

What a statement means is intimately bound up with what it refers to. The sentence, 'He let go of the sheet', does not mean the same thing if 'sheet' refers to a sheet of paper, as it does if sheet refers to the rope attached to a sail in a dinghy. Clearly in a case like this, context is an important determinant of reference, both context in the text and in the 'real world' to which the text refers. But regardless of context, acquired reference can change the meaning of a word. We are all familiar with what has happened to the word 'gay' since it has been taken to refer to a particular sexual orientation. Wrong associations tend to get imported into quite inappropriate contexts. Because reference is so important, to imagine that it is possible to pay attention to the 'text in itself' without bothering with its situation or background is in many cases to be gravely mistaken. It might be possible in the case of poetry, but it is certainly not possible in the case of a text like 2 Corinthians (see further Chapter 5). The meaning of the text is determined to a very large extent by what it refers to.

(i) REFERENCE TO MATTERS OF FACT

There are many examples of texts in 2 Corinthians whose import eludes us because we do not know what the factual reference is. This has already been illustrated in our earlier discussion of the background situation, that is, what precisely was going on in Corinth. It is the reason why so much study of this letter has been concentrated upon reconstructing that situation. What letter is referred to in 2.4? What lies behind 2.5–8 and 7.12–13: who did what to whom, and are we right to presume that both passages refer to the same incident? Is it necessary, as some commentators maintain, to take it that the term 'superapostles' in 11.5 and 12.11 refers to the 'pillars' in Jerusalem? Or is it an ironical reference to nondescript interlopers? Precisely where does Paul allude to charges brought against himself?

Is it true that certain passages in the epistle represent answers to rival claims and doctrines? It makes a good deal of difference whether we think the midrash in 2 Cor. 3 is Paul's own work, or imagine it is an adaptation of his opponents' material. We feel sure that Hickling's arguments against the latter hypothesis are sound,[19] and the midrash is part of Paul's own way of defending his apostolic vocation: the only thing we can glean from it is that Paul's apostleship has been attacked – the direction of the polemic is personal not doctrinal. That estimate inevitably alters the way we read the passage and understand it compared with some other exegetes, and the reason for this difference is that we do not accept that there is any reference to opposing doctrines. Meaning and reference are closely related.

And what about the 'thorn in the flesh' as it is traditionally described? Is this a reference to illness, as has so often been assumed? If so, what was the trouble? Eye-disease? Epilepsy? Malaria? You name it, someone will have suggested it! But all the hardships Paul refers to in this letter suggest that really he was quite robust. So should we look for other approaches? Was it just a stammer that hampered his preaching? Was it depression following his ecstatic experiences? Or was it the pain caused by the Jews' rejection of the gospel?[20] All these things are guesses, though most have been backed up with some apparently corroborating evidence. We have taken up another not very fashionable solution in the previous chapter, one which would radically change our understanding of the meaning of the passage if it were correct.

Meaning and reference are closely related, and if the reference is uncertain, several different possibilities about meaning may have to be entertained. This does not mean that we can make the text mean what we like. The text once had a quite precise meaning. What it does mean is that we have to be prepared to admit uncertainty, and balance up the relative merits of the various suggestions, treating whatever evidence there is available as responsibly as possible. Once again we are dealing with something that is not simply a subjective process, though the interpreter's judgement is bound to affect the conclusion reached.

(ii) CROSS-REFERENCE

But problems about reference are not confined to an author's allusions to matters of fact which were known to him and his addressees but not to readers outside the situation. There are also problems of cross-reference in the text, and how these are settled will affect the way the sequence of thought is perceived. Take 11.12: to what does Paul refer when he uses the word *aphormē*? What does this verse mean? Furnish translates, 'What I am doing I shall also keep on doing, in order to cut off the opportunity of those who want an opportunity to be recognized as our equals in what they boast about.' By contrast the RSV translates, 'And what I do I will continue to do, in order to undermine the claim of those who would like to claim that in their boasted mission they work on the same terms as we do.' *Aphormē* can mean opportunity, but it also means 'basis' or 'foundation'. In this sense Paul has already used it in 5.12, where he says he is providing a basis for their pride (or boast) in him. Used with a word meaning 'chop down', it surely must refer to such a 'base'. He will continue what he is doing (boasting? defending himself?) in order to 'undermine', as the RSV puts it, the base of those who want a base.

The base they have which Paul wants to chop down is presumably self-commendation, letters of recommendation, credentials of various kinds. Paul's 'base' is his total reliance on God. If we take such cross-reference seriously, then surely it makes better sense of the following clause to take it not as unpacking the purpose of the others, but as continuing to unpack the purpose of Paul: Paul is chopping down their base 'in order that they may be found the same as us in the matter of what they take a pride in', or boast of. In other words, like Paul, they will boast in the Lord, or perhaps since that is another way of acknowledging the power is God's, in their weaknesses, not in themselves. Of course, taking it that way might seem to imply that they are redeemable, and the following verses hardly encourage such a thought! (though see Margaret Thrall's interesting paper suggesting that it is conceivable that Paul was referring to followers of Peter when he uses the phrase 'servants of Satan', just as when he spoke of 'superapostles' or 'servants of Christ').[21] Other ways of taking this verse seem unintelligible, whereas this picks up a possible cross-reference to what seems to be a most important point in Paul's argument. It is surely worth considering. But whatever conclusion is reached, it is clear that the question whether there is a cross-reference or not, profoundly affects our understanding of the meaning of this verse.

(iii) REFERENCE TO TRANSCENDENT REALITIES

But problems of reference are not confined to unknown facts, or uncertainties about consistency. There are also references to heavenly realities, to things taken to be theological truths. Knowing what these refer to means being able to enter sensitively into the thought-world of Paul and/or his readers, a thought-world which we may not share, but must take seriously if we are to grasp the meaning of the text. The more general problem of presuppositions and thought-world we will approach in the next section. But the problem may be quite specific: what exactly did Paul intend to refer to by such and such a phrase? What is the allusion intended in this image or metaphor? The following examples illustrate the sort of questions which can arise, and indicate how the question of reference affects what we take to be the meaning.

(a) When Paul says 'The Lord is the Spirit' in 3.17, to what does each noun refer? Patristic commentators found themselves engaged in Trinitarian discussion, since they assumed the reference was to Persons of the Godhead, and had to explain the statement rather carefully so that no one confused their identity. But even if we dismiss such correlations on the grounds that they are anachronistic, problems of reference remain. Does *Kyrios* refer to the God of the Scriptures – Yahweh – or to the Lord of the Church – Jesus? Paul could certainly have meant either. 'Turning to the Lord' in his Jewish Scriptures certainly meant 'returning to Yahweh', or repenting, and in the specific passage on which Paul bases his midrash, Moses removes the veil when he turns to the Lord, that is, the God of Israel. But Paul almost certainly took it as meaning 'turning to Christ' in his interpretation of this scriptural passage. Probably the right approach is to note that when Greeks quoted words in the process of exegesis, they would signal the quote with the definite article as we signal it with inverted commas. So the cryptic sentence means: when the text uses the word 'Lord' (*ho de Kyrios*), it means the same as when it uses the word 'Spirit' (*to pneuma estin*). In other words, to turn to the Lord is to become part of the new covenant of the Spirit. Once again we can observe how crucial is the decision about reference for determining the meaning: is an exegetical reference involved, or a theological reference?

(b) In 1.22 we find a series of pregnant words: God is said to guarantee us, anoint us, seal us and give us the downpayment of the Spirit. Now anointing, sealing and giving the Spirit were soon associated in the liturgies of the Church with the rite of baptism. Are we justified in making that association, or is it simply anachronistic to suggest that this text makes any reference to such things?

In fact I suspect it is probably not appropriate to allow such a reference here. The reason is that it distorts the line of argument in the text as a whole. Paul's subject is the guarantee of his apostleship. God is the one who guarantees this and the one who has anointed him for the task as prophets and priests were anointed under the old covenant. But the sealing and the giving of the Spirit, we suggested earlier, refer to the common experience of those who have become part of the community of the new covenant: it is 2 Cor. 3 which makes this clear. The same God who has given the Corinthians the Spirit, guarantees for them the apostleship of Paul – in fact the two things are intimately related, since their membership of the new covenant is Paul's testimonial (3.2). The 'we' in 1.22a has a different reference from the 'we' in 1.22b: the first refers to the apostles, Paul being the prime representative of that class, and the second refers to all Christians, Paul being included among them.

Now if that is a correct insight into the sequence of thought, then the whole series of words cannot refer to baptism since the word 'anointing' does not go with the words 'sealing' and 'giving the Spirit'. Undoubtedly the latter refers to what happened when the Corinthians became members of the covenant community, and that may refer to baptism, though Paul does say in 1 Corinthians that he did not baptize many of them, whereas he clearly did 'deliver' the covenant, and can claim to be the 'father' of the community (1 Cor. 1.14; 4.15; 2 Cor. 3.3; 12.14–15). Interestingly enough, Chrysostom does not leap to read baptism into the text here, but speaks of Christians being anointed as prophets, priests and kings, and of the anticipation of the Kingdom of heaven in the gift of the Spirit. He has not distinguished the different reference of 'we' as we have, but he has observed the same kind of reference to inspiration and calling, rather than baptism.

We suggest, then, that to see here an allusion to baptism is to read something into the text which disrupts its flow and distorts its meaning. That is a better reason for rejecting it than simply saying it is anachronistic. Even if we allow some 'playing' with the text, and even if we allow the possibility of later insight into meanings not suspected at the time of writing, indications can sometimes be found in the text that this is not appropriate. So it is not only awkward, but not appropriate to treat 3.17 as a Trinitarian statement (see (a) above). On the other hand, the final grace in 13.13 may well be a text appropriately understood in anachronistic Trinitarian terms. Paul was feeling after truths about the nature of God which he could not himself fully grasp or explicate: later insight can uncover deeper levels of understanding inaccessible to the original writer. If this principle is admitted, it may ease embarrassment about the traditional 'messianic prophecies', all of which clearly had a different meaning at the time of composition. Vision and poetry, metaphor and imagery, have the potential for more than one reference, and hindsight may heighten the appropriateness of reinterpretation. The meaning may lie ahead of the text (see

Chapters 5 and 9). It is not whether a meaning is anachronistic or not that determines its validity, but whether it is appropriate to the text with which the interpreter is wrestling.

(c) But in many cases the test of appropriateness will be profoundly connected with what might plausibly be the meaning at the time of writing, and even with the intention of the author. It may seem surprising, but in the case of 2 Corinthians, the question whether the word '*theos*' always refers to God is actually an issue. The problem text is 4.4, where we appear to have the phrase 'the god of this *aeon* (age/world)', and the action of this being has been to blind the minds of the unbelievers/unfaithful. The majority of commentators leap to the conclusion that the phrase must refer to Satan not God, and texts and translations forbear to use an initial capital. (Originally the whole text would have been written in uncials (= capitals), so there was no such convention to make the distinction clear; it is an editorial decision).

Good reasons for this decision are advanced. In John's Gospel the 'ruler of this world' is 'cast out': clearly that phrase means the devil. We know that contemporary apocalyptic writers, whose ideas certainly influenced Paul as we shall see in the next section, believed that during the present evil age power had been usurped by Satan and his angels. It is far from implausible to suggest that Paul was referring to Satan in the phrase 'the god of this aeon'. But if he did, he is using the word 'god' in a way unparalleled elsewhere in his writings. As Chrysostom points out, God is the God of this world – he is God of Abraham, Isaac and Jacob, not just the God of heaven. How is it then that he has blinded them? Chrysostom is as uncomfortable with the thought as we are, but points out that Scripture often speaks this way when it means he allows these things to happen. For example, 'God gave them up to a reprobate mind'. What else could he do? Force them to believe?

Whatever we may think of Chrysostom's reasoning, he has put his finger on something important. In the New Testament we find the early Christians turning to passages like Isaiah 6.10 to explain lack of response: he has blinded their eyes and hardened their heart, lest they should see with their eyes and perceive with their heart and turn for me to heal them, says the author of John's Gospel (John 12.40). Mark's Gospel uses the same text to explain people's failure to understand the parables (4.12), in a way that suggests that the truth was deliberately concealed in this way. In neither case is this blinding the work of the devil; it is a fulfilment of prophecy, and the work of the Lord. And in fact Paul too uses this material to explain the Jews' lack of response (Romans 11.8–10):

> as it is written, 'God gave them a spirit of stupor, eyes that should not see and ears that should not hear, down to this very day.' And David says, 'Let their feast become a snare and a trap, a pitfall and a retribution for them: let their eyes be darkened so that they cannot see, and bend their backs for ever.'

There are good grounds for believing that Paul meant God when he said God.

But Chrysostom was embarrassed. This was his second explanation. His first was that 'of this aeon' is attached to unbelievers, not God, an idea that does seem to strain the language given the word order. He is prepared to resort to such bad exegesis because of the way the text had been used by groups he regarded as heretical. The Marcionites had indeed identified 'the god of this world' as the 'god of the Old Testament', but of course they regarded the 'demiurge' or creator-god as a different being from the God of our Lord Jesus Christ: the Old Testament was to be dispensed with, together with its god of wrath and justice, now that the revelation of the good God had come. The Manichees said, according to Chrysostom, that the devil is intended in this text: they had claimed that two divine entities, good and bad, were eternally at war. Chrysostom is anxious to outlaw both these dualist heresies, and his exegesis therefore has theological motives. Is he tempted to read the text in an orthodox way, regardless of the original meaning? Is he being anachronistic and reading the text in an inappropriate way? We cannot discount the possibility, but as indicated above, there are grounds for taking some of his observations seriously.

Furthermore, we cannot discount the theological motivations of modern scholars who take the other view. It eases the difficulty about attributing deliberate blinding to a God conceived of as a good loving Father, something we find as difficult as Marcion ever did. It also enables the 'orthodox' scholar to salvage Paul's reputation as 'orthodox' – indeed, as an opponent of incipient Gnosticism, rather than the first and greatest of the Gnostics, as the History of Religions School claimed. If the 'god of this aeon' is Satan, then he cannot be the 'demiurge'; in fact in the succeeding verses Paul clearly identifies the creator God who said, 'Out of darkness light will shine', with the God who has shone in our hearts to bring the enlightenment which is knowledge of God's glory in the face of Christ. Paul's thought-world is not gnostic, but apocalyptic. It suits present-day 'orthodox' Christian scholars to reach this conclusion, just as it suited Chrysostom in his time to reach the other.

Now the succeeding section will show that we accept the apocalyptic characterization of Paul's presuppositions. But we do not believe that this justifies the particular interpretation of this text which is now so widespread. Gnostic exegesis shows that if you admit once that Paul may use '*theos*' to refer to a being other than God, then you can admit it again: Valentinian exegetes believed that *katenanti theou* in 2.17 meant 'confronting' or 'contrary to' god, that is, the demiurge. They read it as saying that we 'speak from sincerity, as from God, confronting God, we speak in Christ', in other words, from the Father confronting the Demiurge.[22] The word does mean 'opposite', but you may stand opposite someone without confronting them, and in accordance with accepted usage, everyone assumes that Paul means 'in God's sight', and the gnostic reading is perverse. Once admit, however, that Paul may not have used the word *theos* consistently, and it is hard to prove gnostic exegesis wrong. Surely it is clear that by God, Paul invariably meant the God of the Scriptures, who is also the God of Jesus Christ.

We submit that that is true in 4.4 as well, and that however theologically uncomfortable we may find it, the sentiment Paul expresses there is one that was current in the first-century Church, even paralleled in his own writings. It is both anachronistic, and inappropriate both to the text and to Paul's views expressed elsewhere to read *theos* as meaning anything other than God. But inevitably the final conclusion will depend on our overall conclusions about Paul's thought-world, and the extent to which he shared apocalyptic or even gnostic presuppositions.

Whatever else this discussion has shown, it is clear that the reference of the text is fundamental to its meaning. There are all kinds of different sorts of referents, and the criteria by which the reference is determined are bound to be varied. Sometimes it may be indeterminable, either for lack of information, or because the language is imaginative and metaphorical. The subjective response of the interpreter may play a crucial role in the conclusions reached, but even in the most open-ended cases, objective knowledge of linguistic, contextual and cultural facts will assist the interpreter to reach an informed judgement. There is always an objective element in the interpretative process.

5 DETERMINING IMPLICIT PRESUPPOSITIONS

All of us have inbuilt assumptions picked up from the learning processes of a lifetime, built into our language and culture. Often we are quite unconscious of the presuppositions with which we work, but they act as axioms, deeply affecting the way we think, and the way we use language, and the way we understand what we hear or read. Increasingly exegetes have come to realize the importance of becoming conscious of our own presuppositions if we are to avoid bending texts to suit ourselves.[23]

But this also means that the original author and readers had their own presuppositions, and in a case like Paul's letters to Corinth, the recipients probably had somewhat different assumptions from the sender – they shared Hellenistic culture in general, but did they share the special 'in-group' culture of Paul the Jew? If we are to understand the text, we need to become aware of the underlying assumptions, conscious or unconscious, which were operating.

Some of these almost go without saying: they inherited first-hand (in the case of Paul) or second-hand (in the case of Gentile converts) the monotheism and the sacred literature of the Jews. Paul also inherited a large number of assumptions about what was acceptable ethical behaviour, but having proclaimed a gospel of freedom from the law, he apparently found it difficult to hand on these standards to non-Jews. It is noticeable that every stance he takes over ethical issues in I Corinthians is the one that would come naturally to a Jew, but rather than asserting these positions as rules, Paul often strives to find persuasive arguments to convince (e.g. the discussion of idol-meat). It is not unreasonable to suggest that Paul had presuppositions his readers did not share, and that herein lay some of the difficulties of mutual understanding which plagued their relationship. A plausible case can be made for all the problems which seem to lie behind I Corinthians arising out of misunderstanding of Paul's own gospel-preaching.[24]

But the work of the History of Religions School has forced exegetes to explore the wider religio-cultural scene. The discovery of new texts, like the Mandaean literature, provoked the hypothesis that prior to Paul there existed a 'gnostic redeemer myth', and that Paul's christological understanding derived from that background. His sacramental teaching was attributed to the influence of Hellenistic mystery religions, and by the conflation of all this material, a whole range of mystical and dualistic presuppositions were attributed to him. His theology was then interpreted in these terms. But new discoveries provoked different correlations: the importance of Jewish apocalyptic for understanding the New Testament had long been recognized, and the advent of the Dead Sea Scrolls reinforced that perception. Paul came to be interpreted in terms of apocalyptic, and the case is very plausible.

However, Paul can be shown to have much in common with the Rabbis, and one thing we do know about him was that he was educated by Rabbi Gamaliel. So do the 'gnostic' and 'apocalyptic' features in his letters come from his opponents? Was Paul 'donning the opposition's clothing'? Were his opponents Gnostics or Jewish sectaries or straight Judaizers? Did he face a coherent opposition orchestrated by the Jerusalem authorities? Or do we meet different groups causing trouble in different places? This whole area has attracted a mass of detective work and conflicting hypotheses.[25] The point to note, however, is the extent to which problems of 'reference' and of 'presuppositions' are related.

The question is how far all these clever hypotheses advance our ability to understand the text. Not only does the multiplication of reconstructions undermine confidence in the validity of any of them, but so often the argumentation is circular. The texts are used to make the reconstructions, and then they are interpreted in the light of those conclusions. To reconstruct Paul's gnostic opposition from the Corinthian epistles, and then claim that certain texts are gnostic glosses,[26] is to build uncertainty on uncertainty.

But there are two further problems which dog the investigator: the first is confusion about definition – what do we mean by 'Gnostics' or 'pneumatics' or 'Jewish sectaries'? Can we define them either doctrinally or sociologically with sufficient precision to make them useful for the exegetical enterprise? Gunther, for example, lists the wide range of proposals that have been made about Paul's opponents, and comments that scholars may well be using different terms for the same phenomena. But his own use of a wide range of texts whose relationship can only be described as uncertain, leaves one wondering whether he has really discovered an existing group of sufficiently clear definition to be instructive. The texts initiate us into a world of strange speculations and peculiar ritual and ethical extremes which are illuminating in general terms for the religious underworld to which the early Church must have belonged (there is no hint of any of it in the 'respectable' literature of the Greco-Roman world);[27] but while the Qumran literature belongs to a specific group, other texts and ideas seem to have circulated among variable fringe groups on the borders of Judaism and early Christianity.

Indeed, it seems likely that Gnosticism in its many and varied forms arose in this way – the idea of a mass movement or 'religion' independent of definable religious groups like the Church and the synagogue seems less and less plausible. The evidence seems to point more and more towards a connection between apocalyptic and Gnosticism, to the importance of Jewish fringe groups in its emergence, in spite of its syncretistic and sometimes philosophical character. The Fathers were perhaps not wildly wrong after all in thinking that gnostic heresies were parasitic on Christianity – at least not if we include a slightly wider Jewish element; and the progressive de-Christianization of gnostic material appears as likely as its Christianization. But the problems of defining 'Gnosticism' have plagued scholarship for a generation or more: first-century texts certainly use language that was picked up by the Gnostics in the second century, but evidence for the existence of significant or influential gnostic groups with anything like the characteristic 'world-view' of the second century gnostic sects is minimal.[28]

Which leads us to the second problem – namely the problem of assessing the significance of apparent parallels: does the use of the same words or images imply the same framework of thought? Cannot the same language be used in such different overall contexts that it simply cannot be regarded as significantly similar? The fact that the same words and phrases can carry quite different significances when placed in different settings, has been interestingly demonstrated and exploited in John Riches' book, *Jesus and the Transformation of Judaism*.[29] It is simply unreasonable to leap to the conclusion that when the word *gnōsis* appears, there must be Gnosticism in the background: other Greeks spoke of 'knowledge', and spoke of it in their own way; Horsley[30] has made a good case for its background being in Hellenistic Jewish circles like those of Philo; we have indicated the possible significance of its use in the LXX (see Chapter 3). That point may seem so obvious that we may be suspected of caricature, but it is worth making the point clear. If we are going to exploit parallels we must compare like with like, and note differences as carefully. We must set the use of apparently significant words and phrases in their total context, as far as we reasonably can.

The whole area is exceedingly complex, and compounded by failure among scholars to reach any kind of agreement as to how to deal with the difficulties outlined. What conclusions can we reach? Let us begin by noticing that Pauline texts were exploited to the full by second-century Christian gnostic sects like the Valentinians: according to Pagels,[31] they did not recognize the supposed 'anti-gnostic' argument of Paul, but claimed him as one of their own. So did the 'orthodox' like Irenaeus and Tertullian. In the second century there existed two different readings of Paul. This suggests that Paul himself belongs to a prior stage in which the lines of battle have not yet been clearly defined. It is not helpful to read first-century material in the light of second-century evidence. The alleged gnostic terminology, as Pagels insists, was appropriated and turned into a technical vocabulary by the gnostic exegetes: it is Pauline terminology exploited by the Gnostics, rather than vice versa.

To understand Paul we must firstly examine with the utmost care what he says, and how he uses language, not leap to the conclusion that because he uses certain sets of words and phrases, he must have been influenced by gnostic usage, even if only influenced to oppose it. Nevertheless, study of extant literature as nearly contemporary and relevant as possible, however hard it is to assess the precise bearing it may have on the interpretation of Paul, is essential. It helps us to move into a world of thought very different from our own, and to see Paul as part of that world. Paul has been 'domesticated' by familiarity, and it is easy to imagine, therefore, that his work is intelligible. But to read unfamiliar texts is to be provided with a new set of spectacles, and to have one's eyes opened to a strange and incredible set of preoccupations. It is fascinating to observe both the similarities and the differences. Paul shares some assumptions, but the central focus of his life and thought is dramatically different. The meaning of Paul is not determined by the contents of other texts, but it is illuminated.

Apart from the rabbinic material, which reveals much about Paul's methods of scriptural argument, and the life-style and interests that must have preoccupied him before his conversion, it is apocalyptic material which can perform this function most effectively. What does Paul share with apocalyptic texts?

It is abundantly clear from certain verses in 2 Corinthians that Paul shared the apocalyptic belief in a final judgement. All things are under God; all will be exposed. This in itself suggests that he shared other eschatological expectations with the writers of apocalypses.

Apocalyptic works are preoccupied with tracing what we might call the grand plan of history. The past is divided into great eras, and each era is regarded as worse than the previous one. Soon will come the final woes – earthquakes, wars, portents, etc. – which herald the end of the present evil age, and the coming of God's Kingdom, or the messianic age, or the new creation. Usually these ages are seen in schematic terms – say, 6000 years to be followed by the millennium – the sabbath-rest for the elect, who will be raised from the dead to participate in this blessed future. It was such schemes that made possible the calculation of when the dénouement would come about. The burden of the apocalyptic message is hope, faith and courage, since present persecution and suffering will be rewarded. The framework of that message is found in the manipulation of dates, prophecies and predictions, so that as one hope fails, it can be reinterpreted in terms of another future. Present misery is attributed to the fact that Satan and his angels have usurped control; but ultimately God's plan will be effected. Already laid up in heaven, waiting to be revealed, is the future Messiah, Temple, Kingdom, etc.

If we survey the Pauline writings with such ideas in mind, we find a number of passages which clearly share that sort of perspective, from the Thessalonian letters to Romans 8. But there is one significant difference. Christ has initiated the new creation. Through his resurrection, he has become the first-born among many brethren, and given a down payment on the future in the gift of the Spirit. If we read the Pauline writings with the assumption that Paul thought that the new age had broken into the present evil age, that it would very soon be consummated, but meanwhile everyone is living through the final days of woes and wrath and judgement, then many aspects of these texts make better sense. By dying with Christ, the believer has died to the old life, the old world dominated by sin and evil, the old self. Entering the new covenant community has meant being re-created, having a changed heart, receiving the Spirit, and life in the Spirit means that now sin has no more hold over the believer, and that future resurrection is guaranteed. In Christ we are a new creation. Already transfer from one realm to another has taken place, even though its full promise is yet to be realized. Paul affirmed the fulfilment of what the apocalyptic writers were expecting imminently, yet he still looked forward to a fuller fulfilment – it is 'now', yet 'not yet'.

For the battle with Satan is still going on. Paul subscribes to a dualism similar to the apocalyptic writers. The present evil age is Satan's dominion. But the people of the new covenant are already in the Kingdom of Christ. Emissaries from the kingdom of evil may get a toe-hold in the life of the Church, so the purity of the community must be protected. In fact, the Christian life is a constant struggle to live *kata pneuma*, according to the Spirit, and not *kata sarka*, according to the old standards of the world.

The two eras are overlapping, and believers are caught in the struggle between the two. In principle, they are the germ of the new creation, but in practice things are far from perfect. In the present, the Church is subject to affliction, and the apostle is called to fill up what is lacking in the sufferings of Christ.

Paul's dualism is not the same sort of dualism as we find in Gnosticism. Creation is not an accident, nor the result of a precosmic fall. Creation belongs to God, and it is God who has subjected it to bondage for his own purposes. Satan at times appears, not as God's opponent, but as God's policeman, as in the book of Job – the sinner in 1 Cor. 5 is consigned to Satan for his ultimate redemption. Nor is the 'spirit' an embodied spark of the divine, anxious to put off this bodily clothing. Rather the Spirit is a divine gift, and redemption is resurrection to the new creation, a putting on rather than a taking off, a renewal of everything rather than an escape from it all. Paul's dualism has its roots in Jewish monotheism, like the dualism of apocalyptic. And the element of predestination in Paul, the calling of the elect, the blinding of the unresponsive, the sense that there are secret plans already prepared and revealed in Christ – these are closer to apocalyptic assumptions than to similar notions in Gnosticism.

But there are many things in apocalyptic which Paul ignores or plays down. He is not interested in the past, schematically contrived or not; he is only interested in the present fulfilment in Christ, and the future of which that is the guarantee. He simply assumes that the whole conforms to the predetermined plan of God. Nor is he interested in elaborate calculations to determine the end, a prime concern of apocalyptic authors; in fact he warns people to get on with life and live in trust and hope, rather than giving up their jobs or otherwise preparing themselves for the cataclysm. Other apocalyptic interests he puts into a different perspective: claims to heavenly journeys in which God's secrets were revealed, he perhaps parodies, certainly plays down.[32] The cross is for him the secret plan of God, the hidden strategy which outwitted the rulers of this aeon. He is not interested in angelology: the only mediator that matters is Christ. In other words he appears to share certain perspectives and assumptions with the apocalyptic writers, but for Paul Christ has challenged many of their preoccupations, just as he challenged the rabbinic preoccupation with precisely how to make sure the law was properly fulfilled in everyday life.

For both apocalyptic and gnostic writers, the world was at present alien to God. God's rule was presently usurped, or never existed. God belonged to the future, or to another world. (In spite of the fact Gnostics sometimes used the word 'God' for the lesser divine being who created and ruled this one, that generalization is not really misleading, since their real 'God' was the higher spiritual being they proclaimed as 'Father'.) Neither took the reality of God seriously, because both were too preoccupied with the reality of evil.

Paul shares their sense of the corruptions of the present order, but the combination of the advent of Jesus Christ and his own 'living in the Scriptures', believing they were fulfilled, gave Paul the unparalleled grasp on the reality and presence of God, bringing life out of death, righteousness out of sin, new creation out of destruction, which pervades his thinking. What he has assumed from apocalyptic is transformed by the arrival of the new creation in Christ. He can 'see the world's evil honestly and still believe in good', to borrow a phrase from John Eaton. Furthermore, knowledge for Paul is not the secrets of the universe, but knowledge of the will and purpose of God. A prime interest, therefore, is ethics, even if the rules of Torah and a detailed *halakah* are abandoned for the obedience of the heart. Obedience to God lies at the centre of Paul's concerns. Thus Paul's life and thought is deeply theocentric, but also christocentric because Christ has made God's call presently real.

The above very general and apparently dogmatic survey, which a serious student would need to test out by acquaintance with both apocalyptic texts and the Pauline letters, has already hinted at points in 2 Corinthians which are illuminated by the assumption that Paul's presuppositions are related to those of the apocalyptic writers. Let us look at one precise example of how understanding may be furthered in this way: suppose we ask how it is that the sufferings of Christ overflow onto us in 1.5. Could it not be that when Paul speaks of the *thlipsis* in the midst of which God encourages, he is thinking of the 'messianic woes' that come before the final victory?

Of course it is quite possible to read this passage

non-eschatologically, and think only of comfort in the afflictions of life, as generations of the pious have done. The background in the Psalms which we have noticed, would encourage that kind of 'timeless' or non-culturally-specific understanding. But suppose Paul thought that the messianic woes began with the cross and the sufferings of Christ overflow into the present experience of the elect, who fill up what is lacking in the final afflictions. There is in fact a sense of conflict running all through the epistle, an on-going struggle with the powers of evil: Satan is mentioned three times, in each case as the source of disruption to the church, or to Paul's mission (2.11; 11.14; 12.7). Could it not be that Paul implicitly relates the struggles of apostle and church with the cosmic struggle in such a way that the trauma of their situation becomes the vehicle of God's revelation?

So we might discern in these verses a deep association between, on the one side, the core of the gospel, the hope of the *eschaton*, the ultimate reality of God and his purposes being brought to fruition, and on the other side, the nitty-gritty of day-to-day problems as Paul and the Corinthians experience them. Perhaps the afflictions in which God brings encouragement include the desperate mess in the church and the dreadful state of the relationship between church and apostle. Even in the midst of a potentially explosive crisis, Paul can rejoice in God, because even the worst situation speaks of the messianic woes, the birth-pangs of the new age, the secret power of the cross. The perception of his underlying apocalyptic assumptions may lead us to a deeper appreciation of how Paul can see the particularities of the situation as the on-going locus of God's ultimate revelation of himself and his purposes.

The assumption that Paul worked with some unspelled out apocalyptic presuppositions, deeply modified by the belief that the end had begun to happen in Christ, throws a good deal of light on other passages – indeed on the meaning of his letter as a whole. No doubt this oversimplifies the very complex set of cultural influences upon him, but it seems to fit the content of the texts better than hypotheses about Gnosticism, and it has some explanatory success. Once again both the judgement of the interpreter, and careful attention to evidence are in play. But we have moved into areas where certainty becomes increasingly elusive, partly because of lack of information about many of the texts relevant to the discussion, and also because what has been preserved and what has not is a matter of sheer accident. All we can do is to be as responsible as possible in handling the material, and in doing our best not to build a house of cards by building hypothesis on hypothesis. This responsibility to the evidence depends on being as objective and self-critical as possible. To suggest that the whole exercise is subjective, is to remove any motivation for such responsible scholarship.

6 EXPOUNDING THE MEANING OF THE TEXT

Exegetical comment is aimed at explaining the meaning of words and sentences, at unpacking the reference of the text, at providing information which will assist understanding, whether of the sequence of thought or the unexpressed presuppositions. It is bound to be problem-oriented; where something is obvious or self-explanatory, no comment is needed. The text should speak for itself. Yet the crown of exegesis is exposition of the text's meaning, through summary and paraphrase, explanation and association, so that the interpreter's grasp of the total meaning is communicated, and the reader or hearer can see the text anew through the eyes of the interpreter. At this level there are bound to be different exegeses, as the insights of each individual are articulated. Different exegeses should be regarded as an enrichment; even incompatible exegeses provoke more careful attention to the text. Ultimately different exegeses must be judged by reference to the text, and their relative adequacy assessed against what is written. Response to a text has a subjective element, and is relative to the interpreter's presuppositions, interests and experience. Yet that does not remove the responsibility of submitting that response to the more objective testing of discussion, comparison, and attention to evidence which we have been observing in the previous sections of this chapter.

In this section we propose to offer a sample exposition. As previously noted (Chapter 1), we have not reproduced in this book the commentary we created as a working tool. A commentary requires comment on every difficulty, and there are plenty of commentaries that provide the basic information.

Besides, our aim has been to reflect on the process of interpretation, rather than add to the list of comprehensive studies already available. Already a number of the classic problems in 2 Corinthians have been tackled as examples of what the commentator has to struggle with. Now we simply reproduce the exposition of one section of the epistle which we arrived at through this process of tackling problems and working through them to try and see what the text overall was driving at. The section of text is 4.7—5.10.

'We have this treasure in earthen vessels.' Not earthly fame, but a mirroring of the radiance of God – that is what lies at the heart of Paul's understanding of the apostolic task, and that is what he has been trying to show up to now. But this takes place in the context of a creation which is groaning and travailing, a world under God's wrath, a church in the midst of affliction (see earlier discussion of apocalyptic background), and an apostle constrained by his bodily frame and earthly weaknesses. For Paul, however, this constraint is itself something to exult in; for it shows that his power is derived from God and not from his own resources.

Commentators have noted that the metaphor Paul uses when he speaks of having treasure in earthenware pots, is not uncommon, and various parallels have been cited. One suggestion which fits the previous verse very well is that of Manson, who drew attention to the common use in antiquity of small oil lamps made of cheap earthenware. But maybe it is superfluous to search for a precise allusion; rough earthenware pots were used to store all kinds of valuable things from wine to silver to books (as the discoveries at Qumran and Nag Hammadi illustrate). Indeed, books may be suggestive: written documents carefully preserved in pots have been replaced by the Spirit in the hearts of equally fragile and unprepossessing human beings. But this is hardly explicit. Allusions to biblical texts have been suggested, but most are not immediately convincing or promising. Perhaps it is not totally irrelevant that the one place in the LXX where the phrase *skeuos ostrakinon* occurs is in Leviticus, when an earthenware vessel may be used as a receptacle for killing or boiling sacrifices, and careful instructions are given about breaking those contaminated in any way, especially those used for sin-offerings. Maybe the sacrificial suffering of the apostle-martyr is somewhere in the background of this passage; though it seems a bit far-fetched to press the allusion, even if Paul does hint in this passage that the apostle bears the brunt of persecution and affliction so that life may be communicated to others (4.12).

Paul's language about affliction and God's power anticipates 12.9–10: God's grace is sufficient, power is perfected in weakness, and weaknesses are what Paul boasts of (exults in). It also recalls the opening section of the epistle, especially 1.8, where we find many of the same words used in a rather different way. These interlinkages between the various parts of the epistle are striking, and tend to confirm the view that it is a unity. In 1.8 Paul moves from his being overwhelmed by affliction, to his brush with death and the life-giving power of God: here he makes a parallel move and produces his most extended reflection on death and resurrection in the epistle.

Which makes one wonder whether there are not further resonances in the 'earthenware vessels'. One recalls Jeremiah's visit to the potter, which Paul will take up in Romans 9, and the description of the creation of humanity in Genesis 2: clay is shaped and God breathes his Spirit into it. The clay pot is destructible; if it is imperfect it may be refashioned, broken, even replaced. But it may also be God's vessel, full of God's Spirit. Paul has already suggested to the Corinthians that their bodies are temples of the Spirit (1 Cor. 6.19), and that the Spirit gives life (2 Cor. 3.6). Is the treasure the life-giving power of the Spirit breathed into the vessel fashioned in clay? Precise linguistic references do not exist to establish this link, but often Paul surely invites imaginative and creative associations.

So Paul is afflicted, oppressed, persecuted, bearing everywhere in his body the killing of Jesus. But this is the means of communicating life. His very sufferings prove that the life he has is not his own but that of Jesus. His vocation is to play out over and over again the death and resurrection pattern. And the purpose is to absorb affliction, destruction and death, to fill up what is lacking in the sufferings of Christ, so as to communicate power, life, the Spirit. It is for the sake of the Corinthians; its purpose is the overflow of grace into more and more people, causing an overflow of thanksgiving to God's glory (4.15). Once more Paul is picking up the language and themes of his previous discussions, and the principal drive of his mission is encapsulated in phrases pointing not to worldly success but to the glory of God in worship.

So with the confidence of the Psalmist (see Chapter 3), and reinforced by the power of the resurrection of Jesus, Paul refuses to be daunted, in spite of everything that happens to him. Continuing his explanation of the mode of his apostleship, he again asserts (as he did in 4.1), that he does not give up, and does not give up even though subject to death. By comparison with the eternal weight of glory to come – for we are being transformed from glory to glory (3.18) – the present affliction appears trifling. Paul had said the affliction was excessive (*kath' hyperbolēn*) and beyond his strength (1.8); but now he regards the glory as excessive (*kath' hyperbolēn*) and ever more so (*eis hyperbolēn*) (4.17). So he keeps up his courage in the midst of the travail of the world, determined above all that his life will be well-pleasing to the Lord (5.8–9); for the ultimate reckoning is what matters, not what men think of him now.

Fundamentally this seems to be Paul's line of argument up to 5.10. He is relating what he has said about the basis of his apostleship to the actual conditions in which he works, refusing to accept that his apparent weakness is a denial of what he claims, turning his brush with death into a forceful affirmation of his hope in God. But what he actually says bristles with difficulties, and much of it has been treated as digressive by commentators. The principle reason for this is that what Paul says here has distracted the minds of his readers from the point of what he is saying, and focused them on certain profoundly difficult questions which his remarks seem to provoke. So commentators become anxious to determine Paul's doctrine of the after-life, or the development of his thought about the parousia and the resurrection, or the nature of the false doctrines he is supposed to be countering.

These problems are undoubtedly of great importance, but we refer serious students to the standard commentaries and other relevant literature for discussion of these matters. It is certainly true that in 4.16–18 Paul drops into language more characteristic of Plato and his Hellenistic admirers than the Scriptures, that his phraseology is susceptible of dualist interpretations and suffered these in the ensuing centuries, that at first sight he seems to speak of the dissolution of the body rather than its resurrection and to have dropped the idea of the parousia, thus shifting his position from that in 1 Cor. 15. He almost seems to envisage an inner spiritual self being freed at death to be with the Lord (as Gnostics would). His language in 5.4 is reminiscent of Wisdom 9.15: 'for the perishable body weighs down the soul'. So it appears that Paul, like the Book of Wisdom, has been influenced by Platonic dualism. Yet he does not quite adopt the standard Platonic vision of the liberated soul now gloriously naked, since he emphatically repudiates the idea in favour of a heavenly covering, a new clothing (5.2). Furthermore, the 'weight' he refers to would appear to be afflictions, rather than any inherent grossness of the body.

Be that as it may, to concentrate attention upon these questions is perhaps to lose sight of the real dynamics of Paul's argument here. Paul is still thinking of the reality of life in the midst of death, the re-creating activity of the Spirit which is going on in the realm of the flesh, the tension between the old age persisting and the new age dawning, the groaning of a creation in labour, in the final throes necessary to produce the new order. It is interesting that the language of 5.2–5 will be picked up in Romans 8. Here, as there, we are involved in this groaning and this longing, yet already renewal is being experienced (4.16), and the new creation is anticipated in the downpayment of the Spirit (5.5). In other words the apocalyptic dimension to Paul's thought, sketched earlier, is the most important backcloth to understanding this passage, and it remains integrally related to Paul's overall understanding of the situation in which he, and indeed churches like that at Corinth, find themselves.

So what is the 'inner man' that is being renewed? What is the 'outer man' that is being destroyed? (This is in fact the only passage anywhere in which Paul draws this contrast, though he speaks of the inner man in Romans 7, and the phrase is found again in Ephesians.) What are the things that are visible and temporary? What are the things that are eternal and invisible? (This language is again confined to this passage in the Pauline material.) Surely the 'outer man' and the temporary, visible realities, belong to the present age which is passing away; but as it passes it gives birth to a new eternal reality, at present invisible but to be revealed in the future. Through the Spirit that new creation is already in germ within the hearts of believers, and day by day inner renewal is happening. Thus Paul's recurring antitheses are part and parcel of this paradoxical situation. The old covenant which is passing away, is a written code bringing death and condemnation, the old world is dominated by affliction, sin, hurt and destruction; it is under the dominion of Satan and even Christians are not yet permanently immune from these dangers. But the new covenant is being delivered by Paul, even in the midst of enemy territory, a covenant which is life-giving, eternal, engraved on the heart, deep within a humanity being renewed by the Spirit, binding together a community living under God with joy and thanksgiving, despite the decaying and destructive environment in which they still exist. The Church is the anticipation of the new creation. Paul is struggling to outline the paradoxical double existence of the believer. He has seen the desperate prayers and joyful confidence of the Psalmist through the spectacles of his apocalyptic perspective, and identified with them.

Now the Psalms speak a great deal of dwelling in the house of the Lord, sometimes describing it, with respect for the wilderness tabernacle, as a tent (e.g. Ps. 60.5). Jewish writers, and not just the Platonically-inclined Philo, spoke of the earthly temple as a copy of the true temple in heaven not made with hands (*acheiropoiēton*). The one place in the New Testament when this word is found, apart from 2 Cor. 5.1, is Mark 14.58: 'I will destroy this temple made with hands and in three days I will build another not made with hands.' Later this dominical saying (ascribed to false witnesses in Mark, but attributed to Jesus in John) would be interpreted as a reference to the resurrection of Jesus (John 2.21). Paul has just associated believers with Jesus' resurrection (4.14); he certainly thought of the Christian's body as the temple of the Holy Spirit (1 Cor. 6.19). Perhaps various notions of this sort have been floating around in Paul's mind, have cross-fertilized each other, and come to fruition in the opening sentence of 2 Cor. 5. Already in this life, Paul suggests, the Christian's body is, as it were, a temporary dwelling of the Spirit, and at the resurrection it will have a solid building erected around it, fit for eternity. Switching his metaphor in 5.2–4, Paul speaks of putting on additional clothing, of the mortal being consumed by life.

All this suggests that Paul's ideas are not developed as polemic against some hypothetical Gnostics; nor is he making the same point as in 1 Cor. 15. Rather he is affirming the eschatological character of the transformation already begun, and weaving a new set of images out of traditional material. Precisely when this will be accomplished (at death or at the parousia), is not his explicit interest here. As long as one is in the temporary dwelling, the struggle, the groaning, the longing goes on. Faith and trust alone are the basis of confidence; for heavenly realities are invisible, and one is dwelling apart from the Lord. Paul acknowledges he would rather leave the body and be in the Lord's presence. Perhaps as a result of his brush with death (1.8), he now envisages the possibility that he will not survive until the parousia, and this will happen at his death. There is in fact no fundamental contradiction between this idea and the apocalyptic vision of 1 Cor. 15: for in the apocalypses we find portrayed a heavenly paradise already existing, alongside visions of a future kingdom to be established on earth at the end of time.[33] But Paul is not explicit about this here. The only thing he really cares about is to give satisfaction to his Lord, whatever the state in which he is living. Ultimately all will be brought to light, and whatever the Corinthians think of Paul, the necessity of facing Christ's judgement seat must determine his behaviour as the minister of the new covenant.

So in this passage, Paul acknowledges the consequences of his refusal to act *kata sarka*, and his determination to focus solely upon proper *doxa* – the glory God gives, and the glory due to God. The consequences are trials and tribulations, misunderstanding, persecution and hardship. His mission is not an obvious triumph. Yet in another sense the weakness and suffering through which Paul communicates life, are themselves a testimony to the fact that his mission is entirely grounded not in his own strength or qualifications, but in God's commissioning and the all-sufficiency of God's power. It is the eschatological promise already partially experienced through the Spirit, anticipated in the resurrection of Christ, which puts the whole thing in proper perspective. Faith in God is fundamental, as it was for the Psalmist. Nothing matters beside the fulfilment of God's will, and ultimately all will be made clear. Whatever the Corinthians think of Paul, he can do no other than obey God. This is what he goes on to speak of in the following verses, hoping that

the Corinthians will be persuaded that this gives ground for
pride in him, rather than criticism, doubt or rejection.

7 THE TEXT AND THE INTERPRETER

The exposition of part of the text involves some understanding
of the whole, and of the role that the part plays in the overall
argument. We have been particularly concerned to make this
plain in the specimen of exposition we have offered, eschewing
questions which might seem to distract us from the main line of
argument. For some this interrelationship between whole and
part so that you cannot understand one without understanding
the other, makes interpretation as circular as that other notorious circle – the problem that an interpreter can only read a text
in the light of his or her own presuppositions. We hope that by
concentrating on the practicalities of discerning meaning in a
particular text, we have illustrated the fact that neither circle is
impenetrable. By the disciplined acquisition of relevant skills
and information, objectively significant advances can be made in
determining the meaning of a text. By constantly relating
specific points to context, and testing the perception of the
whole against specific details, real progress can be made. In fact,
responsible exegesis creates a 'spiral' of understanding. One
need not be trapped in a circle.

Nevertheless, the interpretative process can never be entirely
objective. Indeed, total objectivity with no personal involvement would surely deprive the whole enterprise of any real
value. However objective the research, the researcher needs to
be inspired by a passionate need to discover the truth, and by an
appreciation of the beauty of new discoveries. That implies
personal commitment to the enterprise, and is true of any
genuine scientist. The truth about the meaning of a text has
objectivity, but the interpreter should not be dispassionate
about it. The disengaged interpreter presumably couldn't care
less, and such a person is unlikely to contribute much to understanding its meaning. But it cannot be simply the subjective
response of an individual either. Not only must the interpretation be constrained by the objective realities of the text, but
the individual's understanding has itself been formed by the

public language of the cultural community to which the person belongs, and is being exposed to contact with another such language community. The subtle interaction of the human subject, formed by the cultural reality of language and attending to the world external to the self, represented in this case by the text, is explored further in Chapter 5.

If interpretation is to have integrity, it must attend to these complexities, and be critically aware of presuppositions inherent in the interpreter as well as in the text. The interpreter with dogmatic interests invested in the outcome, is likely to distort the meaning to suit personal or community interests. The interpreter must care about honesty and integrity, and that means adopting some measure of objectivity, being prepared to submit vested interests to the bar of discussion and evidence. It is true that a sympathetic interpreter often has a deeper appreciation of some aspects of the text – even more one who shares, at least to some degree, the author's outlook or faith. But a responsible interpreter who does not agree with what the text says, should have as much to contribute as the one who does. Each will see different aspects of the text because they approach it from different standpoints, and their profoundly different value-judgements will be illuminating.

So will be the different reactions of people who come from difference cultures, and begin with different assumptions. African interpreters can help Westerners to appreciate some things which we no longer share with biblical culture whereas they do. But the scholar with specialist expertise is essential, as we have repeatedly seen in this chapter. Good interpretation involves debate, and also sensitivity. Interpreters are privileged in different ways because they come to the task prepared in different ways. This does not mean that relativity rules, but that subjectivity, objectivity and community have to be kept in balance, that we must be prepared to admit that there is no definitive interpretation, and meaning must be sought through ongoing discussion, as well as disciplined study. Interpreters need the humility to be 'subjected' to the text, and to listen to one another.

Interpreters also need to be aware of themselves. Perhaps this interpreter should confess to having had a high degree of personal involvement in the particular exercise of studying

2 Corinthians. This was not planned or foreseen, but it so happens that just as Paul 'lived in his Bible', so this interpreter has 'lived with Paul' during a period of unusual sensitivity to the experience of vocation. Awareness of the insidious spiritual dangers of the desire for personal fulfilment, of the need to and difficulty of sorting out motives, of the ambiguity of a self-recommendation which is and yet is not a recommendation of self, has been accompanied by the excitement and terror of stimulating response through preaching and the pain of causing offence. Inevitably there has been a degree of self-identification with Paul.

Living through this has produced a sense of being caught in a web of human weaknesses, pride, anxiety and reluctance on the one hand, and on the other hand being upheld by the riches of God's mercy and providence, and empowered by the gift of the Spirit; this has been a source of insight into the tension between living *kata sarka* and *kata pneuma*. The experience of human suffering and awareness of the world's deep-seated evils and injustices, has stimulated a respect for Paul's thoroughly realistic grasp of the 'between-times', the present evil age evident in the corruption of church and society, in the corporate sin in which we are all unintentionally implicated, shot through with rays of God's glory, germs of the new creation, gifts of sheer grace. They are there if only we have the eyes to see, and even if we reject the apocalyptic world-view, the tension of the 'now' and the 'not yet' can surely be felt in our Christian existence.

The process of 'correlation' that has contributed to the interpretative exercise has been two-way. It is not just that the interpreter's perceptions and experiences have influenced the interpretation of Paul, but also that Paul has moulded the interpreter's perceptions. Perceiving a meaning in the text has made possible new insight into the reality being lived. This means that in spite of this confession, there is much more than subjective response going on. Of course there is a large subjective element. Of course the interpreter's interests have affected the perception of what is significant. But the examples in this chapter should have made it quite clear that responsible interpretation always and unavoidably involves a large amount of objective handling of data.

Personal insight and judgement must be informed and critically tested against the insight and judgement of other informed interpretation. Given this dimension, progress in understanding is a real experience. Meaning is in principle determinable, even if in practice we have to live with large areas of uncertainty, and even if we refuse to restrict it to authorial intention. Debates about meaning are not always settlable, but they are debates about objective realities. There is a difference between eisegesis and exegesis, and the more informed we are, the more it is possible to sense where the line is to be drawn.

NOTES

1   e.g. J. G. Davies, 'Subjectivity and Objectivity in Biblical Exegesis', *BJRL* 66 (1983), 44–53, following Ricoeur. See further Chapter 5.

2   J. Dupont, 'Le Chrétien, miroir de la grace divine, d'après 2 Cor. 3.18', *Revue Biblique* 56 (1949), 392–411.

3   Commentaries by Barrett, Bultmann, Furnish.

4   Furnish.

5   A. T. Hanson, 'The Midrash in II Corinthians: a reconsideration', cit. sup.

6   J. A. Fitzmyer, 'Glory reflected on the face of Christ (2 Cor. 3.7—4.6) and a Palestinian Jewish motif', *Theological Studies* 42 (1981), 630-44.

7   *TDNT*; V. C. van Unnik, 'The Christian's Freedom of Speech in the New Testament', *BJRL* 44 (1962), 466–88; '"With unveiled face", an exegesis of 2 Corinthians iii.12–18', *Novum Testamentum* 6 (1963), 153–69; and 'The Semitic Background of *parrhēsia* in the New Testament' in *Sparsa Collecta*, Novum Testamentum Supplements 30 (Leiden 1980); S. B. Marrow, 'Parrhēsia and the New Testament', *Catholic Biblical Quarterly* 44 (1982), 431–46.

8   Bultmann; Marrow, art. cit.

9   Marrow, art. cit.

10 Loc. cit.

11 S. C. Mott, 'Reciprocity in Hellenistic Benevolence', in Hawthorne, ed., *Current Issues in Biblical and Patristic Interpretation*, Tenney Festschrift (Grand Rapids 1975).

12 Gordon Fee, ΧΑΡΙΣ in II Corinthians 1.15: Apostolic Parousia and Paul–Corinth Chronology', *NTS* 24 (1978), 533–8.

13 H. D. Betz, *Der Apostel Paulus und die sokratische Tradition* (Tübingen 1972).

14 F. M. Young, 'Note on 2 Cor. 1.17b', *JTS* NS 37 (1986), 404–15.

15 Schlatter; see list of commentaries on p. 277.

16 M. E. Thrall, '2 Cor. 1.2: *ΑΓΙΟΤΗΤΙ* or *ΑΠΛΟΤΗΤΙ*?' in J. K. Elliott, ed., *Studies in New Testament language and text*, Novum Testamentum Supplements 44 (Leiden 1976).

17 See commentaries, and the articles cited in Chapter 3, note 5.

18 Hooker, art. cit.

19 Hickling, art. cit.

20 See the articles cited in Chapter 3, note 4.

21 M. E. Thrall, 'Super-apostles, servants of Christ, and servants of Satan', *JSNT* 6 (1980), 42–57.

22 E. H. Pagels, *The Gnostic Paul: Gnostic Exegesis of the Pauline Letters* (Philadelphia 1975).

23 G. N. Stanton, 'Presuppositions in New Testament Criticism', in I. H. Marshall, ed., *New Testament Interpretation* (Exeter 1977).

24 M. E. Thrall, 'Christ crucified or Second Adam', in Lindars and Smalley, ed., *Christ and Spirit in the New Testament*, Moule Festschrift (Cambridge 1973).

25 See e.g. W. Schmithals, *Gnosticism in Corinth*, ET (Nashville, Tennessee, 1971); D. Georgi, *Die Gegner des Paulus im 2 Korintherbrief* (1964); J. J. Gunther, *St. Paul's Opponents and their background*, Novum Testamentum Supplements 35 (1973); and many articles, some cited elsewhere.

26 Schmithals, op. cit.

27 F. Gerald Downing, 'Ears to hear', in A. E. Harvey, ed., *Alternative Approaches to New Testament Study* (London 1986).

28 R. McL. Wilson, *Gnosis and the New Testament* (Oxford 1968); and many other publications.

29 London 1980.

30 R. A. Horsley, 'Gnosis in Corinth: I Corinthians 8.1–6', *NTS* 27 (1980), 32–51.

31 Pagels, op. cit.; also B. Pearson, *The PNEUMATIKOS–PSYCHIKOS Terminology in I Corinthians* (Missoula 1973).

32 R. P. Spittler, 'The limits of ecstasy', in Hawthorne, ed., *Current Issues in Biblical and Patristic Interpretation*, Tenney Festschrift (Grand Rapids 1975).

33 A. T. Lincoln, *Paradise Now and Not Yet*, *SNTS* monograph series 43 (Cambridge 1981).

5

Hermeneutics and 2 Corinthians

2 Corinthians is a fascinating focus for hermeneutics, the art and theory of interpretation. Hermeneutics both reflects on what is involved in interpreting a text and also tries to interpret it. In previous chapters we have been doing this usually by starting from the text or parts of the text. In this chapter we will start each section with a question rooted in hermeneutical theory. Often that theory seems remote from actual texts, so we will try to bring it into dialogue with 2 Corinthians.

The main aim in doing this is to help in re-reading 2 Corinthians today. That simple aim embraces a host of complex and disputed issues of far wider relevance than just this letter. We have already opened up some of these: the nature of translation, key issues in the determination of meaning and reference, and the importance of genre. Future chapters will deal with the significance of metaphor, the contribution of social description and analysis, and the role of the tradition of interpretation. This is the sort of thing that hermeneutics needs to do, coming at the text from various angles and at different levels, taking it whole and taking it in short sections. It is a task of aiding understanding by showing connections and amplifying resonances, allowing diverse fields of meaning and methods of analysis to interact with each other.

The outcome is neither a vindication of one method nor the production of an authoritative overview of the text. Yet, for all this anti-totalitarianism, we are not wanting to offer fragmentary and disconnected insights. The aim, as stated above, is to help the re-reading of the letter. That is arrived at through many detours, both practical and theoretical, in the course of which it is hoped that the understanding which is gathered can finally serve the event of re-reading. Reading is somewhat like the performance of a piece of music, in which a vast variety of skills, practice, tradition and interpretation are focused, but which still needs to be a unity, an event, over and above the sum of its components. The most perceptive musicological analysis, the best teachers and instruments, and years of patient learning and practice still need to be taken up into the living event of performance. That will never be definitively final, but it must not be prevented from 'coming together' by the pluralism of interpretations.

So we are trying to help the reader's 'performance' of 2 Corinthians. We do it partly by putting forward strong positions which are bound to be controversial but which may stimulate the sort of debate in which the text can live more fully. We hope that each reader will risk re-reading the letter as a whole in the light of our translation and essays, and if the general level of performance is improved even a little by our efforts that will be sufficient. There may be all sorts of other results as well, and the content of 2 Corinthians may inspire other types of performance – reading is not the goal of living! But 2 Corinthians is a text which challenges one's way of living, so that issue is built into the task of more adequate reading.

Finally, the event of reading should not be isolated at the end of a process. The better one's performance the more likely it is that fresh questions will have been raised. One's new reading is drawn on into further interpretation and living. One becomes part of the history of the effects of this text being worked out in new periods and situations (Gadamer's *Wirkungsgeschichte*).

1 HOW IS HERMENEUTICAL THEORY RELEVANT TO 2 CORINTHIANS?

The theory of hermeneutics reflects on the process and implications of interpretation and so provides a set (or rather various sets, as the field is full of competing theories) of questions, concepts and possibilities which may inform the practice of interpretation. The theory is especially helpful to us in making sure that important perspectives are not ignored and that rules grounded in wide experience and reflection are at least given a chance to be tested in relation to 2 Corinthians. The first draft of this chapter was written some years ago after our initial joint exploration of the text. So the other chapters have incorporated as far as possible many of the ideas given here, as we will point out.

The obvious danger with theory is that it will be too far abstracted from any actual text needing to be understood. We hope our focus on 2 Corinthians avoids that. But there is an opposite danger too, that theory is ignored in favour of practice. We do not offer here a complete theory, but we hope that an interpretation informed by some of the theoreticians of hermeneutics will prove richer than if they had not been consulted. Going through some of the often extremely abstruse writings on the subject is an operation that itself entails something usually recommended by the theory: it is a detour from the direct handling of the text of 2 Corinthians in order to enlarge one's horizon, make new connections and see the text in a new perspective. The relation between the theory and the text can never be systematic, owing to the text's particularity (and the more interesting the text the more this tends to be true), but in the course of climbing dizzy theoretical heights and wandering in the dark forests and caves that 'strategies of suspicion' lead into, certain hermeneutical muscles and perceptions may be trained that help in exploring 2 Corinthians. The theory itself may also be illuminated by being focused on one example, for 'examples are the final food of thought'.[1]

Our use of theoreticians such as Gadamer and Ricoeur does not entail agreement with all their theories and will not satisfy their close followers. We try to use them in a low-level way, finding many of their concepts helpful in dealing with this letter, but the implications of their complete positions for theology would probably lead to rather different conclusions from ours in, for example, Chapter 9.

2 OF WHAT SIGNIFICANCE IS IT THAT 2 CORINTHIANS IS CONSTITUTED BY LANGUAGE?

One of the most interesting features of hermeneutics is that it undercuts the split between theory and practice. Speaking and writing are eminently practical activities, through which most of the world's business is transacted and lives shaped. They are actions and events, sometimes with far-reaching effects over centuries. Reflection on them is itself inevitably expressed in more speaking and writing. So hermeneutics, handling language through language, is a very practical form of philosophy, affecting the reality through which our thought, communication and action are formed.

There has been an explosion in the study and philosophy of language in this century. Some has been mainly analytic and empirical in its approach,[2] some has been more existential,[3] and there have been many radical and extreme positions. It has come as a novel and often disturbing experience to realize how closely our identity, our possibilities and our very awareness and contact with reality are bound up with language. In hermeneutical theory the constitutive importance of language for our humanity has frequently been affirmed. There is no 'innocent' perception of self or world. Our experience comes through the categories, concepts, symbols and whole worlds of meaning which we have internalized. These in turn are inseparable from our culture, our behaviour, our values, hopes and fears. And all of this is the product of a long history still in process. We never start from scratch, and language is the most intimate form of our involvement with history and society – even to think about it we need to use it.

Such a view[4] rejects any crude notion of language as merely a means of expressing independent entities called thoughts, feelings or perceptions. Language is not just a convenient labelling of the 'real' world. Rather it is itself a unique, pervasive constituent of our reality, and is dynamic and even creative as it mediates our relationships with each other, the world and ourselves. How far does our interpretation of 2 Corinthians reflect this?

The answer is: very far indeed. This view supports close attention to the Greek text, detailed concern about grammar, syntax, context, nuances of meaning, and rhetoric, and insistence on putting all this in a historical perspective which includes not only the time of the letter's origin but also ourselves and the intervening period. By following through the metaphors of law court and economy we have discovered essential features of the letter and further illustrated the nature of language (see Chapters 2 and 6). Paul too is in no doubt about the importance of language: his proclamation is an event of decisive importance, the gift of bold, confident speech is crucial to his Christian experience, and he fills his language with the resonances of Scripture and of Corinthian culture, while also innovating in words, phrases and metaphors.

But our interpretation has also implicitly criticized extreme positions on the significance of language. The main factors to be taken into account are language itself, the user of language and the reference of the language. However intimately related these are, it is unwise not to distinguish them. In the history of thought there have been attempts to use each of them to swallow up the other two. The classic mode was to have a theory of 'reality' (the reference of language) as an all-embracing ontology or metaphysics. In more recent centuries there have been some philosophies which saw everything in terms of the human subject. In our century both those traditions persist and have been joined by theories that conceive both self and world in terms of language. None of these totalitarianisms seems convincing, and certainly in the practice of interpretation we have found it wise to differentiate language, self and world.

The result is that we try to do justice to the linguistic nature of the text and our understanding of it; but we also investigate the people involved in this communication: Paul, the Corinthians, the Church and others down the centuries, and ourselves; and we explore the reference of the text in various directions, including its historical context and God.

3 WHAT IS THE IMPORTANCE OF THE FACT THAT 2 CORINTHIANS IS A WRITTEN TEXT?

This may seem a strange question, but there has been a lot of reflection on the change that is brought about by language being committed to writing. 'Hermeneutics begins where dialogue ends', says Paul Ricoeur,[5] and he and others have stressed the importance of the difference between speaking and writing. It can be said that Paul's letters are 'a substitute for his presence',[6] but what is the particular nature of this substitute?

Obviously one key difference between Paul's presence and his letters is that Paul is not there to explain what he means, answer questions and objections, or respond to new developments. He is at a distance. That has disadvantages, and it is clear that Paul gives precedence to the oral word.[7] But it also has advantages, as Paul was well aware (cf. 1.23–4; 7.8–11; 10.1–2; 13.2), because there are situations that are better handled from a distance.

This distancing has even more important implications. Writing fixes language so that it survives, and so can cover temporal as well as spatial distance. Paul's absence then from Corinth enables his presence to us now through his letters. This fixation in a relationship of distance therefore somewhat frees the meaning from its original situation. The text gains a certain autonomy: Paul is no longer there to interpret it, so it is freed from his intentions and opened up to many interpretations. It reaches places other than Corinth and may well be fruitful in ways undreamt of by Paul and the Corinthians. It can also be placed in the canon of Christian writings with consequences discussed in Chapter 8. It can be misunderstood and misused. Such are the dangers of writing. It is an action whose consequences can go far beyond the intentions of the agent. But all this points to the role of interpretation, especially of an 'occasional' writing such as 2 Corinthians, in attempting to make the distancing productive. One opinion in Corinth was that Paul was more powerful in his letters than in person (10.10), and in church history it is arguable that he has been more powerful in other ages than in his own.

Allowing the separation from Paul and his intentions and situation to become productive is the other side of a hermeneutical task which also has to take account of the difficulties posed by the distance. These include many matters, from deciphering manuscripts in which there are no word divisions, punctuation or paragraphing, to translation, determining the proper function of Paul's intention and the other issues dealt with in other chapters. The tension between these two sides can be resolved or maintained in different ways, and the whole of this book represents our proposal.

4 WHAT IS THE IMPORTANCE OF THE GENRE OF 2 CORINTHIANS?

It was through discussing a paper on the theory of hermeneutics in a seminar on 2 Corinthians, that we first pressed the question of its genre and began to move towards the position in Chapter 2. Genre in its widest meaning embraces all the conventional forms in which language may be shaped, from prose and poetry through all their subdivisions (history, fiction, love letters, scientific treatises, epic poems, sonnets, haiku, etc.) down to commands and questions. Genre indicates something of how a piece of writing or speech is to be taken as a whole. It makes a great difference to the way a piece is understood whether its genre is rightly grasped. E. D. Hirsch even claims that 'valid interpretation is always governed by a valid inference about genre',[8] and suggests that disagreement over genre is the main source of conflict among qualified interpreters. As we try to understand the parts of a discourse in sequence, it is vital what conception we have of the whole. Our way of construing all the details is influenced by our guess about its genre.

Some sharp conflicts in biblical interpretation give support to Hirsch's claim. Are the stories in Genesis 1—2 history, science, myth, saga, liturgy, theology? Where does prophecy fit into the forms of public discourse in Israel? How does it affect its theological meaning if a book or part of a book is decided to be wisdom or law or hymn or apocalyptic? In the New Testament field there has been fierce debate over the Gospels in relation to the genres of history, biography, myth, testimony, kerygma, ethical teaching and others. Paul's writings have generally been accepted as letters, but that is a very wide category, since many types of discourse can be conveyed in epistolary form.

Our conclusions about 2 Corinthians have already been given

in Chapter 2. We see it as a letter primarily akin to the common ancient genre of the written legal defence. Paul modifies this greatly to his own ends, and to suit the 'family' context, but the main lines of the genre are there and help to grasp the unity and meaning of the letter.

This is the genre in which 2 Corinthians seems to have been written and read by its first recipients. Yet in the continuing existence of a text the genre of reading need not be the same as the genre of writing. Gibbon's *Decline and Fall of the Roman Empire* was first written and read as the most authoritative history of the period; nowadays it tends to be read as a major work of literature filled with historical wisdom, but not as a rigorous academic treatment. While we must recognize the original genre of 2 Corinthians, we must also do justice to the fact that down the centuries it has functioned as part of the genre of canonical Scripture, where, like a quotation in a new context, it has been read in new ways. More recently it has been read as a historical document, figuring as part of the historical reconstruction of early Christianity. It can also be read as theology, and then we meet the many problems of the inter-relation of genres; it is by no means clear, for example, what status in theology a letter should have in relation to a narrative or a hymn or a credal statement.

To all of these 'reading genres', we argue, the 'writing genre' should be important, not as a constriction, as if we could be confined to how the Corinthians might have read it, but as a constraint on arbitrary interpretation and misconstrual. This is part of the wider issues of the hermeneutical gap and subjectivity treated below, and of the relation of interpretation to the author's intention, to which we now turn.

5 HOW RELEVANT TO THE MEANING OF 2 CORINTHIANS IS PAUL'S OWN INTENTION?

We have argued in Chapter 4 for the relevance of Paul's intention to the interpretation of 2 Corinthians. One attack on that line is that it is a form of 'psychologism': that is, it postulates some non-linguistic psychological reality in Paul called an intention, which may or may not have been successfully put into words. That sort of occult entity separate from language is not entailed by our position. By intention we mean the probable original sense of the words and constructions of 2 Corinthians when understood in relation to whatever else we know of Paul, his language and his environment. Both the overall thrust and the sense of each section and sentence are best approached first of all under the unifying hypothesis that Paul did mean something and that it is worth trying to establish this. On this view, Paul's intended meaning need not all have been conscious. For example, we do not need to know how far he intended consciously to make use of the genre of the legal defence or of economic metaphors so long as they can be understood as related to an intention about which he is explicit.

Another, often related, attack on the notion of author's intention is based on the autonomy of the text. This holds that the author's intention is irrelevant to the interpretation of his work: the meaning is to be found only in the text, which, once launched, leads a life of its own independent of its author's purposes. This is often associated with literary criticism,[9] and that is significant, because literary texts are likely to be more complete in themselves than are, for example, histories, news articles, washing machine instructions or letters. The 'immanence of meaning' will vary with various types of text. We have already argued for some independence of the author's intention in the distancing that happens in writing and the later career of the text. But, as Chapter 4 holds, the intention of Paul still is a vital ingredient in interpretation. No general theory can be allowed to rule out what seems to be appropriate to this particular text. 2 Corinthians is a functional link in a specific chain of communication between Paul and the Corinthians, and the intention of Paul is a key element in this. In fact, Paul's intention has several dimensions. The meaning of the language and form of the text is part of his self-defence, which is itself inseparable from his aims of building up the church and bringing glory to God.

In modern biblical interpretation and theology the intentions of biblical authors have often been used polemically. Scholarship often aimed to get behind traditional spiritual or doctrinal uses of Scripture and discover the original meaning, variously identified as the history behind the text, the consciousness expressed in it or the author's intention. What was discovered was often seen to undermine traditional positions. In response the Churches often rejected or attacked biblical criticism. We are trying to get beyond that now arid debate. Our proposal about Paul's intention is that it is right both to try to determine it and to go beyond it. But going beyond it is only justifiable on condition that that original intention is always present in informing and confronting the further meaning that emerges. Any new interpretation must embrace this dialogue, trying to listen to Paul's intended meaning as far as possible, but not ruling out fresh meaning and truth which Paul certainly could not have intended. In short, the aim is only to go beyond Paul's meaning by going through it; or, better, by taking it along as a constant partner to be questioned, listened to and criticized. The greatest challenge in this is yet to come in the final chapter: Paul's intention was centred on God, and the truth of God cannot be bracketed out of the interpretation of his writing.

6 HOW IMPORTANT FOR ITS INTERPRETATION IS THE CONTEXT OF 2 CORINTHIANS?

We have tried to show in practice in other chapters the many ways in which the context of 2 Corinthians is relevant to understanding it. Two main uses of 'context' appear there: within 2 Corinthians the context of any word, verse or section of the letter is primarily the rest of the letter; and beyond that is the wider use of context to refer to the connection of this letter with the rest of Paul's letters and the whole first-century environment, language and history.

Hermeneutical theory goes further than this and points out that every context has its own wider context, and so the process of contextualizing is infinite. Within this vast horizon the historical context of the text through successive generations leads to what is often called the problem of the 'hermeneutical gap' between different periods, which we discuss in the next section. Another dimension of this is that we ourselves are part of the context of the text, so that raises the question of the subjectivity of interpretation, discussed in section 8 below. We deal there with one aspect of the 'hermeneutical circle', according to which we, the interpreters, inevitably bring to the text our own ideas and presuppositions, which are therefore in circular fashion reinforced by what we read. A more embracing concept of the hermeneutical circle is of the relation between part and whole. How can one understand the part without its whole context, and how can one understand the context without understanding its parts? This is the most adequate brief statement of the key question of hermeneutics, since the 'whole' includes other periods and the interpreter as well as the immediate context of the text at its time of writing.

It is that latter narrower context that we focus on in this section. In taking this as seriously as we do in other chapters we are finding our way between two extremes, not because of a prejudice that that is always where the truth is to be found, but because it is what seems most appropriate to 2 Corinthians. The first is what Ricoeur calls 'the ideology of the absolute text'. This stresses the autonomy of the text in a way already rejected in the previous section, and sees its intrinsic meaning distorted or misconstrued by contextualizing it. We are sympathetic to the intense concentration on the internal structure and relations of the text that this encourages. But, while its more extreme forms may be suited to certain literary texts, the content of 2 Corinthians itself requires a wide-ranging contextual investigation in order to be more fully understood.

The other extreme is to dissolve the text into its context by explaining it completely in those terms. This would make 2 Corinthians merely a product of its times and so conditioned by them that as a distinctive entity it witnesses only to a temporary confluence of causes and interactions. History, sociology, psychology, economics and other disciplines could all contribute to this. We are sympathetic to the concern to do justice to the historical particularity and 'situatedness' of 2 Corinthians, but also affirm its ability to transcend its context. It is a whole in itself, carrying a new meaning which must not be flattened into the sum of its origins and dimensions. Re-reading it is an event that is unique and could never be replaced by general accounts which claim to include its truth. It can speak over against its period (cf. Chapters 6, 7, 8 below) and over against other periods, and it resists reductionist explanations. Its situatedness is not in competition with this integrity. Context and content interact with each other and the result is not a circle but a hermeneutical spiral. Our studies try to show how the deeper we explore its historical particularity the more we find its potential meaning liberated beyond that time and place. Ultimately this is linked to the theological understanding of incarnation and the Holy Spirit in which specific historical events and expressions continue to have relevance and power. But this truth itself, in true incarnational fashion, is inseparable from the problems of periods, prejudices and appropriate interpretation with which hermeneutics (as well as a great deal of ordinary life) is concerned.

7 CAN THE 'HERMENEUTICAL GAP' BETWEEN OURSELVES AND 2 CORINTHIANS BE OVERCOME?

The distance between ourselves and 2 Corinthians is partly a matter of different periods, cultures, languages and presuppositions. It can easily be exaggerated, and a reasonably open modern reader could gather a great deal from a good translation of the letter. Paul is talking about many things that have analogies in the experience of most people: misunderstanding and conflict with those to whom one is deeply attached; attempts at self-justification; suffering, forgiveness, hope, fear, death; collecting money for a good cause; religious belief and experience. In all this he takes what one might call a 'middle distance' perspective on life,[10] neither dwelling too much on private internal states or experiences, nor on grand overarching concepts and viewpoints. This perspective is the most common one in day-to-day public existence from one generation to the next, and so is well suited to conveying much of its meaning into different cultures and centuries. It is the same perspective that the Gospels, especially the first three, take on the life of Jesus. Paul's letters are in many ways the application of this typical Christian perspective to the life of his churches. People and events in interaction in local circumstances are what this perspective mainly focuses on. This produces writings that are both irreducibly particular in their meaning and also extremely durable and capable of transcending barriers that block more private, more privileged or more abstract meanings.

Yet there is also a strangeness about 2 Corinthians, and dozens of questions that cannot be given a commonsense answer because our commonsense does differ from Paul's. We have tackled many of these, from the biblical and cultural resonances of his language to the sociological and economic conditions (see below Chapters 6 and 7). Even when we are clear about the translation of words such as 'God' or 'church' or 'apostle' how do we know that we are not meaning something very different from Paul? The text resists easy domestication in our understanding, and at times the strangeness intensifies into painful alienation. One task of hermeneutics is to see how this alienation (or, as it was called above, distancing) can be productive.

A helpful concept here is Gadamer's 'fusion of horizons'.[11] In this metaphorical use 'horizon' means the range of our understanding, intentions and questions. This is not fixed but moves with us and invites us to advance further, and is the context within which we understand things in their relationships and relative importance. Whatever we are dealing with, we try to make sense of it within our horizon. This may lead to our horizon being challenged, and the result may be a transformation of our worldview.

2 Corinthians also has its horizon. The aim of understanding is not so much to enter into that horizon (which would ignore the fact that we can never separate ourselves from our own), as to unite the two horizons in such a way that justice is done to the text's integrity and otherness while it is also allowed to question and expand our understanding. It attempts a fusion without confusion, and it produces something new. Every reading takes up the past into a new present, where 'old and new continually grow together to make something of living value'.[12] Hermeneutics tries to improve the quality of this reading.

Gadamer's approach has many strengths. It rejects any notion of neutrality in interpretation. Our very questions to the text are formed within our horizon of expectations and prejudices (prejudice is a term Gadamer tries to rehabilitate by going back to its original meaning of pre-judgement with prior understanding, which must be the basis of any future understanding even if it is transformed in the process), and we attain a proper openness not by ignoring these but by bringing them into play as consciously and critically as possible. There is a discipline of reflecting on ourselves which must go along with reflection on the text because we never start with an empty head able simply to see and assess what is there. This subjective pole of interpretation will be discussed further in the next section.

Gadamer's 'fusion of horizons' also insists on the text's claim to truth being taken seriously. Interpretation which tries to divorce meaning from truth is criticized, and treating the text historically is never allowed to mean analysing and explaining it in such a way that the question 'Is this true' is ignored. This too we discuss below.

Above all, however, the advantage of the concept in discussing the hermeneutical gap is its link with the idea of the 'history of the effects of the text' (*Wirkungsgeschichte*, cf. above p. 140). There is in fact no gap. The past is not a closed circle with a periphery, and neither is the present. They are both part of a continuous history mediated by language. This is the tradition, a community of interaction and interpretation down the centuries. Even a judgement that there has been a major discontinuity in the text's interpretation can only be made from within this community and taking account of it. Our horizon today has been formed partly by 2 Corinthians and the tradition in which it has participated. Our interest or lack of interest, our questions and their presuppositions, and our whole modern situation are partly the result of positive and negative response to that tradition. 'Gap' is therefore a misleading image, suggesting some neutral buffer zone separating us from the past. The truth is of a much more complex dynamic interrelationship. In this there can be no self-contained past or present. There is rather a continuing responsible participation in the history of the text's effects as we try to fuse our horizons without confusing them.

8 HOW SUBJECTIVE IS OUR INTERPRETATION OF 2 CORINTHIANS?

All interpreting is done by human subjects, and so is bound to be subjective in that sense. But subjectivity can be of varying quality. The aim in interpretation is not to eliminate subject-ivity, which is impossible, but to become critically aware of it, to train it and to check it out as thoroughly as possible. The objection to 'subjective interpretation' is not that it is subjective but that it is capricious, arbitrary or purely private.

The crude picture sometimes implied by 'objectivity' is of a person in front of an object which can be clearly seen and verified by anyone else who can see. Even in relation to that situation one would want to say a good deal more if 'taking a look' is to be converted into knowledge.[13] But, in relation to a document of the past of which the only visible evidence is marks on a page, the visual image is especially unsuitable. What is understood from those marks will depend on the way the subjectivity of the reader has been shaped through learning or not learning the language as well as through a host of other factors. Meaning is an odd reality, if our criterion for reality is pots and pikestaffs. It has to be internalized, it lives through the medium of lan-guage, and it carries with it a rich history. This means that no one is an isolated 'subject' as regards meaning, no one is 'innocent' or neutral, but each finds him/herself in a world of meaning with no possibility of starting from scratch. So the division between subjectivity and objectivity is undercut by this view of meaning as linguistic, historical and intersubjective.

Why then do we insist on the importance of objectivity in Chapter 4? The issue there (as is explicit at the end of the chapter) is not a contrast with an excluded subjectivity but the insistence that the subjectivity of the interpreter be disciplined in ways appropriate to this text. It is not a matter of rejecting subjectivity but of the need to recognize constraints on the range of acceptable interpretations. These constraints include the disciplines of philology, history, theology and other fields, the need to listen to other interpreters past and present, and the effort to take account of our own biases as far as possible. Even such intersubjectivity is not, of course, infallible, and whole communities and traditions can become distorted or divided, but responsible learning from others is the minimum insurance against arbitrary subjectivism.

Yet talk of constraints and disciplines can seem too grim and methodical. It makes subjectivity seem like a wild, negative force which must be repressed and dominated by more reliable elements. Our view that the best subjectivity for interpreting 2 Corinthians goes through such disciplines by no means rules out creative interpretation which gives scope to imagination and 'plays' with the meaning. For the intensity of life and reality expressed by Paul to be comprehensible we need to have our imaginations opened up. Excursions such as Chapter 6 on 'The Economy of God' are a vital ingredient hard to quantify. Often such suggestive play goes on without being admitted in the interpretations that reach print. Biblical commentators are often so caught in the conventions of a falsely 'scientific' idea of their task that they fail to take the risks needed to help readers appreciate an explosive subject-matter that stretches our imaginative as well as other capacities. Yet for the best scientists, artists and human beings discipline is not a negative concept, but is the servant of a subjectivity liberated for truth and creativity in community.

The word 'responsible' used above points to another ingredient in interpretation, the ethical. It is often presupposed by theories and rarely made explicit enough.[14] There are decisions and value-judgements made all through the process, without which respect for the particular text (and, necessarily, the decision not to respect some texts – there are some horizons with which it is right not to fuse one's own), commitment to the immense labour of understanding, and willingness to allow oneself and one's truth to be changed would never occur. Reading itself is an activity that can be done immorally, and one function of the scholarly community is to try to maintain standards, while also reflecting on what those standards should be.

The ethical dimension in turn underlines another vital fact about interpretation: for all its concern with texts of the past it is an activity in the present oriented to the future. It cannot responsibly ignore this. With 2 Corinthians this is intensified because the content of the letter makes fundamental claims about the future of all of us. If Jesus Christ is risen and we are to be judged by him, if with him a 'new creation' has begun, and if the God who raised him cares about our response to Paul's message and is even involved in our interpretation of it, then the aim of our interpretation will be to participate more fully in the future that the letter opens up. This challenge to our whole conception of what we are part of and how to regard the future brings the question of subjectivity to its sharpest point where no scholarly consensus can help. The interpreter of this theological text must be prepared to face the questions of God and the gospel as they affect his or her own horizon.

9 WHAT IS THE TRUTH OF 2 CORINTHIANS?

Do we find truth? Do we fashion it? Most approaches to truth tend towards either a 'finding', correspondence, discovery concept, or towards a 'fashioning', coherence, inventive and constructive concept.[15] Our task of interpreting 2 Corinthians has used and tried to show the need for both approaches, often in complex interplay. The whole interpretative process clearly has to do with truth – it is not an issue that appears at the end after meaning has been discovered. The truth is not just one thing. It has levels, aspects, subjective and objective poles, a history, a present, and a future; and new questions can elicit new answers. The crude objectivist picture of truth is no more adequate here than it was in understanding how language relates to reality or how human subjectivity is related to understanding. Yet we hold that that objectivism can be rejected without falling into the relativism of which hermeneutics is frequently accused.[16]

Since the whole process of interpretation is in question here, this is the right place to say what we find the best way of describing that process as appropriate to 2 Corinthians. This will be given in the form of theses with some explanation.

(i) The process is most helpfully seen not in a linear way but as dynamic interaction between the key elements of text, original context, reference, history of interpretation, and modern readers and their context and interests. This whole ecology needs to be taken account of, and in fact is a description of what goes on anyway in interpretation: hermeneutics tries to allow it to be the subject of reflection and debate. Within this holistic, historical conception, it is helpful to differentiate aspects, as the next three theses do, but it should always be remembered that these aspects are coinherent – that is, each needs to take account of the other two, and cannot see itself as an independent point of departure for a linear development, or as a foundation on which the others are built.

(ii) Understanding (in the sense of Gadamer's *Verstehen*) is the most adequate term for this dynamic process.

(iii) Explanation guided by various methods can play a vital role in this. Gadamer is too dismissive of method in hermeneutics. He is too fearful of the totalitarian tendencies of methods, which are often tempted to dictate in advance what a text may say, or to dominate it in some more subtle way. Ricoeur[17] corrects this, and we have tried to learn from him in applying various methods to 2 Corinthians.

(iv) Assessment in terms of truth and value is going on through-out.[18]

(v) The conceptions of truth as 'finding' and as 'fashioning' are inadequate to this process of understanding, explanation and assessment: we need to take them up into a more historical and future-oriented concept discussed below.

(vi) That view of truth is needed to do justice to 2 Corinthians, and this need for hermeneutical concepts to be appropriate to particular texts is both the last and the first word in the theory of interpretation. As the first word it of course presupposes some understanding of the particular text, and so we are back with our earlier theses.

We will now outline the concept of truth mentioned in (v) and (vi) above. In relation to the text of 2 Corinthians it means that its reference points are not only behind it in the intention of Paul, or around it in its historical context, or within it in its structured language and message for its recipients, but also ahead of it. This is obvious insofar as it had immediate effects in Corinth. But a more comprehensive idea of 'ahead' points to the way the text opens up a world of meaning ahead of each reader, conveying possible ways of understanding, believing and acting. As it is read through history by people who are unavoidably oriented to the future it interrupts their orientation and challenges it. Its truth comes as an interruption to the continuity of life.[19]

We all understand ourselves, implicitly and partly explicitly, as part of a story with a past, present and future.[20] Reading 2 Corinthians is an event in that story that has the possibility of opening a different future. So the truth of the letter is an event of meaning inviting a response in terms of our whole understanding and way of being. This conception of truth is in line with the content of the letter. Its prime orientation is to God and his future for the world. This is mediated by the gospel and dynamically worked out by the Spirit seen as the realizer of God's future. The main events of its overarching story are creation by God, Israel's history with God, the life, death and resurrection of Jesus Christ understood as the 'Yes' to God's promises and the inauguration of a 'new creation' in the midst of the old, the present time of conflict between old and new, and the future judgement and consummation. In all this the urgent stress is on the future being opened up and the implications of this good news. So any view of the truth of the letter which fails to face its challenge to our most fundamental orientation is inadequate.

Is this really true? Is it not an outmoded mythological framework? Should not the challenge of this text be rejected? We try to face the issue of the framework in our section on appropriation below, and we devote the final chapter to the most important matter of all, God. For now we will conclude by discussing the accusation of relativism.

The awkward point of this criticism is that given our view of history, language, subjectivity and truth it is hard to see how one can have criteria of validity in interpretation. It may be conceivable enough in some philological and historical matters, but in the bigger issues we seem condemned to a vast pluralism of interpretations. We have dealt with this subject from one angle in section 8 on subjectivity. There it was admitted that in a broad sense relativism seems inevitable, since all interpretation is done by historically relative interpreters in specific communities. But we have also argued throughout against any unlimited pluralism. There are constraints on validity in interpretation which we have tried to observe and reflect on. This does not mean that there are universally appropriate objective criteria. That would be again to want a crude objectivism which is especially inappropriate to texts and meaning. Criteria too have their presuppositions, history and values. The attempt to step outside the continuing debate about them and set up a clear objective standard is to have adopted a criterion of truth which can probably be traced to a misunderstanding or misapplication of the method of certain natural sciences.

The most we can do is to make assessments in line with our best efforts at understanding and explanation, trying to be as honest and self-critical as possible. Our unavoidable relativism should (if we are responsible interpreters) be constantly opening up to better understanding, explanation and assessment, but that by no means rules out claims to truth now. Our final chapter is such an affirmation about the theological content of 2 Corinthians. And it is because of that content that a certain sort of relativism is seen to be required for theological as well as hermeneutical reasons. For God and his future for the world relativize every past and present affirmation, and the event of truth among us now is unavoidably incomplete: 'for we walk by faith, not with the vision before our eyes' (5.7).

10 HOW SHOULD THE 'HERMENEUTICS OF SUSPICION' BE APPLIED TO 2 CORINTHIANS?

So far we have mainly considered what is sometimes called the 'hermeneutics of retrieval'. This has a largely positive attitude to tradition, recognizing that, for example, 'long before we understand ourselves through the process of self-examination, we understand ourselves in a self-evident way in the family, society and state in which we live'.[21] Part of our finitude is that we can never attain an independent overview of all this in order to assess it, and even our criticisms and rebellions presuppose it. Hence Gadamer's attempt to rehabilitate the ideas of prejudice (in the sense of pre-judgement which may or may not be subsequently grounded), authority (distinguished from violence and domination) and tradition, and so to establish our inextricable involvement in a history of language and meaning. For Gadamer we belong to a dialogue with the past and our basic attitude is one of respect which yet does not rule out criticism.

Criticism can be given a far more important role in hermeneutics than this. There is another tradition (or anti-tradition) which has been called the 'hermeneutics of suspicion'. The

Enlightenment demand for the reason for everything, its attack on the authority of the past, Descartes' programme of systematic doubt, critical history's sceptical approach to evidence and the reconstruction of the past, and the modern masters of suspicion, Marx, Nietzsche and Freud, all contribute to a devastatingly powerful set of weapons threatening Gadamer's project and ours. A tradition can dominate and oppress the present. It can be an ideology that rationalizes the interests of the powerful in order to support them. We may need not to retrieve it but to be liberated from it.

Ricoeur's discussion of the controversy between Gadamer and Jürgen Habermas (one of the Frankfurt School of 'Critical Theory', leading practitioners of 'suspicion') makes out a convincing case that both approaches are needed and are able to contribute to each other. Yet he concludes that the two cannot be synthesized in one integrated perspective.[22] This is true to our experience with 2 Corinthians. We have clearly found retrieval to be the most appropriate main approach. This is not, we hope, an arbitrary decision, but one that is cumulatively justified through the chapters of this book. There are other texts to which we would find a predominantly suspicious approach justified, though even there the assessment depends on retrieval.

So we find the tradition of Paul worth retrieving, though not uncritically. But there is a crucial twist to this because of the content of 2 Corinthians. Its message is itself one of radical suspicion and liberation. There is a cry of freedom from the tradition of Moses in Chapter 3. The dominating categories of prestige, power and recognition are rejected. Paul himself boasts of his resilience in the face of legal punishments and other pressures to abandon his undermining of the old order. In the church he resists the claims of apostles who probably had on their side the authority of a tradition going back to Jesus' own words.[23] His appeal throughout is to the supreme critical instance, the death and resurrection of Jesus Christ. That is a drastic critique of all tradition and signifies a new freedom and the breaking in of a new and hopeful future. It is a 'dangerous memory', and its content forbids any past-oriented, antiquarian retrieval. Paul has an apocalyptic hope for the future in relation to which the tradition is interpreted.

Therefore any adequate retrieval of this message finds itself challenged by a tradition with explosive possibilities for critique of both other traditions and its own developments. Yet it can of course itself be suspected. The most fundamental form of this is directed at the content of Paul's gospel. What if God is a human projection adequately explained by psychological needs, political and economic usefulness or moral weakness? What if God exists but is nothing like what Paul imagined? What if Jesus did not die or rise, or if the gospel about him basically misunderstood him and his significance? What if the maxim of strength in weakness is an ideology well suited to allow inadequate people like Paul to exercise power? Does not the whole framework depend on an expectation of the end of the world which was manifestly mistaken? Surely Paul's interpretation of the OT is a twisting in comparison with which Jewish exegesis then or now makes more sense? Is not the supreme illusion or delusion of the letter Paul's preposterous identification of his message with God's truth and judgement?

Such questions show both how there can be no synthesis between retrieval and thoroughgoing suspicion, and also how unavoidable in the interests of truth it is to face up to the issues. There is no security against them and part of the continuing history of the text is the way it provokes dialogue about them both between interpreters and within each one. The problem is that one's whole horizon is at stake, so the attempt to answer them involves a complete programme of interpretation and theology, not to mention one's values and way of living. Some of these we do deal with in this book, and in particular Chapter 8 deals with the suspicion of Paul's power and authority. Others are dealt with by us elsewhere.[24] But we must be very wary of 'innocent' suspicion, which refuses to face up to the fact that it is itself by no means neutral. Strategies of doubt and suspicion need themselves to be suspected and to have their assumptions and interests examined. One fundamental issue in this is the demand for self-certainty and human autonomy. For Paul this would be a clear instance of living 'at the human level' (*kata sarka*), whereas living by grace in faith (*kata pneuma*) comes from a security placed in Christ. There is here a transformation of the self through love which makes certain sorts of suspicion as inappropriate as distrust in a good marriage. But not all marriages are good, and in the modern types of doubt in religion the depths of distrust and meaninglessness have to be tackled, without in the process allowing to pass unchallenged the often unspoken assumption that this faithless understanding is somehow more 'realistic' than trust in God. It is certainly more respectable in many circles, but maybe that should make it all the more obliged to face Paul's sustained critique of the world's ways, backed up by his way of life.

Besides the suspicion of the main content affirmed by 2 Corinthians, there is another, related suspicion directed at the communicational process of which the letter has been and is a part. Should we take the rhetoric of 2 Corinthians at face value? What hidden personal or ecclesiastical motives might Paul have had in writing such a letter? How far is Paul determined by gnostic ideas, mystery religions, an apocalyptic world-view, Jewish culture or mystical religious experience? How far can the whole situation be explained in sociological terms? How far have other books in the New Testament and the tradition of Christian interpretation distorted the message of 2 Corinthians? How far is our own perception of the letter conditioned by the various ideologies and theologies in which Paul's writings have been enlisted, and by a host of personal and cultural distortions and corruptions? Following up such questions is inevitably the other side of responsible retrieval of the letter, and we have at least begun to answer them in this and other chapters.

So the short answer to this section's question is: strategies of suspicion are to be applied as a critical part of the overall strategy of retrieving 2 Corinthians and allowing it to inspire constructive theology. This is itself an assessment of the truth and value of 2 Corinthians which can be suspected, but that suspicion we would in turn question as we defend our approach in continuing debate.

11 HOW CAN 2 CORINTHIANS BE APPROPRIATED AND APPLIED BY READERS?

In appropriation the interpretation is focused on the performance of re-reading the text. This is a new event which is not adequately described as entering into the text's original meaning and context. The objectivist, historicist binding of a meaning to one time and place misses the possibility of its going beyond its origin and enabling its world to inform other worlds of meaning, beyond what Ricoeur calls the limited horizon of the author's own existential situation.[25]

The realization of this possibility requires a freedom to let the two worlds play together, experimenting to find and construct the right fusion without confusion. It also demands the self-awareness and self-criticism of the reader, what Ricoeur calls 'the purification of the network of appropriation', in order to let the reader really confront this text rather than just reading into it preconceptions and biases. Ricoeur even speaks of the 'revelation of new modes of being', and of the reader's accompanying letting-go of the self and its narcissism in the face of the new being manifested in the text. The reader is not in control of the text but needs respectfully to be open to something different and new, whose effects cannot with integrity be limited in advance.

Interpretation of the Bible has suffered terribly from the extremes of subjectivism and objectivism. We have proposed a subjectivity which both recognises constraints beloved of the objectivists and also allows itself through these to be transformed and liberated by the content of the text. We have therefore taken account of the strengths of objectivism without accepting its constriction and reification of meaning. That whole approach shows itself naively unaware of the claim to power and of the immense ethical and theological implications involved in its alleged neutrality.

Our aim, then, is a responsible reading, as alert as possible to our own subjectivity and to all the other elements treated in the previous sections, and also open to the content of the text, which cannot be reduced to either Paul's intention or our present appropriation. That involves challenges at many levels and the appropriation and application will of course vary from period to period and situation to situation as the history of the text continues 'in the Spirit'. But that history has an essential factor for which general theories of hermeneutics understandably have little place: the Church as the community continually appropriating and applying this text. It is of the utmost importance for appropriation and application that 2 Corinthians became part of the canon used by the Church, and Chapter 8 needs to be understood as part of the present topic.

One final problem is Paul's alleged 'apocalyptic framework'. Here we need to remember Karl Popper's warning: 'The Myth of the Framework is, in our time, the central bulwark of irrationalism. My counter-thesis is that it simply exaggerates a difficulty into an impossibility.'[26] We have already discussed Paul's apocalypticism in Chapter 4 and shown how critical he is of the prevailing forms of it. The difficulty it poses for modern appropriation was eased by such considerations. It is further qualified by questioning the appropriateness of the term 'framework' for what is all-encompassingly important for Paul: God. The final chapter will show how Paul's understanding of God is not at all inaccessible or irrelevant today.

12 CONCLUSION

We have sketched some ways in which 2 Corinthians and hermeneutical theory might be mutually illuminating. The identification of key issues and the scheme of understanding, explanation and assessment are just one approach to distinguishing aspects of a process in which they should continually coinhere in mutual integration. Matthew Lamb describes the importance of theory in a way which agrees with what we have found in studying 2 Corinthians:

> Theory is not an impoverished abstraction away from that reality. Instead theory as critical is a profound effort to understand processive reality ever more adequately. Theory, then, does not move away from the concrete, only to be returned to it in the form of some sort of practical application. Instead theory is continually moving toward the complexity of the concrete and, in the measure that it is correct in indicating the underlying concrete and contradictory tensions in reality, is capable of guiding the transformation of reality.[27]

Or, put more briefly by the grandfather of hermeneutical theory, Aristotle, it is the search for *phronēsis*, that wisdom which has to do with the contingencies and particularities of life and of texts as part of life.

NOTES

1   John Wisdom, 'A Feature of Wittgenstein's Technique', *Paradox and Discovery* (Blackwell, Oxford, 1965), 102.

2   For a good survey and a contribution to this approach see Simon Blackburn, *Spreading the Word. Groundings in the Philosophy of Language* (Clarendon Press, Oxford, 1984).

3   Martin Heidegger has been the most influential in this line.

4   Perhaps best summed up by H.-G. Gadamer, *Truth and Method* (Sheed and Ward, London, 1975), in the related concepts of 'linguisticality' (*Sprachlichkeit*) and 'historicity' (*Geschichtlichkeit*).

5   *Interpretation Theory: Discourse and the Surplus of Meaning* (Fort Worth 1976), 32.

6   N. A. Dahl, *Studies in Paul* (Augsburg, Minneapolis, 1977), 77.

7   Robert W. Funk, *Parables and Presence, Forms of the New Testament Tradition* (Fortress, Philadelphia, 1982), Ch. 7, analyses the 'apostolic presence' of Paul, the three media of his authority in descending order of importance being his personal presence, his emissaries and his letters.

8   *Validity in Interpretation* (Yale University Press, New Haven, 1967), 113.

9   Notably that of T. S. Eliot and the 'New Critics' such as Monroe Beardsley and W. K. Wimsatt; and also by structuralism. For a critique of this see E. D. Hirsch, op. cit.; and *The Aims of Interpretation* (University of Chicago Press, Chicago and London, 1976). For a critique of Hirsch and a survey of the field of hermeneutics from the standpoint of Gadamer see David Couzens Hoy, *The Critical Circle. Literature, History and Philosophical Hermeneutics* (University of California Press, Berkeley, Los Angeles and London 1982).

10 cf. David Ford, *Barth and God's Story. Biblical Narrative and the Theological Method of Karl Barth in the 'Church Dogmatics'* (Peter Lang, Frankfurt and Berne 1981, 1985), Chapter 4.

11 op. cit., 217, 273ff., 333ff.

12 ibid., 273.

13 cf. Bernard Lonergan's critique of 'naive realism' throughout *Insight. A Study of Human Understanding* (Philosophical Library, New York, 1970); and his integration of his epistemology into theological method, including hermeneutics, in *Method of Theology* (Darton, Longman and Todd, London, 1972).

14 One exception is Werner Jeanrond, *Text und Interpretation als*

Kategorien theologischen Denkens (Siebeck, Tübingen 1986), to whom this chapter is also indebted for much input through discussion in person.

15 For a profound reflection on the significance of these positions in theology and philosophy see Donald MacKinnon, *Explorations in Theology* 5 (SCM, London, 1979), Chapters 10, 11.

16 Hoy, op. cit. (n9 above), gives a sensitive justification of a position that rejects both objectivism and relativism.

17 See especially *The Conflict of Interpretations* (Northwestern University Press, Evanston, 1974), and *Paul Ricoeur, Hermeneutics and the Human Sciences*, ed. John B. Thompson (Cambridge University Press, Cambridge, 1981).

18 Lonergan, *Method in Theology*, op. cit., sees assessment on two levels, judgement and decision, oriented in theology towards what he calls the 'functional specialities' of history and dialectics. We see hermeneutics more widely than he does, but the difference need not be serious: Lonergan's method is by no means linear but recognizes the sort of coinherence that we find. His great value is in his insistence on the elements of judgement and decision in relation to *Verstehen*.

19 See E. Jüngel, 'The Truth of Life. Observations on Truth as the Interruption of the Continuity of Life', *Creation, Christ and Culture*, ed. R. W. A. McKinney (T. & T. Clark, Edinburgh, 1976), Chapter 16.

20 Narrative theology makes a good deal of this, but it is an insight of much broader currency and comes under the general concept of the 'historicity' of human existence.

21 Gadamer, op. cit., 245.

22 See *Paul Ricoeur, Hermeneutics and the Human Sciences*, op. cit., 63–100.

23 See below Chapter 6, p. 182.

24 Daniel W. Hardy and David F. Ford, *Jubilate. Theology in Praise* (DLT, London, 1984); Frances M. Young, *Can These Dry Bones Live?* SCM, London, 1981), and *Face to Face* (Epworth, London, 1985).

25 op. cit., 191.

26 Quoted in Hirsch, *The Aims of Interpretation*, op. cit., 170. Hirsch quotes this in the context of a rejection of Gadamer's and others' alleged relativism. We can take his point without his misconstrual of Gadamer, who is better understood by Hoy, op. cit.

27 'The Challenge of Critical Theory', in *Sociology and Human Destiny. Essays on Sociology, Religion and Society*, ed. Gregory Baum (Seabury Press, New York, 1980), 203.

6

The Economy of God: Exploring a Metaphor

When Paul says, 'We are Christ's aroma to God' (2 Cor. 2.15), or 'Our letter is you' (3.2), or 'We have this treasure in earthenware pots' (4.7), he is clearly using metaphors. A metaphor is, in very general terms, 'the application of an alien name by transference'.[1] It is typical that metaphors are needed to describe what metaphors are: 'teaching an old word new tricks', or 'a calculated category mistake', or 'an affair between a predicate with a past and an object that yields while protesting'.[2] Metaphors pervade our language, and there has been a great deal of controversy about their nature and status, especially as regards expression of truth. Some have seen them as purely rhetorical or ornamental, in sharp contrast with 'literal' expression. Others have seen them playing a variety of more important roles in conceiving, discovering and doing justice to the truth. So Mary Hesse writes about their use in science: 'Acceptance of the view that metaphors are meant to be intelligible implies rejection of all views that make metaphor a wholly non-cognitive, subjective, emotive or stylistic use of language.'[3] We agree with Hesse's line. In this chapter we want to keep close to the text of 2 Corinthians and explore one metaphor, or family of metaphors, to see how our understanding of the letter can be enhanced. But before moving into the text we will make some further remarks about metaphor.

1 ASPECTS OF METAPHOR

Generalizations about metaphor easily become vacuous because of the sheer richness, variety and particularity of the subject. Besides, metaphors as such can be dead, misleading, banal, unsuccessful, awkward and much else. What we say here is oriented especially towards what we will try to show as Paul's vivid, strong use of certain metaphors, and while this will be more widely relevant, we mainly want it to illuminate 2 Corinthians.

Chapter 4 treated metaphor in passing, and the discussion below is really a special instance of what was discussed there. Metaphor has certain distinctive marks and capacities. Chapter 4 discussed the fact that 'meaning inheres not just in words but in the relationship between them', and that is especially true of metaphor. Its minimum unit is not the word but the phrase or sentence, and, as with the key metaphor discussed in this chapter, the meaning may only emerge by allowing the metaphor to resonate through a whole text and beyond. Metaphor sets up an 'interanimation' between words, images, concepts and whole ways of conceiving reality in which the reader's work of passing back and forth, discerning new relationships and receiving insights, is the only way of trying to do justice to the dynamic relationality of the metaphor. This does not mean that there are no controls on the meaning – Chapter 4 has been at pains to demonstrate this. Rather it necessitates an attentiveness which tries to be sensitive to metaphorical dimensions of meaning, and in these areas too to maintain, for example, the priority of the meaning at the time of writing. So in what follows we will not just examine the various economic metaphors as they function in the text but will refer to the sort of material economy that is the context for Paul's usage.

This could easily be a pedantic deflation of vigorous metaphor. What, hopefully, prevents this is the attempt to enter into the dialectic of familiar and unfamiliar that goes on in metaphor. This will be seen to work both ways. It leads to fresh ways of conceiving the gospel and God's activity through economic metaphors, but it also leads to ordinary economic concepts being transformed in accordance with the new metaphorical reference.

The peculiarity of metaphor is perhaps sharpest in the issue of its reference. It is easy to see how a mode of expression which claims X is Y, when it clearly is not, could be dismissed as ornamental or secondary where correspondence with reality is concerned. Yet we are persuaded by recent studies which insist on the referential importance of metaphor.[4] Metaphor challenges any simplistic idea of language as, on the one hand, words, and, on the other, the reality to which they either do or do not correspond. Any such naive correspondence theory of language should have been undermined by the previous chapter, and investigating metaphor is just one way of developing the point. To say 'We are Christ's aroma to God' is to disrupt the literal reference of 'aroma'. Out of the ruins of the literal meaning a new reference arises, one not simply reducible to paraphrase in literal terms. The very use of metaphor is itself an event in 'reality'. Areas of discourse are related in a new way, new possibilities of conceiving our relationship with God are opened up, and the interaction between speech and reality is seen to be one of interanimation which is very different from a static correspondence.

This does not mean that metaphor is not referential, rather that if our ideas of reference are based only on literal usage, they are inadequate. We need to expand our notion of reference to include that of metaphor. In a world which includes coinherence, change, possibility, novelty, and transformations of many sorts, we need to be able to do justice to this in our conception of language as part of this reality. Metaphor in particular allows us to reach beyond the actual, disclosing something beyond the familiar world, yet using the familiar to get there. The way metaphor works leads us to find realistic reference beyond correspondence. This happens partly through bringing to light new relationships and forms of coinherence whose very perception is inseparable from understanding the indirectness of the metaphor. Partly too it draws our notion of reference beyond both correspondence and coherence theories into that strange aspect of temporal existence, the reality of possibility. What is actual does not exhaust reality, and metaphor works powerfully at the boundaries of the actual, opening it up to new possibilities.[5] So metaphor is highly practical, as persuaders in politics, education, religion and other areas have long known, and it is not surprising that it should be a major part of Paul's appeal to the Corinthians.

Finally, there is the relationship of metaphor to other aspects of the text. We hope that the discussion to follow will show that our way of understanding the role of metaphor is not in competition with the other approaches we use. Meaning is not so monochrome or on a single level that there cannot be more than one way of exploring even the same phrase or sentence: our earlier investigation (above pp. 128ff.) of 'treasure in earthenware pots' in no way conflicts with our reflections on its metaphorical meaning below. On the contrary, just as Aristotle's *Poetics* saw metaphor as integrated into the text as a whole through its being one of the parts of *lexis* (diction, modes of language) which in turn is subordinate to the *mythos* (plot, dynamic thrust uniting the work) and all of this is in the service of *mimesis* (poetic representation of reality), so we see metaphor as playing an important but subordinate role in the overall meaning of 2 Corinthians. Just how all the parts come together was the theme of the previous chapter on hermeneutics.

One pervasive family of metaphors, that associated with the law-court, has already played a crucial role in Chapter 2. We find the metaphors of economy similarly pervasive and important but in a very different way. To miss their role would not obscure the main thrust of the letter, and so far as we know nobody has drawn attention to it before in this way. But meaning is not just about a separable 'main thrust', and we offer this exploration as a way of enriching and deepening our understanding of 2 Corinthians.

2 PAUL AND ECONOMY

Paul very clearly suggests the appropriateness of economic analogies in 2 Corinthians. The Spirit is called a 'downpayment' or 'deposit' (1.22). Paul's work as an apostle is called a *diakonia*, meaning 'ministry' and 'service' such as that of a slave who waits at table or acts as a messenger, a common form of labour in the economy of the time; and he sees himself as a poor man who makes many rich (6.10). The Gospel, as summed up in 4.5–6 is called 'this treasure' (4.7) and chapters 8—9 show the connection between 'real' economics and the gospel's 'economy of God', interweaving them inseparably in relation to the practical issue of the collection for the Jerusalem church, backed up by a basic reformulation of the gospel:

> For you know the grace of our Lord Jesus Christ, that for you he became poor though he was rich, so that you might become rich through his poverty (8.9).

Much else of relevance will emerge below, but we are not just interested in noting how often such links can be seen. We want to explore the whole letter in terms of the basic metaphor of 'economy of God'. This is one way of understanding the text more fully. It sets a model (that of an economy) alongside 2 Corinthians in order to help some of the letter's features to be noted and related. It 'plays' with the text by transposing it into this language in the hope that the reader too can join in and as a result return with enriched understanding to the text.

The Greek word from which economy comes is *oikonomia*, which extended its original meaning of 'household administration' to embrace administration in general, stewardship, treasurership, management, governing, provision, organization, direction, regulation, sustaining, distribution, planning and adaptation of means to ends. In the NT it is used by Paul to describe his own ministry (1 Cor. 9.17) but in such a way that it is inseparable from its content, the gospel as God's way of dealing with the world. This content is in Col. 1.25 summed up as the '*oikonomia* of God', again inextricably linked with Paul's ministry, and Eph. 3.2 continues this dual focus. In Ephesians (which we take to be closely linked to Paul, if not by Paul) the term has become an established way of referring to God's plan and administration of salvation (1.10; 3.9). This prepares for the widespread patristic use of it to refer to all of God's dealings with his creation, in shaping the natural order, in providence, in the old and new covenants, in the sacraments and above all in the incarnation.

Clearly *oikonomia* was a very fruitful metaphor in Christian expression, and the history of its derivations has continued in interesting ways. The most recent development has been the rise of 'economics' and the immense attention paid to the state of the 'economy', understood as the way in which goods and money are produced, distributed and regulated. This was part of the meaning of the Greek word too, especially when limited to the household, and we will focus on connections with this area in 2 Corinthians. This means a concern for resources, work, money, production, distribution, value and exchange, together with the processes and relationships that these involve. Corinth was a major commercial centre, Paul himself was a craftsman who manufactured, bought and sold, and probably (see 7 below) integrated his ministry and his daily work. So it is not at all remarkable that his gospel was expressed partly in economic language.

3 GOD'S WORK, THE CENTRAL RESOURCE

One notable mark of 2 Corinthians, further discussed in Chapter 9, is its theocentricity. In economic terms this means that it is God who has set up the economy of salvation. He has done something which has produced a resource comparable to the most fundamental resource of all, the creation (cf. 4.6; 5.17). The nature of this work of God is the key theme of Paul's gospel. He sums it up in various ways, all of them focused on the Christ-centred activity of God (cf. 1.3–11; 4.4–6; 5.14–15; 8.9; 13.4). Such statements point to Paul's basic given, 'this treasure' (4.7), which is to him a stupendous resource, something overwhelmingly good, of universal effectiveness and capable of transforming all of life. Faced with it, he affirms it, rejoices in it, exults in it, thanks God for it:

> Thanks be to God, who in Christ... (2.14)
> The whole thing comes from God, who...through Christ... (5.18)
> Thanks be to God for his inexpressible gift! (9.15).

Such expressions of celebration and appreciation frequently slip into his speech, woven into more direct statements of content. They show how central is his recognition of God as the one who has produced and now sustains this new life. It is all simply given by God: that is the most astonishing fact about this economy, summed up in his use of 'grace' (*charis*). God has done something and offered it freely, and this availability of grace, life, the Spirit, glory, reconciliation, freedom, wealth, or however else it is described, determines both Paul's work and the new state of affairs of the whole world. There is now a new agenda set by the need to distribute this resource and to let it flow through all hearts and relationships. This can be called 'co-working', 'collaboration' with God (6.1; cf. 1 Cor. 3.9).

4 THE ECONOMICS OF ABUNDANCE

Most economies are characterized by their ways of coping with scarcity, but Paul's vision is of more than enough of the central resource. Bruce Malina describes the material economy of which Paul was a part as a 'limited good' economy.[6] It was pre-industrial, with city dwellers making up perhaps 10% of the population. Overall probably about 2% were the élite who took no part in production but exacted taxes and maintained order, and 8% were engaged in manual work, mainly handicraft manufacturing. There was a roughly stable, limited amount of resources, which meant that more for one meant less for others. Unlike our industrial economy with its capacity to generate wealth, there was no way of greatly increasing the 'cake' to be divided, and the dominance of the élite meant that for 98% of the population (including Paul) most goods were in short supply. Subsistence with stability was the main aim of economic activity for most people, and the right to subsistence was closely bound to one's family and its inherited place in society. It was an economy in which equilibrium, not growth, was the ideal. This was supported by a network of relationships based on informal reciprocity, enforced by the powerful appeal to honour and shame. This picture underlies the contrast with the divine economy as described by Paul.

The theme of abundance and overflow runs all through the letter. Paul describes the intensification of both suffering and blessing initiated by Jesus Christ's death and resurrection.

> For just as the sufferings of Christ overflow onto us, so through Christ even the encouragement we receive is overflowing (1.5; cf. 7.4; 11.23).

There is no steady equilibrium here, no careful regulation of limited goods. The basic fact is 'the extraordinary (surpassing) grace of God' (9.14).

This grace overflows in a variety of ways. It is both the content and the power of Paul's 'bold power of free speech' (3.12), his confidence and courage in spreading the gospel. It is the cause of his exultation (pride, boasting) which continually wells up in this letter. It flows between Christians in love, joy, new life, forgiveness and generosity, and it 'overflows through the multiplication of thanks to God' (9.12). The whole economy is one of free receiving and free giving resulting in new sorts of relationship.

Four main extended passages make this abundance explicit. There is the opening in 1.3–11, an extraordinarily intense expression of mutual reciprocity in suffering and encouragement. Paul sees himself part of something that leads far beyond stoic acceptance and endurance into confidence 'in God who raises the dead' (1.9) and into the accompanying expansion of celebration and thanks, as requests to God are answered and give more and more cause for gratitude (1.11).

In chapters 3—4 there is the description of the new covenant 'overflowing with glory' (3.9). This climaxes with the supreme image of free distribution, that of light (4.6), followed by reference to the 'extraordinary (transcendent, surpassing) power of God' (4.7), and later a summary of this economy and its aim:

> For everything is for your sake, so that grace abounding through more and more (of you) may cause thanksgiving to overflow to the glory of God (4.15).

'More and more' is the dynamic symbol of this God and of Paul's mission.

The third key passage, discussed separately below, is chapters 8—9, where the logic of Christian overflow is followed through in relation to finances. The fourth is Paul's 'exultation' in chapters 10—12, where the combined pressures of his vocation and the opposition to it produce a passionate self-defence. Here the specific logic of this grace is made most paradoxically explicit:

> And he has told me, 'My grace is sufficient for you; for power is perfected in weakness.' Gladly then will I take a pride in (exult in) weaknesses, that the power of Christ may be pitched like a tent over me (12.9).

This identifies the strange exchange through which power is generated in this economy, recalling many similar statements earlier and later in the letter (1.6,9; 2.14; 4.7–12; 6.3–10; 11.23–30; 13.4). This is an economy of abundance at the heart of which is an exchange that requires to be re-enacted in appropriate ways in new circumstances if the abundance is to be shared properly.

5 THE CHRISTIAN ECONOMY

This exchange is crucial to Paul's argument in 2 Corinthians. It is the transaction conditioning all relationships in the new economy. It is essentially something done by God through Jesus Christ, as stated in most detail in chapter 5:

> ...one has died for all – so all died; and he died for all so that those who live should no longer live for themselves, but for the one who died and was raised for them... On our behalf he made into sin the one who knew no sin, so that we might become the righteousness of God in him (5.14,15,21).

In conformity with this Paul sees his ministry as a process of exchange informed by the death and resurrection of Jesus:

> For just as the sufferings of Christ overflow onto us, so through Christ even the encouragement we receive is overflowing. So if we are afflicted, it is for your encouragement and salvation; if we are encouraged, it is for your encouragement... (1.5–6);

> For always we who live are being handed over to death for Jesus' sake, so that Jesus' life too might be made apparent in our mortal flesh. So death is at work in us, but life in you (4.11–12).

This ministry in turn enables the Corinthians to take part in the exchange:

> And our hope is firm in your case, knowing that as you are partners in the sufferings, so also you are in the encouragement (1.7).

A dynamic mutuality, such as is summed up in Romans and 1 Corinthians by 'the body of Christ', is in 2 Corinthians expressed in the imagery of sharing, generosity, free communication and the flow of grace, life, joy, prayer and material goods. The whole letter aims, as the complement of the attempt to persuade the Corinthians to recognize the authenticity of Paul's ministry, at persuading them also to the sort of reciprocity that is intrinsic to that ministry. The unity of the church ('in Christ', in relation to Paul, and in their relations among themselves) depends on this mutuality informed by the central, generative exchange of Christ's sufferings and death.

How is the exchange described in economic terms? It is a *katallagē* (5.18, reconciliation), which originally meant the exchange of money, a money-lender's profit, or merchandise. It then came to mean the exchange of enmity for friendship, and so reconciliation. This exchange is costly (8.9) and it produces a new sort of wealth: '...so that you might become rich through his poverty' (8.9). This wealth can also be described as 'power perfected in weakness' (12.9). The exchange of Christ, his costly work, which involved suffering the most intractable realities of sin and death, has generated 'the power of Christ' (12.9), a new creation, a new currency which can through the downpayment of the Spirit, be spent now in living the sort of life which Christ's pattern of humility and weakness laid down. This is straining the monetary implications of 'downpayment', but the very lack of appropriateness points to what is different about this currency: it is 'the Spirit in our hearts' (1.22); 'the Spirit makes alive' (3.6); this is the power of God realizing the new age in the midst of the old. The unit of value that the Spirit represents is that of each person's life revalued in Christ into 'a new creation' (5.17). To have the Spirit is to spend oneself. Jesus himself gave his life in exchange for the new life for others. Paul takes a pride in his own life given for his churches. The very lives of the Corinthians themselves are seen by him as his only letter of recommendation, 'written, not with ink but with the Spirit of the living God' (3.3). The Macedonians are praised because the heart of their financial generosity was that 'they have given themselves first to the Lord and then to us through the will of God' (8.5). This theme is not stretching the economic language of the time very far, because slavery, trade in people, was a major element in it, and Paul in 1 Cor. 6.20 can say, 'You were bought with a price'. But in 2 Corinthians when Paul sums up the idea most clearly it is with reference not to slavery but to another major economic factor, inheritance. He says that in visiting Corinth, 'I don't want your goods, but you. Children ought not to make a fortune for their parents, but parents for their children. But I will gladly spend and be spent on your behalf (lit. on behalf of your souls or very selves)' (12.14–15).

The economic cycle in which all this takes place is bounded by 'the day of our Lord Jesus Christ' (1.14). The Spirit is the life of that day anticipated now, given by God with the aim of producing (*katergasamenos* 5.5) a final product: people prepared for the ultimate exchange before Christ where 'each may receive his due for deeds done through the body, whether good or bad' (5.10). The aim of Paul's ministry to the Corinthians is likewise this ultimate testing of selves as the units of value, 'as you will fully acknowledge that we are your pride and joy, even as you are ours, on the day of the Lord Jesus' (1.14; cf. 13.5). That final joy is Paul's basic standard for reckoning cost-effectiveness in his ministry, which he describes in the language of measuring-scales:

> For this immediate trifle of an affliction produces for us, in extraordinary quantities, an eternal weight of glory... (4.17).

This vision of the final glorious state of abundance relativizes all other values, both personal and material. But it is not only a vision: it is possible even now to live in the Spirit, 'in God's grace' (1.12). This new resource in the midst of the old sets up the tension already discussed above under the heading of eschatology (pp. 122ff.) and worked out in economic terms in section 7 below.

6 GOD'S FINANCES

'He expresses himself in a way which is impossible to translate', says Dahl about chapters 8—9 and their terminology for the collection which Paul was making for the church in Jerusalem.[7] In our terms, Paul here interweaves inextricably the 'literal' and the 'divine' economies through the words and ideas he uses. In our translation we have strained to bring out the ways in which the same words are used in various senses, and some awkwardness is inevitable. The collection itself is called *charis* (grace, gift of grace, favour, benevolence, gracious work, 8.6,7,19; cf. 8.1,9; 9.14; 1 Cor. 16.3), *koinōnia* (partnership, sharing, fellowship, 8.4; 9.13; cf. Rom. 15.26), *diakonia* (ministration, service, relief work, 8.4; 9.12,13; cf. 8.19,20 (the verb *diakonein*), and Rom. 15.31), *eulogia* (open-handedness, blessing, liberality, willing gift, 9.5; cf. 9.6), *leitourgia* (service, voluntary public service, priestly religious service, 9.12; cf. Rom. 15.27), *haplotēs* (single-minded commitment, simplicity, generosity, 8.2; 9.11,13), *hadrotēs* (large sum of money, plenitude, liberal gift, 8.20), *perisseuma* (overflow, abundance, 8.14), *endeixis tēs agapēs hymōn* (proof of your love, demonstration of your love, 8.24), *sporos* (seed-corn, seed, resources, 9.10; cf. 9.6), and *ta genēmata tēs dikaiosynēs hymōn* (the offshoots, harvest or yield of your righteousness, 9.10; cf. Hosea 10.12). Even this limited focus shows the collection linked into key terms in Paul's gospel and in 2 Corinthians. The ordinary word for collection, *logeia* (1 Cor. 16.1,2), is not used at all here. The chapters are certainly about money and basic attitudes to possessions and prosperity, but these are inseparable from the character and glory of God, the practice of faith and love in the church and the dynamic reality of grace. The metaphorical application of economic terms to the gospel is given a new development, as key gospel concepts, including economic ones, are in turn directed at reconceiving financial attitudes and relationships.

The background to what Paul says is a Hellenistic urban society whose economy, as mentioned above, was one of 'limited goods' mainly supported by agriculture. Within this, benevolence was virtually an institution, closely identified with the patron-client relationships through which so much of the wealth, power and influence in Hellenistic cities was channelled. The main feature of this benevolence was reciprocity, and as Stephen C. Mott, who has made a thorough study of this, says: 'A worthy recipient was considered to be one capable of making a concrete return of gratitude.'[8] The word grace, *charis*, was used in this context both for the benevolent gift of the patron and for the gift or act of gratitude in return.[9]

Another aspect of the background to what Paul writes is a long Jewish tradition of teaching about possessions. This, like that of many Greek moralists, was concerned about honesty, working for one's living, meeting economic obligations, resisting the temptations to greed or avarice, and giving as generously as possible to those in need. There was also the centrality of God as the giver of all good things and the encourager of generosity with what he has given.

Paul takes up a great deal in both of these strands, Hellenistic and Jewish, but they are woven into something different. The rest of 2 Corinthians shows how lightly he sits to versions of the patron-client relationship when he sees them interfering with his ministry. He will not, for example, be dependent on 'letters of recommendation', nor will he necessarily accept the support (which would have implications of patronage) of the Corinthian church – or rather, perhaps, of the wealthy within that church. In his refusal of dependence and insistence on carrying on his trade, there are hints of the Cynic and Stoic way of handling this society by aiming at independence, self-sufficiency and content-ment (*autarkeia*). For them the wise man was as independent as possible of external conditions and relationships, which was a radical rejection of the reciprocity of social relations. But even though Paul uses some of their language, including *autarkeia* in 9.8, he is not in line with them either. For Paul the content of *autarkeia* is an economic provision which, far from enabling an isolated self-sufficiency, is given by God in order 'to overflow into every act of goodness' (9.8), and is continually dependent on the grace of God.

Paul's implicit critique of both the current patterns of re-ciprocity and the Stoic form of protest against them is rooted in his own positive position, which also carried with it a trans-formation of the common Jewish approach. His position, as suggested above, embraces much of both Greek and Jewish economic ethics but they play their part in a very different whole. It is most significant, as Dahl argues, that 'Paul never looks at an individual's relationship to money in isolation. Refer-ences to money are always part of a total context, which includes the attitude to its use.'[10] This context is what we are calling 'the economy of God'. All human relations of reciprocity are relativized by the God who 'enables every grace to overflow into you, so that in every way and all the time you have total self-sufficiency to overflow into every act of goodness' (9.8). In the face of what this God gives, calculations of reciprocity are pointless: one simply gives freely in the spirit of the God who does likewise. The embodiment of grace is Jesus Christ (8.9) whom the Macedonians have imitated by generously giving out of 'the overflow of their joy and extreme poverty' (8.2). The Macedonians' trust in God, as they give despite their poverty, is the most graphic illustration of what happens when prudent worldly economics meets the gospel of this God and his paradoxical combining of vulnerability with abundance. Yet Paul does not urge that the Corinthians risk poverty like Jesus Christ and the Macedonians. All he asks is that they aim at equality between the congregations seen as economic units:

> For there is no intention that relief for others should bring affliction to you; but for the present time, on the basis of equality, your overflow should make up their shortage, so that their overflow may make up your shortage, that equality may prevail (8.13–14).

This is clearly the minimal appropriate response to God's generosity, in line with much ethical teaching about equitable distribution in Judaism and the Greek moralists. But in the context there is no danger of misunderstanding it as a static or legalistic ideal: the Macedonians are the leading example, and the emphasis on the poverty of Jesus Christ together with the need for free, cheerful giving means that there is no measureable limit to what may be inspired by God, both in thanks to himself ('inexpressible', 9.15) and in generosity to others.

This is an economy in which freedom is precious, and Paul is trying to encourage a free response in the Corinthians. Therefore, his appeal is both a celebration of God's grace and an invitation to the Corinthians to recognize afresh what they are part of and to draw the practical consequences. Vis-à-vis Hellenistic reciprocity, what seems to have happened is that the inexhaustible generosity of God places everyone in the position of his clients and therefore owing him thanks; but among the clients themselves there is no basis for anything other than equality or uncalculating generosity, and so all patron-client relationships are relativized.

The positive relationship which Paul recommends is that of *koinōnia* (partnership, communion, sharing, fellowship), one of the words used for the collection. 'The poor and the rich have the same Lord, who gives both groups a share in his bounty and who joins them in the same church; this is the strikingly new element in Paul's thought. The congregation becomes the decisive social reality for the Christian way of life, and communal life by necessity involves the use of possessions'.[11] We explore this further in our account of church and society in Corinth in Chapter 7 below.

Another major factor in the economy of God that was

mentioned above is that of eschatology. The relevance of this to economics is clearest in 1 Corinthians, where those who do business are told to live as though they had no goods, because 'the appointed time has grown very short' (1 Cor. 7.29–30). Again, the effect is a radical relativizing, in this case superficially like the detachment of Cynics and Stoics, but very different because of its eschatological motivation.

In 2 Cor. 8—9 all of this is concentrated on the one particular issue of the collection. It is given extraordinary importance and breadth of implication by the very terms Paul uses to name it. This is borne out further by reference to it in 1 Corinthians, Romans and Galatians. As well as being an effort in relief work for the Jerusalem church it obviously had immense symbolic importance. This money seems to function like a sacrament of both the unity of Jews and Gentiles in the Church and the validity of Paul's apostolate in relation to the original apostles in Jerusalem. It also, as we have been describing, represents the 'new creation' in operation, in which money, one of the basic aspects of ordinary life, is taken up into life in the Spirit. It may even relate directly to Paul's understanding of eschatology, as a sign of the final gathering of the nations to Jerusalem (Munck). There is a large literature about the collection, as there is about the opponents of Paul. In both cases it would certainly help to know what the situation was, but even without needing to adopt one of the reconstructions as correct, a great deal can be learnt from the text. In this section we have shown how closely integrated it was with Paul's most characteristic ways of conceiving his gospel and his mission, and how it expresses the coinherence of the financial and divine economies: the mutuality of spiralling giving and thanksgiving culminates in the ultimate value, the glory of God (8.19; 9.13), to which the constant overflow of thanks attempts to do justice without ever succeeding (9.15).

7 TWO SYSTEMS IN COMPETITION

The economy of God has competitors, both outside and inside the church, symbolized by Satan (2.11; 11.14–15). It is taken for granted that the whole Church is in constant tension with another mode of being in the world.

In 2 Corinthians Paul does not pay much attention to the situation of non-Christians or the relations between them and Christians. His focus is rather on the ways in which the economy of God in the church can go wrong, both in community life and in sharing the gospel. If the dynamics of overflow in the church are blocked, then Satan takes advantage (2.5–11 on forgiveness). In sharing the gospel, Paul's opponents are accused of being 'traders in the word of God' (2.17, *kapēleuontes* means 'offering for sale', or even 'huckstering' or 'diluting the product'), of being 'false apostles, workers who cheat' (11.13), and even of being directly in the service of the opposition (ministers of Satan, 11.15).

The competing systems are most commonly called by their basic principles, *sarx* (flesh, the human level, which is sometimes used neutrally but generally in a negative sense, contrasting with what is in right relationship with God) and *pneuma* (spirit) or *charis* (grace) or simply 'the Lord'. Nothing is exempt from being understood or used either *kata sarka* (at the human level) or *kata pneuma* (in the Spirit): money, time, plans, boasting, other people, the law, the gospel and Jesus Christ. So it is very important to note that this is not a distinction parallel to those between the material and the spiritual, or body and spirit, or secular and sacred. Rather *sarx* can qualify each side of those dichotomies just as *pneuma* can, and the most helpful dualism with which to relate it is that between the old age or order and the new (5.17). It is the overlap of the ages that is at the root of the conflict and of the urgent demands to discriminate that run through 2 Corinthians.

The economy of God described above is an abstraction from the dense language of conflict and self-defence in the letter. The economic resonances could be amplified by considering the role of promises (1.15–22, especially v. 22) and of trust and mutual confidence (e.g. 6.11–13, with *antimisthian*, exchange or recompense). And, as with the collection, it seems that actual financial issues were at stake between Paul and the Corinthians in the conflict over his apostleship. He protests his innocence of corruption and greed (e.g. 7.2) and carefully involves other reputable Christians in the collection (8.16ff.). Above all there is his need to defend the fact that he earns his own living (11.7–9; 12.13–14).

Paul's means of subsistence could be a pointer to a larger tension within the church of his time, as Gerd Theissen suggests.[12] It may be that Jesus himself and the early Palestinian church missionaries relied on trusting in God to provide support through local generosity. This was in Palestinian society where 'charismatic begging' was common and demonstrable poverty in the name of God suggested the authenticity of an itinerant preacher. The sphere of operation was a network of rural villages within a day's walking distance of each other, so that rejection in one place could be met by moving on to the next. When this pattern was applied in the Hellenistic cities it required already existing Jewish or Christian groups willing to provide support and, as a guarantee of authenticity over long distances, letters of recommendation. Paul, however, was part of a missionary movement to cities where there was no previous Christian group and where the content of his message antagonized the organized Jewish community. He was primarily an organizer and sustainer of new communities. Letters of recommendation were not much use (he wanted his to be written in the form of the results of his evangelism, 3.1–3); and to have independent means by working at a craft was an advantage, greatly increasing the freedom of his proclamation.

Yet for Paul to work to support himself was controversial. Other missionaries saw it as part of their own legitimation that they trusted in God and the generosity of others. So Paul could be seen as evading both the command of Jesus (cf. 1 Cor. 9.14) and the risk of charismatic poverty that it involved. His financial self-support could be interpreted as living *kata sarka* (at the human level, 2 Cor. 10.2), trusting in his own efforts rather than in God.

So the issue can be seen again as how the 'economy of God' relates to actual economics: what is it to support oneself as an apostle 'according to the Spirit'? Paul had no objection in principle to being given support, and there were times when he accepted it (especially from a church which was willing to finance the next stage of his travels, *propempein*, after leaving them), but he was also determined not to be bound legalistically by the tradition when new circumstances of mission made a more flexible arrangement desirable. The central thrust of his argument is that his whole apostleship is in line with the heart of the divine economy, the death of Jesus. He is not evading rigorous demands but is equal to any missionary in what he suffers and does for the gospel. For someone founding new communities in urban centres against considerable opposition there was plenty of opportunity for risk, trust in God and going the way of the cross without making a shibboleth out of one form of subsistence. And as Ronald Hock argues, Paul's daily work justified him in seeing it in conformity with the weakness and humiliation of his Lord:

> More than any of us has supposed, Paul was *Paul the Tent-maker*. His trade occupied much of his time – from the years of his apprenticeship through the years of his life as a missionary of Christ, from before daylight through most of the day. Consequently, his trade in large measure determined his daily experiences and his social status. His life was very much that of the workshop – of artisan friends like Aquila, Barnabas and perhaps Jason; of leather, knives and awls; of wearying toil; of being bent over a workbench like a slave and of working side by side with slaves; of thereby being perceived by others and by himself as slavish and humiliated, of suffering the artisan's lack of status and so being reviled and abused.[13]

So Paul translates the radicalism of the Palestinian mission into a practice which could claim to be just as radical (both in its consequences for himself and for an ordinary Christian life lived *kata pneuma*) but which grappled with the problem discerned in a new situation. The main issue was whether this transformation was a betrayal of the gospel. Paul's appeal to conformity with Jesus Christ crucified was to have a lively history in Christianity, most dramatically in the Lutheran Reformation. It authorized a fruitful paradigm, neither 'conservative' nor 'liberal', for prophetic change in Christianity. It looked to the crucifixion of Jesus as the legitimation of discontinuity in Christian tradition. The fact that Jesus was a circumcised Jew could not be used to argue against Gentiles becoming Christians without circumcision, and the fact that he had given certain instructions about the support of missionaries did not mean they were to be legalistically followed for ever after. Here was a tradition with the principle of its own radical adaptation and transformation, and Paul maintained that it was his apostleship's conformity to the central reality of the death of Jesus that legitimated his mission, for all its innovation.

It is in Paul's peroration in chapters 10—13 that all of this

comes to a head. The section is introduced by his appeal against
the accusation of living *kata sarka* (10.1–2) and in its most
daring rhetoric it plays with the accusation, perhaps ironically.
He engages in boasting *kata sarka* like his opponents (11.18).
He tries to beat them at their own game, then goes one better by
listing his sufferings. He repeats the gambit in chapter 12,
again trying to explode the opposition's case from the inside. It
is like a new version of the exchange of Christ, who on our
behalf was made into sin. It leads into his most vivid statement
of life *kata pneuma*: 'My grace is sufficient for you; for power
is perfected in weakness' (12.9). followed up by another
expression of its economic consequences for his ministry
(12.13,17). He is clear that the highest stakes are at issue and he
ties the local matters inextricably into the heart of his gospel. The
use of metaphor is just one way in which he does this, but it does
have a vital role both in taking up all of life into the movement
of the gospel and in elucidating the meaning of the gospel
itself.

NOTES

1   Aristotle, *Poetics*, 1457b, 7–8.
2   N. Goodman, *Languages of Art. An Approach to a Theory of
     Symbols* (OUP, London, 1969), 69, 73. For a theological reflection
     using Goodman and others mentioned below see Colin Gunton,
     'Christus Victor Revisited. A Study in Metaphor and the Trans-
     formation of Meaning', in *JTS*, NS 36 Pt 1 (Apr. 1985), 129–
     45.
3   *Models and Analogies in Science* (Sheed & Ward, London, 1963),
     164.
4   Notably that of Paul Ricoeur, *The Rule of Metaphor* (University of
     Toronto Press, Toronto, 1977).
5   For a good discussion of this in the work of a contemporary
     theologian, see John Webster, 'Eberhard Jüngel on the Language
     of Faith', in *Modern Theology*, vol. 1, No. 4 (July 1985), 253–
     76.
6   *The New Testament World. Insights from Cultural Anthropology*
     (SCM, London, 1983).
7   N. A. Dahl, *Studies in Paul* (Augsburg, Minneapolis, 1977), 31.
8   *Biblical Ethics and Social Change* (OUP, Oxford, 1982), 57. Cf. his

essay, 'The Power of Giving and Receiving: Reciprocity in Hellenistic Benevolence', in *Current Issues in Biblical and Patristic Interpretation*, M. Tenney Festschrift, ed. G. Hawthorne (Eerdmans, Grand Rapids, 1975), 60–72; and *The Greek Benefactor and Deliverance from Moral Distress* (unpublished Harvard University Ph.D dissertation, 1971).

9 cf. Gordon D. Fee, 'XAPIN in II Cors. 1.15: Apostolic Parousia and Paul-Corinth Chronology', in *NTS* 24.4 (July 1978), 533–8; and Mott, op. cit. (1982), 32.

10 op. cit., 24.

11 Dahl, op. cit., 26.

12 *The Social Setting of Pauline Christianity. Essays on Corinth.* (Fortress, Philadelphia, 1982).

13 *The Social Context of Paul's Ministry. Tent-making and Apostleship* (Fortress, Philadelphia, 1980), 56.

7

Church and Society in Corinth

The very first verse of 2 Corinthians points to many of the issues
dealt with in this chapter:

> Paul, apostle of Christ Jesus through the will of God, and Timothy the
> brother, to the church of God in Corinth, with all the saints who are in
> the whole of Achaea...

What is 'the church'? What sort of place was Corinth in
Achaea? What does it mean that these people are called
'brother', 'saints'? What was the relationship between Paul and
Timothy and the church in Corinth? Given that 'Christ Jesus'
indicates Jewish origin, what is the connection between this
group and the synagogue?

Such questions about what the Corinthian church and its
context were like are unavoidable. Yet inevitably most of the
answers were taken for granted in the letter itself. The Corinthians did not need to learn about Corinth, but we do, so this
chapter explores the social context of the letter. The aim is, at
the least, to prevent misunderstandings, and, at best, to throw
new light on 2 Corinthians and on how it is relevant today.

This will lead us into a major growth area in recent scholarship, what is variously called the 'sociology', 'social history',
'social description', 'social setting', 'social aspects' or 'social
world' of early Christianity.[1] Paul's letters are especially
valuable for these studies because they are the earliest surviving
documents of the church, and offer a good deal of information about various local communities. His first letter to the
Corinthians is the most helpful of all. When this is combined
with a considerable amount of other material that throws light on

life in Corinth and other cities of the Roman Empire at that time we find that it is possible to give a more adequate account of the church and wider social background of 2 Corinthians than of any other New Testament document.

1 THE CHURCH AS PART OF CORINTHIAN SOCIETY

Paul founded the church in Corinth around AD 50. He probably wrote 1 Corinthians in AD 54 and 2 Corinthians in 56. So this was a very young church trying to cope with a radical trans-formation of life and unprecedented problems. Paul's letters show that to be a Corinthian Christian was to maintain one's identity in a field of forces which included pressures from the rest of society, an intense church life and the arguments and attractions of other forms of Christianity. In this section we will describe the wider social realities of the city itself and such basic features as class, status and institutional life as they bear on the church. This will be more general than section 2 in which we attempt an account of the community of the church.

Corinth in the time of Paul was a new city, just under a hundred years old. The ancient Corinth had been levelled to the ground by the Romans in 146 BC for its leading part in a Greek revolt, and it was not rebuilt until 44 BC by Julius Caesar. It was a Roman colony, and the new settlers came from many parts of the Empire. A majority of these were freedmen (former slaves) who, as settlers in a Roman colony, became Roman citizens. Corinth was therefore more Roman in character than other native Greek cities, and eight of the seventeen extant names of Corinthan Christians are Latin.[2] But its common language was Greek, it shared in the cosmopolitan culture of the cities of the eastern Roman Empire and since its foundation it had attracted many different types of people to live in it.

There had been a political, social and cultural revolution begun by Alexander the Great in the late fourth century BC when he conquered vast areas of the Mediterranean lands and those further east. Its chief mark was the founding or refounding of cities with a common Hellenized culture and their own system of education and self-government. When the Romans conquered much of the same area they produced widespread disruption at first but by the time of Paul the *pax* of Augustus had produced stability and prosperity.

The Romans based their control mainly on a network of cities, many of them colonies. Corinth was part of this network and is a good focus for discovering what happened to Christianity when it made its transition from rural Palestine to the cities of the Empire. The mission of Paul and his circle was completely urban, and they and their churches must be understood in this context. The overarching features of it were the political control of Rome and the common Hellenistic culture. It was also a mobile society, with a well-developed system of roads and sea-routes. The churches that Paul founded were on important trade routes. The possibilities and necessity for travel in the Empire facilitated the spread of Christianity and supported the Church's common identity through communication, while also allowing disputes and divisions to spread far beyond their origins.

Corinth itself[3] stood at a vital junction between the Peloponnese and the rest of Greece to the north, and for sea traffic it was on an isthmus opening onto both the east and west of Greece. It was in an economic boom at the time of Paul. Many streams fed its prosperity: expanding trade, reliable banks, exports of craft manufactures, the tourist trade (partly due to the revived Isthmian Games, which would have been good for tentmaking), and its political and administrative importance as the governing centre of the province of Achaea.

Archaeology has shown that there was a great deal of new building, public and private, around the time of Paul. The size and close proximity of the private houses points to a densely packed population, which may have numbered more than 100,000. Most of them would have had little scope for privacy but would have spent most of their time outdoors in company, a noteworthy factor in communication and opportunities for persuasion. Paul's workshop might well have been one of the small artisans' shops in the North Market. This was built not long before he arrived in Corinth, and was made up of a series of shops around a square. Each shop got its light through its doorway, so was always open for social and business contacts with the many passers-by.[4]

How far can the concept of 'class' help to understand this

society? Rohrbaugh's perceptive survey of the debate about this and its methodological problems concludes that it is helpful to focus on the intersection of political power with the economic system. In the Empire wealth tended to follow power rather than vice versa and those with political and military authority had wide scope for enrichment through various forms of taxation or confiscation. Wealth which was not supported by power was precarious in this society, so many of our habitual expectations about status and power relative to wealth are unreliable.[5]

The number of people who had the political power that was essential for control of the economic system (especially in the sense of being able to appropriate its surplus) was very small, and had become smaller under the Empire. The vast majority was powerless in this regard. The Roman Empire in the first century AD was stratified and largely stable, with a narrow apex to the pyramid of power. At the very top were the Emperor, the small senatorial and equestrian orders, the larger decurionate, and members of the wider élite who in each city combined power and wealth and made up in all perhaps two per cent of the population of the Empire; at the bottom were slaves on farms and in mines. In between were those from whom the Church drew most of its members, neither the highest nor the lowest, but all alike in being unable to control the economic system and so not part of the dominant class. If there was anything approaching 'class consciousness' it was perhaps expressed in the widespread sense of 'fate' in which fear of losing wealth and well-being in an arbitrary way reflected the precariousness of those who were largely powerless. The message of Paul met this pervading anxiety not with an analysis of the class situation or proposals to change it, but with trust and hope in a radically alternative future already tangible in social form in the Church. Its relationship to the division that might be termed 'class' was therefore one of drawing its membership almost completely from a class with little power and offering a new group identity in which vital aspects of the consciousness usually associated with that class (such as anxiety and powerlessness) were transformed.

Status is a common companion to class in the interpretation of social relations and structures. It is especially valuable in looking at one local situation, as it is more attuned to gradations, nuances, individuals, and the complex interaction of various factors, some of which may seem irrelevant within a broad, structurally-oriented concept of class, but which may be crucial in the functioning of one group in a particular city. There are dangers in trying to decode the often subtle signs of status in a very different society,[6] but the illumination gained from a thorough attempt to do so seems to us to be one of the major recent contributions of scholarship to the understanding of the early Church and in particular of Corinth.

The Roman Empire was a very status-conscious society in which the criteria and categories of status were in many ways different from modern Western society. A key value in terms of which status was measured was 'honour', with associated concepts of reputation, dishonour, shame, glory, blame, insult, reproach, praise, etc. Honour symbolized a person's rightful place in society. The dominant orientation was towards maintaining one's inherited status, so that birth, marriage and household were fundamental, and one's status was deeply embedded in kinship groups whose concern was mainly for continuity and stability.

The dynamics of the culture were what cultural anthropologists sometimes call 'agonistic', which means that there was constant challenge, conflict and assessment focused on matters of honour, and social interactions were often seen as contests for honour.[7] This is part of the background (the other part of which is the OT and Judaism, discussed in Chapter 3 above) of Paul's 'pride' and 'boasting' in 2 Corinthians and of the prominence of rhetoric in the culture (cf. Chapter 2 above). When Paul uses the cross as his criterion for glory and ironically surpasses conventional grounds for boasting by placing his pride in his humiliations and weaknesses he is hitting at the heart of this culture – or, as he puts it, at 'pride in achievements at the human level' (11.18).

Economically, wealth was seen as of limited quantity (see previous chapter), and so excessive accumulation was a threat to the established order of society. Honour as regards money attached largely to the defence of inherited means of livelihood, maintaining oneself at one's social level and entering into the necessary work, alliances or contracts necessary for this and compatible with other criteria of honour. Since the élite had the power to make or break their inferiors, but also needed the honour granted by the inferiors, there was a network of patron–client relationships through which the classes interacted. Letters of recommendation were one way in which one's 'honour-rating' was communicated to new people and groups. So in refusing both letters of recommendation and Corinthian financial support Paul was avoiding being tied into a form of patron–client relation.

Within this general picture the gradations and nuances were complex and Meeks had taken account of many attempts to conceptualize the various indicators of status in offering his description of the situation.[8] The chief indicators were: official rank or *ordo* (senatorial, equestrian, decurion, plebeian, slave – the vast mass of the population in the last two categories); public offices and honours; citizenship; personal liberty (slave, free or freedman); wealth; occupation; ethnic origins; age; sex; education; religion. These could of course be combined in various ways, and a person could have higher status by some indicators and lower by others – this is called 'status inconsistency'.

Our information about the seventeen named Corinthian Christians is very fragmentary, but going on clues about offices held, services provided for the church, and sufficient wealth for travel and for owning houses, it would seem that nine have high status of some sort. They also seem to have been disproportionately important in the church and to have been its leaders and patrons. Among them too there is much 'status inconsistency', being high by some indicators (wealth, public position) but lower by others (race, slave origins, sex, occupation). For example, Erastus (Rom. 16.23) was the 'city treasurer', a position that might possibly have been a fairly low one held by a trusted slave but is more likely[9] to have been a high office equivalent to that of quaestor which was held prior to the top office of aedile. There is an inscription from Corinth that shows an Erastus as aedile around this period. It does not mention his father, so Erastus may have been a freedman; it does say he financed the laying of a pavement, so he was wealthy; and his name is Greek. So he may well have been a Greek freedman who rose through becoming wealthy in commerce.[10]

Prisca and Aquila (Rom. 16.3; Acts 18.2,18,26; 1 Cor. 16.19) seem to have been independent artisans wealthy enough to operate on quite a large scale, but not of high status in terms of occupation and ethnic and religious origins (Eastern Jewish tent-makers). What this means is that the most prominent Corinthian Christians were able people who did not fit neatly into any social niche. Their membership of the new community gave them a strong social identity and the opportunity to exercise their abilities.[11]

Yet these were 'not many' (1 Cor. 1.26). How many were there in the congregation? They could all fit into the house of Gaius (Rom. 16.23) and if estimates based on excavations of the houses of wealthy Corinthians and others at the time of Paul are accurate this means a maximum of fifty people crowding into the two large public rooms.[12] Meeks sums up much interpretation of detail about the majority of the congregation by saying that the 'typical' Christian, 'the one who most often signals his presence in the letters by one or another small clue, is a free artisan or small trader'.[13] There were also slaves (though not, it seems, a large number), but no evidence for those who were at the very bottom of the social scale – destitute, hired menials who did not even have the security of belonging as slaves.

This community was nevertheless an unusual mixture of social levels and backgrounds, and members carried into the church many of the divisions and problems of the wider society. 1 Corinthians deals with meat-eating, sex and marriage, legal disputes, how to handle discrimination between rich and poor at the eucharistic meal, the role of women, and various ethical issues. Theissen[14] shows how many of those problems were probably connected with the sociological diversity and tensions of the new group. Paul's responses show an interesting combination. On the one hand, the gospel of Christ crucified radically relativizes the divisions, and upturns notions of status and importance by which society lives (e.g. 1 Cor. 1.10–31). In 1 Corinthians he is attempting to transform the understanding and practice of the community regarding status and the differences between people over a wide range of issues, only one of which is his own apostleship. In 2 Corinthians the main focus is on his own ministry. But in both the implications of the crucifixion are the key to changing social reality. On the other hand, there is no encouragement to change one's status in society either upward or downward (the end is too near for that to be worthwhile – 1 Cor. 7.17–31), and Paul's practical advice is often traditionally Jewish.[15] The main change in society is the presence in it of this 'body of Christ' living differently.

How differently? How did the church compare with other groups in Corinth? This might be termed the issue of institutional identity, with 'institution' understood as an organized group enduring over time. The two fundamental institutions of this society were the state (*politeia*) and the family (*oikonomia*). We have already seen how Paul's language in 2 Corinthians draws on both these spheres, the public including the law courts and the private including the economy (for unlike our society in which the economic often dominates public life, in ancient society the economy was considered part of private life). We will look at each of these spheres and show how the church compared with them and also represented something new.

Religion is the main area of comparison in public life. As regards the state religion, the gods and cults of Greece and various other cults represented by the many temples of Corinth,[16] there could be no confusing of the church with them. The distinctive features of the church discussed below were very sharply in contrast with such religion, and it had no discernible influence on the form of the new community. There were no significant sociological parallels. However, there was some overlap in language and activity which gave rise to boundary problems. These were concentrated in the area of sacrifice and worship and in particular revolved around the question whether it was acceptable to eat meat offered to idols (1 Cor. 8 and 10).

Closer parallels exist with the mystery religions, which on the one hand overlapped similarly with the public religion insofar as rituals were expected and on the other hand involved the individual in a private religious choice and commitment. The offer of salvation through initiation and sacrament uncannily resembles the early Christian religion, but resemblance to the Church as a social reality is less obvious. Though some comparison with voluntary associations has been made (see below), initiates did not become members of a close-knit society like the Church, and certainly did not feel excluded from all other forms of religion by their initiation into a particular cult. The degree of valid comparison in terms of belief and practice is hard to ascertain, since secrecy was at the heart of a mystery religion and the secret was well kept. However, when Justin Martyr suggested in the second century that the Devil imitated the Christian mysteries in the cult of Mithras one can hardly deny that parallels were perceived, probably with considerable justification.[17]

Far more important is the relationship to Judaism. The background to Paul's comparison of Jewish and Christian worship in 2 Cor. 3.12ff. is that there was a synagogue in Corinth. It has been estimated that Jews made up about a seventh of the population of the Empire at this time, with at least five million living outside Palestine. In most cities they were not citizens but were allowed a measure of self-government and were exempted from civic duties that conflicted with practices such as keeping the Sabbath, observing food laws or avoiding idolatry. The synagogue was therefore an institution with legal powers over its members. Paul's statement, 'From the Jews I've received the thirty-nine lashes five times' (2 Cor. 11.24) is a vivid reminder of this. What this means is that Paul, for the sake of his mission, was both a Jew to Jews and like a Gentile to Gentiles (1 Cor. 9.19–23). He chose, when he could have opted out of the jurisdiction and the punishments of the Jewish authorities, to keep open his access to the synagogue at the cost of frequent punishment for his sharing in Gentile life.[18]

Socially and economically, the Jewish community seems to have had members at most points in the scales of status such as wealth, occupation and education, and so could act as a partial model for the diversity of the Christian community. It was also a network covering the Empire, and offered a total way of life and belief which emphasized worship, teaching, study of Scriptures and an ethical code largely the same as that of Paul. Yet the synagogue, despite the acceptance of some proselytes, was mainly an ethnic group. The difference over entry requirements and the role of the Torah in relation to purity and holiness was fundamental to the social identity of the Church. The Church was influenced (especially later in its pattern of eldership) by synagogue patterns of organization, but its ethos, as further described below, was so different that it cannot be seen as essentially modelled on the synagogue.[19] Yet its basic self-understanding as reflected in Paul was Jewish, applying the Scriptures of Israel to itself as the people of God in the new age of the Messiah.

In the *oikonomia* the basic social unit of the household embodied key status distinctions and hierarchical relationships. Meeks sums it up:

> Within the household, a vertical but not quite unilinear chain connected unequal roles, from slave to paterfamilias, in the most intimate strand, but also included bonds between client and patron and a number of analogous but less formal relations of protection and subordination. Between this household and others there were links of kinship and of friendship, which also often entailed obligations and expectations.[20]

The church met in the setting of a household, it used much household and family terminology about itself, and its own households formed a network of hospitality for travelling Christians. Indeed it was probably due to the division into household-centred units that it was so easy for factions to develop. The 'opponents of Paul' may be partly explained by picturing various households being influenced by visiting Christians to whom they have given hospitality. But the social form of the church was little like the household. Its worship and ritual were unlike anything in pagan domestic religion. The authority of the head of the household in which a group of Christians met was subject to that of the wider Church, represented by apostles, and also to the guidance of leaders, prophets and other charismatics in the congregation. Embracing all this was the sense of belonging to a wider fellowship spanning the Empire, all members of the Church living in fundamental equality as children of God in a way which had no parallel in the household.[21] Later on, as Theissen describes,[22] the Pauline churches adopted far more of the structure of the household, but this was not yet true in Corinth. There the situation was one of complex interaction in the one geographical space where meetings happened. There were divisions and ambiguities as regards the boundaries of church and household, with Paul's tendency being on the one hand to support the conventional roles of men and women, slave and free, and on the other hand to try to relativize even these basic distinctions in the light of the gospel.[23]

As an economic centre Corinth also had many groups related to manufacture and commerce, and those in the same trade would have been gathered in their own quarter of the city. Paul as a tent-maker would have had a ready-made set of contacts in his fellow-tradesmen such as Priscilla and Aquila, with whom he worked and lodged (Acts 18.2–4). But the church itself was not comparable to a trade guild.

Beyond all these groupings, however, there were new developments in the Hellenistic world at this time. Neither the *politeia* nor the *oikonomia* and their component institutions were meeting the needs and hopes of many people. What is today often called 'alienation' was widespread and part of the response was the creation of new sorts of groups.[24] There were intellectual efforts to conceive the 'good life' afresh, such as the Stoic rational, ethical commonwealth. Teachers of such philosophies travelled around and even set up schools, and their instruction and communication network had some similarities with the Church. Malherbe's conclusion is that 'there can be no doubt that Paul was familiar with the different types of philosophers, and that he took great care, on the one hand. to distinguish himself from some of them and, on the other hand, to describe himself in terms commonly used to depict certain ideal philosophers'.[25] And throughout his letters there are signs of Stoic and Cynic ideas, as Malherbe himself shows in his study of the military imagery of 2 Cor. 10.3–6.[26]

But there was another more widespread and popular development which was far more significant for the Church. This was the spread of voluntary associations (in Latin, *collegia*), bound together by the principle of *koinonia*, voluntary sharing or partnership. These had mushroomed and usually had some special interest, such as politics, religion, a craft, a profession, philosophy or sport. Their main function was usually social – holding meals and festivals – and they were an important part of the social identity of many people. Often they had members of diverse backgrounds, were about the same size as the Corinthian church and had some religious ritual in their meetings. To many observers the church must have seemed like another such association, and the church gained in attraction by meeting the same sort of needs. Yet the differences were on closer inspection even more striking. The church claimed a member's whole commitment and loyalty; it had a much greater mixture of backgrounds than any known associations; its special terminology and its self-understanding do not seem to be indebted to the associations; and it was also distinguished by its Empire-wide network.

The striking result of this survey has been that while the church in Corinth had a great deal in common with a variety of institutions it was nevertheless an original creation as a whole, and was by no means simply the development or combination of existing forms. How can this be understood further? We must go beyond the rather external and formal approach so far and attempt to give more of an insider's view.

2 INSIDE THE COMMUNITY

All along you've been thinking that I was making my apology to you. Before God we speak in Christ: everything has been for your building up, my beloved (2 Cor. 12.19).

If we take that statement of the main intention of the letter seriously then the sort of community that Paul was building up is central to grasping its meaning.

'My beloved' is a good place to start. In 2 Corinthians it is striking how much of the language of love, affection, intimacy and warmth – both in pain and joy – is used, often incidentally. There is the family language of children, brothers, parents, betrothal. Compound words are used to express the closest joint involvement: '...as you too join as collaborators in efforts (*synhypourgountes*) on our behalf in prayer' (1.11); 'we are fellow-workers (*synergoi*) for your joy' (1.24); 'you are in our hearts so that we die together (*synapothanein*) and live together (*syzēn*)' (7.3). The use of 'you', 'us', 'we' and 'all' is worth noting as a sign of the mutuality and solidarity, which is sometimes made explicit at length: 'So if we are afflicted it is for your encouragement and salvation; if we are encouraged it is for your encouragement, encouragement that produces endurance of the same sufferings which we also suffer' (1.6; cf. 2.2–4; 3.18; 5.10; 13.13).

What must the church have been like for this language to have been current in it? Clearly too it was not only a matter of language, but of suffering, giving money and hospitality, praying, obeying, forgiving, trying to overcome 'strife, jealousy,

passions, disputes, slanders, tale-bearing, posturing, rebellion'
(12.20), and of greeting one another 'with a holy kiss' (13.12).
So what was going on in this community?

In Paul's letters we see the signs of a new cultural and linguistic entity being formed through faith in the gospel. It had
'in' language, such as 'saints' and 'in Christ', it used a few
foreign words such as *Abba* and *maranatha*, it had formulae for
greetings, blessings, thanks, praise, and concise expressions of
the gospel. It had hymns and songs to Christ, and favourite
passages from the Septuagint (the Greek translation of the
Jewish Scriptures) together with its own ways of interpreting
and applying them.[27]

The issue of the boundaries between Church and world was
crucial, but Paul would not permit the Jewish solution of keeping to the boundaries laid down by Torah. So he had to work
out with the churches what was consistent with the gospel. The
solution was a positively-defined social identity sustained by
rituals which focused on the death and resurrection of Jesus
Christ. The boundary issues were treated with reference to this
new identity, which in its key features was no invention of Paul,
since the two central rituals, baptism and the Lord's Supper,
were inherited by him.

1 Cor. 6.11ff. is a good summary of the main themes of baptism: washing, sanctification, justification, the name of Jesus
Christ, the Spirit of God, union with Christ and the fact of
redemption. Paul appeals to all these in order to show the
distinctiveness in being a Christian, assuming that his readers
acknowledge that baptism was a decisive break with their previous lives. As regards the Lord's Supper, participation in this
common meal, remembering the death and resurrection of
Jesus, communing with him and expecting his return comprised
a fundamental form of identification very different from, for
example, those defined by such matters as legal purity, or doctrinal orthodoxy, or some other form of separation from the
surrounding society (dress, ethics, living place). It was flexible
and adaptable to local conditions. It made good sociological
sense in a city like Corinth, enabling a resilient, intimate fellowship in a pluralist setting. As Paul urged against the abuses of the
Corinthians, this fellowship gave the possibility of dignity and
a lively 'family' life to all, including those of low status.

What features of the church are especially prominent in 2 Corinthians? We have already mentioned the intimacy, mutuality and intensity, which were also illustrated from another angle in the previous chapter as part of a new sort of 'economy'; and in the next chapter we will deal with how power and authority in the church are key themes in the letter. We have also seen how important the wider Church is to the local Christian identity. The collection is the main occasion for noting this in 2 Corinthians but there is also the importance of Paul's co-workers. They play a vital role in communication and instruction, and those most prominent in 2 Corinthians are an apt symbol of the diversity of the Church: Titus is Gentile, Silvanus is Jewish, and Timothy is half-Greek and half-Jewish.

We conclude this section by examining a complex and fundamental characteristic of the church that this letter shows. This is the role of knowledge and its communication. Banks surveys well the centrality of knowledge (and similar concepts such as wisdom, truth, discernment, understanding, testing and thinking) in Paul's ideas of faith, hope, love and community.[28] 1 Corinthians shows knowledge to have been a specially contentious issue in Corinth, and we have already discussed the biblical and contemporary background to this.[29] In 1 Corinthians we get a fascinating insight into the worship in which many of the problems came to a head. In a group which pivoted around the Lord's Supper and accompanying worship this was naturally an arena for achieving recognition and status and for demonstrating power. The gifts of the Spirit mentioned (1 Cor. 12.8ff.) were mostly knowledge and speech gifts (utterance of wisdom, knowledge, faith, prophecy, discernment, tongues, interpretation) and even those which seem not to be such (healing, miracles) would probably have been accompanied by inspired prayer. The picture is of a group in which knowledge plays a constitutive and dynamic role. Paul's critique of what was going on maintains the importance of knowledge but insists on the implications of his decision 'to know nothing among you except Jesus Christ and him crucified' (1 Cor. 2.2). This is the true measure of status and knowledge.

In 2 Corinthians Paul sees his whole ministry as spreading 'the incense of his [God's] knowledge in every place' (2.14), the 'treasure' of the gospel is called 'the enlightenment which is the knowledge of God's glory' and the summary of this gospel in chapter 5 is repeatedly introduced by the claim to knowledge (vv.1,6,11). The boasting competition with his opponents (chaps. 11—12) is concluded by boasting of a relevation which undercuts all claims to be able to boast about revelations (12.9) and reasserts the cross as the key to this strange knowledge.

We will take up this vital theme again in Chapter 9, but for now will draw some of the conclusions relevant to church and society in Corinth. The knowledge of the gospel was intrinsically social. It involved knowing the will and purpose of God in Christ and that divine economy included a new covenant community. That community was the instrument of an information explosion in which its own life and behaviour were vital. It was to be a place of free communication in word and love, a process which is the reflection of God's glory (ch. 3). And at the heart of this communication was the symbol of the cross and the suffering of Paul and others. Here was a 'social construction of reality' in which the most negative realities could help to create community and at the same time act as a radical critique of the rest of society.

3 THE CONTRIBUTION OF SOCIAL DESCRIPTION TO THE INTERPRETATION OF 2 CORINTHIANS

What is the value of this social historical approach for the interpretation of 2 Corinthians? The basic value is to enable us to enter further into the 'common sense' of the world of 2 Corinthians, which was largely taken for granted by the author and readers of the letter. On this basis we have been able to attempt a portrayal of the church in its context. The picture has been of a strong and in many respects original group identity, subject to many conflicting pressures, and shaped by certain rituals, language and habits of behaviour, all of which were part of a new social embodiment of the gospel. Issues of boundaries and status were being worked through in relation to a gospel which was itself understood in various ways, and the definition of roles, authority and power was inevitably fluid and often controversial. This was the setting for Paul's defence of his apostolate. In taking this approach there has been no tension with the traditional scholarly and historical disciplines, and overall the main contribution has been to enrich the understanding which they have had the major role in forming.

Beyond this there is the further possible question of what relevance these results have today. One could within the contemporary Church take Paul's message to the church at Corinth as a norm for the modern urban church. The broad parallels in dynamics and problems (for example as regards status) could be taken as support for parallel solutions. The irony of this is that Paul himself was refusing to take over other forms of the church but was insisting on transforming it in a new context.

If one recognizes more adequately the particularity of the Corinthian situation, which makes it seem almost as strange in some ways as it is familiar in others, then one might try through it to go deeper into the interaction of gospel and context. This is likely to yield a modern application that is less legalistically tied to the reconstruction. It might insist on the need to go through the reconstruction and so far as possible enter into that world, while denying that lessons for today are directly deducible from the letters. Rather, relevance would be seen in the discernment of issues, principles, challenges, options and horizons, and it is worth stating what some of these might be.

If Paul was controversially breaking with other Christian practice in order to deal with a new context, it is likely to be more appropriate to do what he was doing rather than apply as a rule what he said. More profoundly, Paul is preaching a gospel which in the crucifixion has at its heart a reality that radically criticizes attempts to live by 'the letter' or 'the law'. This frees his letters to be more relevant. They may, of course, sometimes have direct lessons for modern situations, but there is no rule that they must. The problems of status distinctions in the church, of the boundaries of the church, of powerful élites which simply mirror the world's way of running organizations, of authority outside the local congregation, of order and freedom in worship, of innovation in tradition, and much else are perennial.

Yet, even where there is quite a close parallel in some respects, the overall 'ecology' is likely to be different. Detailed social description helps to show this and so to guard against treating the letters as contemporary documents. But illumination may be by contrast as much as by similarity, and part of the value of retrieving this ancient social world is to show how Paul deals with another perennial Christian issue, the indigenization of the gospel. Seeing the Church in different contexts helps to illuminate what the gospel is. There is no gospel in general, it is always rooted in particular contexts, language, conflicts, interests. It is a social and linguistic entity which can no more be communicated in general than a language can be spoken in general. Yet, as with a language, its 'grammar', its basic codes, can be elucidated. Grammar can never give the content to be communicated in a situation, but it can act as a second-order guide which is especially helpful in teaching the language to others and extending range and fluency.

So in order to appreciate the 'grammar' of the gospel one needs to do justice to the social transformation envisaged by Paul, which he articulated through the specific conditions of his churches. Especially if one is concerned with the contemporary performance of the gospel it is desirable to have understood Paul's performance with attention to its sociological dimension. Such immersion in a classic in all its specificity is the way to prepare for new classic performances appropriate to different conditions. There will be similar grammar even though the sentences are very different. Later Christian understanding of Paul usually failed to see how concrete social conditions and relationships are intrinsic to every form of the gospel.

So the social historical approach can be taken up into the larger project of theological retrieval. It can also fuel a hermeneutic of suspicion. This can take various forms. The most radical would offer a framework of understanding within which any reference to God would become meaningless, or, more usually, would be seen as an aspect of ideology with social and psychological functions which adequately explain it. Such reductionist explanation needs to be grappled with by anyone hoping to arrive with integrity at an alternative position – our test case will be the question of authority in the next chapter. But it also must beware of 'innocent criticism' whose own presuppositions need to be examined. For its sociological method is informed by a world-view and interests through which vital issues raised by Paul are already prejudged, and the debate must be carried on as much at the level of overall world-view as of the interpretation of Paul.

Yet there are other, less totalitarian, ways of suspecting the appearances of Paul's letters and churches. So one can show what Weber called the 'elective affinities' between the social reality of the churches, on the one hand, and the gospel of Paul on the other. Is it not likely that those with high 'status inconsistency' would be attracted to a gospel whose central figure represents a paradox in status, the Son of God crucified? Might not the strong emphasis on eschatology, with its radical change and intense expectation, be correlated with the need of the young community for clear boundaries and enthusiastic commitment? Does not the pluralist, mobile urban situation in Corinth make the family characteristics of the church seem a sensible response to a social and psychological need felt by many ordinary people? Besides, the fairly rigid social structure of the Roman Empire might make the church attractive to those with ability and initiative who would be frustrated in the wider society but in the church could find security, scope for leadership and a call to energetic living in response to an ultimate vision. Likewise the internal problems of the church can be correlated with social factors, and it is possible to conjecture what more information might help us to explain.

Such affinities are neutral as regards fundamental conclusions about the truth of Paul's gospel. They may lead one in a re-ductionist direction, or they may illustrate the incarnational nature of the gospel, always inextricable from particular con-ditioned situations. But they certainly call in question some ways of using the letters in theology. A gospel about a person involved in ordinary physical existence to the point of death, and which is then maintained through his 'body' in history in ways that include travels, dangers, arguments and money as well as for-giveness and hope in God – this is not likely to be done justice to by a theology which, for example, abstracts truth content from historical particularity or locates primary experience of God in the interiority of immediate consciousness. An essential ingredient for an adequate interpretation and theology must be social and cultural understanding, informed by the particulari-ties of the Bible, history and tradition in order to come better prepared to the task of being faithful and innovative in the present situation.

Peter Winch, discussing the problems faced by anthropologists trying to understand another society, concludes:

> My aim is not to engage in moralising, but to suggest that the concept of 'learning from' which is involved in the study of other cultures is closely linked with the concept of 'wisdom'. We are confronted not just with different techniques, but with new possibilities of good and evil, in relation to which men may come to terms with life.[30]

Learning from a letter of Paul has similarities to such primitive societies, and wisdom is a good term for the sort of unsystematic, highly particular and nuanced appreciation, insight and assessment that may result. The 'hermeneutical gap' can be crossed, just as it is in the wealth of otherness and 'gaps' that make up any pluralist contemporary society, and the results of sharing in the common sense and unusual sense of another culture are not controllable or predictable.

NOTES

1   For surveys see Thomas F. Best, 'The Sociological Study of the New Testament', *SJT*, vol. 36 No. 2 (1983), 181–94; Abraham Malherbe, *Social Aspects of Early Christianity* (Louisiana State University Press, Baton Rouge and London, 1977); John H. Schütz, 'Introduction' to *The Social Setting of Pauline Christianity. Essays on Corinth*, by Gerd Theissen (Fortress Press, Philadelphia, 1982); Robin Scroggs, 'The Sociological Interpretation of the New Testament: The Present State of Research', *NTS* 26 (1982), 164–79; Richard L. Rohrbaugh, 'Methodological Considerations in the Debate over Social Class Status of Early Christians', *JAAR*, vol. lii No. 3 (Sept. 1984), 519–46; Robert Banks, *Paul's Idea of Community. The Early House Churches in their Historical Setting* (Paternoster Press, Exeter, 1980).

2   Theissen, op. cit., 99: Aquila, Fortunatus, Gaius, Lucius, Priscilla, Quartus, Titius Justus, Tertius.

3   For more details see Victor Paul Furnish, *II Corinthians* (Doubleday, New York, 1984), 4–22; Jerome Murphy-O'Connor. *St. Paul's Corinth. Texts and Archaeology* (Michael Glazier, Wilmington, Delaware, 1983); Theissen op. cit., 99ff.

4   Murphy-O'Connor, op. cit., 167ff.

5   Rohrbaugh, op. cit.

6   cf. Bruce J. Malina, *The New Testament World. Insights from Cultural Anthropology* (SCM, London, 1983); Wayne A. Meeks,

The First Urban Christians. The Social World of the Apostle Paul
(Yale University Press, New Haven and London, 1983), which is
probably the best overall treatment of the subject; also Rohrbaugh, op. cit., who questions the method of Meeks. The criticisms are most relevant to analysis on a larger scale than one city.
Within such a context Rohrbaugh is right to point to the risk of
subjective weighing of the various elements in a synthetic judgement of status; but that seems to us, as to Meeks, a risk worth
taking.

7   See Malina, op. cit., Ch. 2, especially pp. 32f.

8   op. cit., Chaps. 1, 2.

9   See Theissen, op. cit., 75ff.

10   J. H. Kent, *Inscriptions 1926–1960. Corinth: Results*, vol. 9 Pt 3,
     (Princeton University Press, Princeton, 1966), 100.

11   Meeks, op. cit., Chaps. 2, 6.

12   Murphy-O'Connor, op. cit., 153ff.

13   op. cit., 73.

14   op. cit.

15   For example on the role of women. Several of the Christian
     women mentioned in connection with Paul's churches had high
     'status inconsistency'. They included some who, untypically for
     women, seem to have been independently wealthy (e.g. Phoebe,
     Rom. 16.1); carried on business (e.g. Lydia, a dealer in purple
     textiles, Acts 16.14ff.); and have been heads of households (Lydia;
     Chloe, 1 Cor. 1.11, though she may not have been a Christian).
     Women prayed and prophesied in the worship of the church (1
     Cor. 11.5). Paul's teaching in 1 Cor. 11.2–16 means in social terms
     (which is not to deny other dimensions of its meaning) that he
     affirms the practice of women taking initiatives in worship but
     wants them to maintain conventional sexual differentiation in
     dress and hairstyle. The background seems to have been that the
     new social freedom of the church attracted and gave a welcome
     identity to some able, unconventional women. Some of these went
     to what Paul considered extremes in breaking with the surround-
     ing norms, provoking his characteristic response: he affirms a
     traditional Jewish position while allowing for Christian content.
     In this case, that means affirming the subordination of women to
     men while allowing them to play leading roles in worship. His
     instruction to women to keep silence (1 Cor. 14.34–6) seems to
     have been a response to a specific problem of disorder. The wives
     were interrupting worship with questions about it to men. Public
     discussions between men and women were frowned on in that
     culture. So the double concern for order in worship and the im-
     pression made on visitors explains Paul's instruction (see Banks,

op. cit., 125f.; on the whole issue of women see Meeks, op. cit., Ch. 2). Another dimension of this is the distinguishing of household from church, all the more important because the meetings were 'public gatherings which assembled in private space' (Stephen C. Barton, 'Paul's Sense of Place: an Anthropological Approach to Community Formation in Corinth', in *NTS* 32 (1986), 225–46).

16 For a survey see Furnish, op. cit., 15ff.

17 The literature on mystery religions is vast. An introduction to the discussion may be found in A. D. Nock, *Conversion* (OUP, Oxford, 1933).

18 See A. E. Harvey, 'Forty Strokes Save One: Social Aspects of Judaizing and Apostasy', in *Alternative Approaches to New Testament Study*, ed. A. E. Harvey (SPCK, London, 1985), 79–96.

19 Meeks, op. cit., 80f.; Malina, op. cit., Ch. 6; Banks, op. cit., 17–19, 49f., 111f., Chaps. 13, 14.

20 Meeks, op. cit., 30.

21 Meeks, op. cit., 75f.

22 See Theissen, op. cit., 37, 106ff.: Ephesians shows this most clearly.

23 See note 15 above, especially Barton, op. cit.

24 See Banks, op. cit., Ch. 1.

25 Abraham J. Malherbe, 'Antisthenes and Odysseus, and Paul at War', *Harvard Theological Review* 76.2 (1983), 172.

26 ibid.

27 For an excellent description see Meeks, op. cit., 88ff.

28 Banks, Ch. 7.

29 See above, Chaps. 3, 4.

30 'Understanding a Primitive Society', in *Rationality* ed. Bryan R. Wilson (Basil Blackwell, Oxford, 1970), 106.

8

The Authority of Paul

The question of Paul's authority is vital to the interpretation of 2 Corinthians for several reasons. The most obvious is that one of the main issues between him and the Corinthians is his authority in relation to them. But, because this letter became part of the New Testament, its treatment of authority and of other matters became authoritative for later Christians too. So we must ask about Paul's authority (especially through this letter) in the context of the canon of Scripture and church history.

Within that history authority has always been a disputed issue, but recent centuries have seen a crisis of authority in Christianity and other spheres which has had fundamental and worldwide repercussions. We are still very much involved in this and it must be taken seriously in discussing Paul's authority. Does Paul in 2 Corinthians have any serious claim to relevance and importance today? Is he not so remote or marginal or discredited that his plausibility as an authority is unrecoverable?

Authority can for the purposes of this chapter be initially defined as a form of the exercise of power which involves the right to power. It entails obedience and so is essentially inter-active, a social relationship whose meaning and interpretation are vital to the nature of any community.

It is not surprising that issues of authority were contentious in the early Church. Whenever traditional forms of exercising power are challenged and new ones emerge there are almost certain to be conflicts. The church Paul had founded in Corinth was only about five years old and was caught in the interplay of the forces described in the previous chapter. In 2 Corinthians authority is the primary social relationship with regard to which the others already described must be understood, and a close examination of this will have important consequences for both the understanding of the letter and its contemporary relevance.

Our approach will be first to discover the signs of Paul's own way of understanding and using his authority in 2 Corinthians, and to relate these to the issue of his apostleship and to his whole context in Church and society. We will then follow 2 Corinthians as it becomes a part of the main written authority of the Church and bring it into dialogue with the way Scripture and church authority developed. Then we will discuss the contemporary relevance of Paul's authority, and will conclude with some remarks about what we see as the central symbol of authority.

1 PAUL AND AUTHORITY IN 2 CORINTHIANS

The whole letter can be seen as an example of Paul's exercise of authority. In Chapters 1 and 2 above we gave our understanding of how this is carried out. We will now analyse it further, paying special attention to how relationships of authority are characterized.

The opening words of the letter give the three main participants in the debate about authority: 'Paul, apostle'; 'of Christ Jesus through the will of God'; and '...to the church of God in Corinth'. Authority is, as we said, relational and interactive, and the key relationships in the letter are between Paul the apostle, God the Father of Jesus Christ and the Corinthian church of God founded by Paul.

We start with God. Whenever authority is an issue Paul's central appeal is to God. His sense of speaking and acting in the presence of God recurs constantly: 'We speak in Christ in God's presence' (2.17); so does his insistence that '...to God we are transparent' (5.11; cf.1.23; 3.4; 4.2; 5.10; 7.12; 8.21). Paul's adequacy is from God (3.5), his power is from God (4.7) and when he summarizes his message and ministry he says: 'The whole thing comes from God, who has reconciled us to himself through Christ and has given to us the ministry of reconciliation.' (5.18).

The vital medium in the relationship of God with Paul and the Corinthians is the 'gospel of God' (11.7). The gospel is knowledge with power from God. It is an ongoing dynamic, realizing the new creation, and it is the measure of Paul's right to authority.[1] If he does not preach it, correspond to it in his life and take responsibility for the Corinthians' faithfulness to it then he forfeits that right. God, Christ, knowledge and the gospel are inseparably united as the source of power and authority: 'the light of the gospel of the glory of Christ who is the image of God' (4.3). That verse also points to a key term for the manifestation of authority in 2 Corinthians, glory. It is through what he says about the glory of God shown in Christ (involving a reconception of who God is – see Chapter 9) and the glory and boasting of himself and his opponents that Paul goes to the heart of the authority issue.

The second aspect of this triangular relationship is that of Paul and the Corinthians. We have already argued (Chapter 2) for continuity between the situations behind 1 and 2 Corinthians. One feature of this is their common concern with power and authority. In these two letters Paul mentions *dynamis* (power) twenty-four times compared with ten in all the other letters that are certainly by him; for *exousia* (authority) and *exousiazein* the figures are fifteen and five. How is Paul's relationship with this church to be described?[2]

If taken at face value the most striking feature of his language is that it is persuasive, appealing, encouraging, pleading. The reason is clear: the only way Paul can have any effective authority is if the Corinthians recognize it voluntarily, from the heart. For this a common basis must be acknowledged in their joint faith. So in an early rebuttal of any misunderstanding Paul says: 'Not that we lord it over your faith; rather we are fellow-workers for your joy – and you stand on your own two feet in faith' (1.24). Paul never conceives his authority apart from his conviction that the Corinthians are called by God, share his faith in God, are 'in Christ' and have the Spirit (1.21–2). His relationship with them is part of a more fundamental joint relationship with God. His appeals are to the shared gospel and Spirit, to the Jewish Scriptures (see above, Chapter 3) and to the common ethos described in the previous chapter. His exertion of authority is through interpreting these in a way which must try to inspire the agreement of the Corinthians, who have already taken the radical step of joining the church, are perhaps fifty strong and know him and each other very well. In such a situation of intimate bonding and many types of informal and formal constraint, the exercise of authority blurs into all the many factors that promote or destroy mutual confidence, and it is always dependent on the mutual recognition of a common higher authority. This is double-edged: it both gives them an independence of Paul, requiring him to persuade and convince them rather than simply order them, and it also gives an ultimate urgency and familial intensity to Paul's self-defence.

Yet for all the joint participation in faith and equality before God the relationship is by no means symmetrical. Paul is different: he is called by God to be an apostle, he has founded the church and he has a continuing responsibility for it. This is the most contentious side of his authority. He is identified with the gospel in a special sense, which means that response to his ministry can be equated with response to God: 'for we are Christ's aroma to God among those being saved and those perishing, to some a stench from death to death, to others a scent from life to life' (2.15–16). This identification takes up his whole life. His 'biography of reversal' enacts it, and he sees his very body displaying it (4.8–14; 6.3–10).

But he also differentiates himself from the gospel. He is simply its servant, its vessel, its ambassadorial spokesman. He is both identified with his gospel and differentiated from it. His own explanation of this is that it is demanded by his vocation and by the gospel, and response to the letter pivots around how this explanation is assessed. In the servant of the gospel, Paul claims, there can be both an ultimate urgency with accompanying authority, and also a self-effacement eliminating any pride in oneself except insofar as one has corresponded to one's message. To be identified with this message is to be in union with one who was poor, humble, weak, and dead. If this is how true power from God comes then it must involve a critique of other sorts of power, authority and effectiveness, and of all boasting and pride. There is a new pivot for all authority, Jesus Christ, in the light of whom not only Corinthian ideas and behaviour but also Moses and apostles can be questioned. For Paul's own apostleship it means that authority can and even

must go together with what seems its denial: a slave-like existence, humiliation, vulnerability and the need to plead and persuade at every point.

The third aspect, and the one around which the authority
issue in Corinth focused, was that of the content of apostleship.
In the early Church at this time there seems to have been no
normative concept of what an apostle was, and apostolic authority was probably not a recognized category. In Paul's letters
we see traces of the various interpretations of apostleship. He
himself stresses the gospel as the criterion of faith and of apostleship. The main content of apostleship seems to be the founding
of Christian communities. Paul's concerns are that God has
called him, that his gospel is right and that his life and work
correspond to it. These are the elements of his authority. Clearly
in the Church there were alternative criteria, such as having
been part of Jesus' ministry or having been a witness of the
resurrection appearances. Paul sees such criteria of legitimacy as
extrinsic to the essential matter of conformity to God's call and
to the content of the gospel – 'for Paul no claim to apostolic
legitimacy could resolve a dispute that centres on authority'.[3]

To understand Paul's apostleship more fully it must also be
seen as a new sort of mission, as already discussed in Chapters
6 and 7 above. He developed his mission through his own
travels, through a team of co-workers who could either ac-
company him or go on visits by themselves, and through writing
letters. His authority was exercised in each of those ways, and in
order to have the most effective sort of ministry he refused to be
bound by precedents which laid down, for example, how a
missionary was to be supported (see above pp. 181ff.). In setting
up his churches he does not seem to have tried to impose any
particular pattern of organization. A great deal, both in govern-
ance and way of life and detailed ethics, was left to each community, with the result that Corinth, for example, seems to have
developed very differently from Philippi. Authority in terms of
leadership and influence over the community can be helpfully
divided into three overlapping types in these churches.[4] First,
there was that which appealed to authoritative figures in the
wider Christian movement – in 1 Corinthians 1 there are mentioned allegiances to Paul, Apollos, Peter and even (perhaps in
an attempt to transcend such appeals, echoed in 2 Cor. 10.7) to

Christ. Second, there was the authority that came with status of
various sorts, as discussed in the previous chapter – those who
provided the places of meeting, who were heads of households,
or had more education, wealth or power. Third, there was the
authority that came with gifts of the Spirit, among which Paul
included apostleship.

The crisis that Paul is answering in 2 Corinthians involved all
three. There were outside Christian leaders who threatened
Paul's standing with the Corinthians. Paul's habits and attitudes
as regards such worldly marks of status as letters of recommendation, how he earned his living, rhetorical ability, and pure
Jewish origins were also an issue. So was the demonstration of
spiritual gifts (12.1–4, 12). These come to a head in chapters
10—13, but the previous chapters can be seen as part of the same
self-defence. In the early chapters Paul is sensitive to criticism
at a number of points (1.12–14; 1.17; 1.23—2.16; 2.17—3.3;
4.1–2; 5.11–13; 6.3; 7.2; 7.8–12; 8.20). His main response there
is to lay out the basic features of his authority (God's call, the
gospel, the building up of the church, the enactment of the
gospel in his life). He describes a complex network of active
relationships through which the quality of his apostolate can be
discerned.

This network's main features are best summed up in 4.5–7.
'For the God who said, "Out of darkness light will shine"...'
expresses the priority and initiative of God. '...is the one who
has shone in our hearts...' points to the shared Spirit revealing
Christ and uniting all equally in him. 'Ourselves as your slaves
for Jesus' sake' combines the apostle as slave, working to build
up the church, with the qualification of prior loyalty to Christ
from which rather un-slavelike language can flow. 'For we do
not proclaim ourselves, but Christ Jesus as Lord', differentiates
Paul from his gospel, and this is carried through into the sphere
of power: 'We have this treasure in earthenware pots, in order
that this extraordinary power may be God's and not come from
us.' At the heart of all this is a key image of ultimate authority,
expressing the content of the gospel: 'the enlightenment which
is the knowledge of God's glory in the face of Christ'. God's
glory, the reality of his authority, is focused in the face of Christ.
Paul's theology of authority has its most significant symbol
here, as the later parts of this chapter and Chapter 9 try to
show.

In chapters 10—13 Paul's passionate peroration recapitulates many of the earlier arguments and themes, and the more explicit handling of sensitive, hurtful issues shows their depths and their ambiguities. Our standpoint on these chapters is his commitment to building up the church which Paul repeats twice in 10.8 and 12.19.

Paul's agonizing dilemma is clear. His aim is to build up the Corinthians, but if they lack confidence and trust in him that cannot happen. To deal with the crisis of confidence he is forced to defend himself, but every aspect of his self-defence is ambiguous when tested by his own gospel. So he engages in this suspect exercise but brackets it between those two statements of what he sees as its only purpose, the building up of the church.

The most obvious ambiguity is over boasting, saying what he is proud of about himself. On the one hand, '"Let him who prides himself on anything, pride himself on the Lord"; for the person who commends himself is not the one approved, but the one whom the Lord commends' (10.17–18). On the other hand, 'Since many take pride in achievements at the human level (*kata sarka*), I too will pride myself' (11.18). By irony and other rhetorical means he tries to have it both ways, managing both to mention the reasons why he is at least the equal of his opponents in their own *kata sarka* terms, and also to undermine such legitimations by taking most pride in the things that seem least impressive but which conform to the gospel. The ballast for this precarious exercise is in the earlier part of the letter, where he has tried to make clear his gospel's relation to glory and reputation in contrast to ways of understanding and living *kata sarka*.

What about the content of the accusations against Paul? The first is to do with the discrepancy between his letters and his presence (10.1,10). This links in with the theme of weakness. As regards the authority of Paul, the most likely of the many suggestions as to what the situation was behind this seems to be Oostendorp's.[5] He argues that Paul was accused of being too weak a disciplinarian in contrast with his opponents. Paul opens his reply by a strong statement of his intention to bring about obedience (10.1–12), and later rejects his opponents' harsh approach to discipline (11.20). Paul insists on the co-operation of the church, and his case is undergirded by his earlier rejoicing

over the success of his methods (1.23—2.11; 7.8–16). He is concerned to show both that there is a weakness, humility and
vulnerability that the gospel inspires and also that this is not
simply weakness. Rather it has precisely the power of the gospel
(10.4–6). Paul is not shy about claiming authority or exercising
power, but it must be in line with the aim of building up a
church through the gospel. If Oostendorp is right, the opening
appeal, 'I myself, Paul, encourage you through the gentle restraint of Christ...' (10.1), points to the heart of the whole
matter as Paul sees it: an authority informed by the Spirit of
Christ.

There are other signs of objections to Paul's unimpressive
way of being an apostle – idiosyncratic speech (11.6), refusal to
demand payment (11.7–9; 12.13,16,17), and lack of reliance on
Jewish credentials (11.22) or on visions, revelations, signs,
wonders and acts of power (12.1–12). And clearly the attacks
threatened his very authenticity as a Christian minister (11.23;
cf. 10.7; 11.4). In response he again builds on the earlier part of
the letter. There is the same stress on suffering witness in being
a *diakonos* (11.23–30) and Paul both identifies himself with
his gospel and differentiates himself from it. The climactic
affirmation of this is 13.1–4:

> ...if I come again, I will not refrain (from judgement), since you seek
> proof that the one speaking in me is Christ. He is not weak in (encoun-
> tering) you but is powerful among you. For out of weakness he was
> crucified, but he lives out of God's power. So we are weak in him, but we
> will live with him out of God's power in (encountering) you.

That is the final knot tying his authority into the heart of the
gospel.

2 WHAT SORT OF AUTHORITY IS THIS?

So far the main standpoint from which authority has been
analysed has been that of Paul's letter. We will complete that
now by trying to characterize Paul's whole approach in
2 Corinthians in general terms before asking some more critical
questions.

It is no accident that the treatment of authority has come after our previous two chapters. Paul conceives his authority as being in the service of the new economy of God and, as part of that, enabling the building up of the church. He is primarily concerned with the 'new creation'; his own authority, for all its importance, is a secondary matter which he is forced by the situation into defending. The key questions therefore are: What sort of authority best serves that economy and community? How can the new social relations described in Chapters 6 and 7 be promoted?

There are several elements in Paul's answer. First of all, he is no idealist in the sense of thinking that the crisis in Corinth is mainly about a clash of ideas or theologies. The Corinthian correspondence shows him very clear about the role of group interest, personal loyalties, power relations in the local and wider church, pressures of culture and society, sex, money, means of persuasion, physical presence or absence, example and shared experience. The thrust of his answer is to locate his own authority firmly within such factors, in all their complexity and ambiguity. His is an embodied authority. Word and deed are inseparably united as regards his own authenticity as an apostle. So he rejects formal claims to legitimation which abstract from the content of the apostle's message and example. Another consequence is that he is willing to engage in all the messy business of conflict and argument over authority, and to use all the practical means of his mission to influence the result. This principle of the embodiment of authority is directly related to the example of Jesus Christ.

Second, for all the stress on his authority and its embodiment, this is by no means an individualist or monarchical concept. Its source is God alone. But how, according to Paul, does God rule? – Through Jesus Christ, by having the gospel shared, by giving the Spirit. It seems that he rules his new creation by distributing his power and authority. So Paul's apostleship is one of many gifts of the Spirit, which are all for service (1 Cor. 12.5; cf.2 Cor. 3) in building up the church, and it is inconceivable apart from participation in this new sociality, with its trust, mutuality and death of the old self: 'He died for all so that those who live should no longer live for themselves, but for the one who died and was raised for them' (5.15). Apostleship is the leading gift of the Spirit because it takes a lead in the sharing of the power of the gospel by founding new churches. The founding and sustaining of his churches inspires Paul's concern to persuade, encourage and appeal, and by the standards of discipline of other institutions lays him open to the charge of weakness. The root of this principle of the distribution of authority is also in the heart of Paul's gospel, in joint participation in Christ and the sharing of the Spirit.

Third, Paul's authority is vulnerable. There are many ways in which he could make it safer or less agonizing, such as reliance on formal legitimation, or having a ministry and message that appealed more to his Jewish credentials, or being less concerned about the quality of church life. But just as he insists several times on the dangerous nature of the rest of his ministry, so he takes the risky way of authority. Essential to it is the trust and faithfulness of the Corinthians, which means that it is constantly being threatened or subverted. This fragility is built into it and it would not be the same sort of authority if it were less vulnerable. So time and again Paul tries to rescue his authority by appealing for recognition that this odd sort of ministry, open to dangers and contingencies from all sides, is in fact the touchstone for true authority, the reason again being at the centre of the gospel: 'For the love of Christ constrains us, in that we have come to this verdict, that one died for all – so all died' (5.14).

Fourth, interpretation plays a crucial role in Paul's authority. Schütz defines authority as 'the interpretation of power'.[6] It interprets both by word and act. It differs from force in needing to be able to give an account of itself acceptable to those who obey it. Paul in 2 Corinthians is primarily interpreting the gospel and his own calling, but this involves the interpretation of Scripture (Chapter 3 above), of events, relationships and motives. The importance of interpretation means that authority can even be described by Friedrich as a 'quality of communication',[7] and this ties in to the present chapter what we have said about Paul's language, rhetoric and ways of arguing. The letter's whole content and form are relevant to its way of exercising authority.

Fifth, Paul's authority is eschatological. It of course draws on tradition, the gospel shared with the rest of the Church, but that message is seen to be about a promise in process of fulfilment.

There can be no absolutizing of past or present in this perspective, and there is a critique of forms of legalism. The Holy
Spirit is a downpayment or guarantee whose truth will only be
demonstrated in the future. Paul sees his ministry as helping to
realize God's future, reflecting a glory that will only be unam-
biguously apparent at the consummation. So every present form
is tested by its openness to that future. The theme of glory, in all
its complexity, is the most helpful for tracing Paul's concept of
an eschatological authority which is also powerful in the present.
We discuss this further in our final chapter.

Finally, the pervasive feature of this authority is its appeal to
God.

So the general picture that emerges is of Paul's authority as
embodied, distributed, vulnerable, interpretative, eschatological
and from God, and each feature can be intrinsically related to
his gospel. But that is seeing it from Paul's standpoint. What
happens when he is viewed with more suspicion?

It is possible to be suspicious in a thoroughgoing way by
holding that, for example, Paul was deliberately using the
gospel as an instrument of selfish power and that 2 Corinthians
is a conscious attempt to manipulate the Corinthians into sub-
mission. Such a position can interpret all the evidence consistently (using the principle of disbelieving anything Paul says
that contradicts it) and there is no conclusive argument against
it. But such utter and cynical lack of sincerity on Paul's part
does not seem the most likely conclusion from reading his letters
and from noting the backing given to him by Acts and the
tradition's early use of his writings as authoritative.

A more plausible and more common accusation is that Paul
was to some degree deceived. He may have been sincere, but
that is no guarantee against the corruption of power. What he
intended and what he actually did may have been quite different,
and as we only have his side of the situation we need to be
especially alert to this possibility. Religion easily acts as an
ideology to justify and enhance our own interests, and it is all
the more dangerous when the ideology is sincerely held to be
unconditionally true. Let us look at each of the six principles of
Paul's authority in reverse order.

The appeal to God is the most easily suspected of all. Everyone
with whom Paul is engaged in the letter (Jews, other Christians)

made the same appeal, and it was well suited to polemical use by all sides. Paul even sharpened the difficulty by refusing to be content with a legitimacy coming from God through scriptural backing or formal criteria of apostleship, and insisting on his personal commissioning 'through the will of God' (1.1), and on an identification of response to his message with response to God. There might even seem to be a confusion of identity between Paul and God, and his immense confidence could be parallelled time and again in the pathology of religious delusion. This could be true even if one does not go further in rejecting appeals to God by doubting God's ability to communicate or even his existence.

As regards eschatology, hopes and promises lend themselves easily to manipulation. Paul can be seen as fostering eschatological anxiety. He may be doing it in good faith, but the function of it is to work on fears and insecurities in order to intensify the urgency of his appeal for obedience. Threats of death and judgement and the offer of privilege in another world lie behind his claims, and the common faith can be an ideal instrument for enforcing personal power.

As regards Paul's authority seen as the interpretation of power, the crucial questionable move is again his identification of the gospel of God with his own authority. This is supported by his way of interpreting Scripture, which can make it appear as his ventriloquist's dummy, saying what he wants it to say. His whole case, using rhetoric to disclaim rhetoric and verbal violence to denigrate his opponents, can be seen as a form of eloquent coercion.

Paul's celebration of his vulnerability could be seen as making a virtue of necessity. His legitimacy as an apostle was suspect by formal criteria such as having been part of Jesus' ministry or one of the original witnesses to his resurrection; once he was committed to the Gentile mission his Jewish credentials were bound to be devalued; and his concern for the quality of church life is inseparable from his desire to remain in control of it. He was in fact in a weak position in Corinth, and the gospel of the crucified Christ allowed him to turn that to his advantage. Nietzsche is the modern thinker who has given most ammunition to Paul's accusers on this point, arguing that Christianity is a means whereby the weak are enabled to rule the strong.

The principle of the distribution of power and authority is shown to be hollow if the previous accusations are true. It makes a fine rhetoric to cover Paul's desire to dominate, on the common political grounds that, for example, the power of some dictator or élite is more secure if it is in the name of 'the people'. For Paul, the Corinthian possession of the Spirit is not a basis for challenging him, but the reason why they should obey him.

Finally, the suspicion of Paul comes to a head in the examination of his embodiment of authority. The case against him so far has been that, however sound the principles in what he says, what he is actually doing can be seen very differently. In line with this, each area of ambiguous involvement can be turned to Paul's disadvantage: he advocates social control by sexual repression, conformity, alienation from the surrounding society, and a group mentality that suppresses dissent; the collection for the church in Jerusalem is used to enhance his own position; and he is intolerant of any competition with himself as the reference person for the community.

Nearly all of the above accusations appear in the most comprehensive indictment of Paul's exercise of authority to appear in recent years, Graham Shaw's *The Cost of Authority. Manipulation and Freedom in the New Testament*.[8] How convincing are they?

Shaw employs a method of thoroughgoing suspicion, with an especially sharp moral concern to expose the manipulative use of power. Texts are consistently interpreted in this light and a damning cumulative case is built up against Paul. The ambiguities are resolved unfavourably to Paul and Shaw sees the ideal of freedom through the gospel corrupted and distorted. It is helpful to compare this with Schütz's approach. His method is what we called in Chapter 6 one of retrieval rather than suspicion. His is a more detailed, descriptive study. He refuses to polarize freedom and authority, and uses sociological categories to characterize the context and content of Paul's apostleship. He follows minutely the complexities of Paul's language and theology, takes account of the various constraints and options facing him, and cumulatively makes moral and Christian sense of Paul's exercise of authority.

The divergence is not one that can simply be resolved at the

level of detailed exegetical argument, even though we would
want to dispute many of Shaw's interpretations.[9] There are also
presuppositions and a whole horizon within which Paul's letters
are being read by each scholar. And as we suggested in Chapter
5 (following Ricoeur), it is probably not possible to have a
synthesis of the methods of suspicion and retrieval. Even
though each can contribute to the other, one is bound to be
pre-eminent. Clearly our own way has been that of Schütz, and
the several chapters of this book are our cumulative case. The
suspicions are sometimes persuasive in detail – Paul was radical
and controversial, he did not pull his verbal punches, and his
embodiment of the gospel was ambiguous and flawed. But the
overall view depends greatly on presuppositions about God
(and the possibility of his commissioning of Paul), about the
gospel, and about authority as conducive to or in competition
with freedom, and also on the way the situation behind the letter
is reconstructed – if, for example, Paul is indeed fighting to
defend a gentler and 'weaker' method of discipline, then many
of Shaw's interpretations are wrong. Our argument against
Shaw is integral to our interpretation in each chapter.

Our conclusion is that, far from being an oppressive authori-
tarian, Paul was working out, with some success, a pattern of
authority that enabled a set of social relations through which
there was new freedom, energy and mutuality. Meeks, whose
study complements that of Schütz by filling out the social
description of Paul's churches, sums up the picture as one 'of
a great fluidity, of a complex, multipolar, open-ended process
of mutual discipline'.[10]

3 2 CORINTHIANS AND AUTHORITY IN THE CHRISTIAN TRADITION

For any institution to last it must have vehicles for its continua-
tion. In the Church two of the most important were the pattern
of ministry and the twofold canon of Scripture, Old Testament
with New Testament. 2 Corinthians is part of the history of
these crucial means of maintaining Christian identity through
authority acknowledged in persons and writings. We will look
briefly at it in relation to the way ministry and the canon devel-

oped, our concern being to sketch a picture in broad lines in order to show the relevance of this letter to assessment and development of the tradition today.

(i) MINISTRY

As regards ministry, we have already situated Paul's apostleship in relation to leadership in Corinth and the wider Church. In sociological terms, during Paul's lifetime ministry in his churches was only rudimentarily institutionalized. There were various types of ministry, all seen as gifts of the Spirit. Paul listed them several times (1 Cor. 12.8–10, 28–30; Rom. 12.6–8) and tried to bring some order into how they were understood and used. The outstanding feature in contrast with later patterns is the general participation of believers in the gifts, without any sense of 'ministers' being a distinct group. In the later letter to the Ephesians, probably not by Paul, the list (4.11) is more select and formalized, and in the post-Pauline letters to Timothy and Titus there are various signs of ministry being institutional-ized – leadership is more special, criteria for office are given, there is laying on of hands, the chief task of leaders is to maintain the teaching content of apostolic tradition, and there is no mention of widely distributed charismatic gifts.

Such institutionalizing might be seen as carrying further what Paul himself had begun in the face of problems of church order, and also as simply obeying the elementary laws of group survival into the second generation. In order to ensure faithfulness to the received gospel there was a formal procedure for recognizing leaders, and these were a more distinct, specialized group with more clearly defined responsibilities. Their authority was still derived through the Holy Spirit, but their ministry was no longer seen as just one among the many charismatic gifts.

This was part of a wider change in the nature of the com-munity, which took on more of the hierarchical nature of the Hellenistic household, and in doing so reflected more of the surrounding society's power relations. Later on many of the Roman Empire's patterns had parallels in the Church. It was a process which has been repeated with variations in many new movements, as the charismatic impetus of the beginning is channelled into routine structures and procedures. In the

Church the general pattern by the end of the first century had moved towards a uniform model of groups of elders (*presbyteroi*, *episkopoi*) as the specialized authoritative ministers. The elders tended to annexe the power of two other sorts of authority mentioned earlier, that of the hosts or patrons of house churches and others with similar positions of secular influence, and that of charismatic figures, such as prophets. This was by no means a smooth process, and in the early period, as all through church history, there were tensions between hierarchical, secular and prophetic types of authority. Edward Schillebeeckx sums up the complex history of the hierarchical developments from the second century as follows:

> In broad outline, the structure of the church's ministry thus develops as follows: along the lines of the New Testament 'brotherhood', to begin with there is still everywhere a very 'democratic', collegial government by presbyters; later, embedded in this college, there is leadership by one individual, after which the joint government by the presbyters gradually loses importance. In some areas a hierarchy of bishops, metropolitans and patriarchs comes into being. By analogy with diets in the empire, synods of all bishops in a particular region come into being, and finally ecumenical councils of all bishops in the empire. Even later, one of the patriarchs – at the end of the fourth century there were five great patriarchates, Jerusalem, Alexandria, Antioch, Constantinople and Rome – became the supreme leader of all bishops and patriarchs in the whole of the church: the Bishop of Rome, patriarch of the West.[11]

For Corinth we have a milestone on this road. Around the end of the first century there was a division in the church there when some elders were deposed by younger (or perhaps newer) Christians in the congregation. An elder in Rome, Clement, wrote the letter called 1 Clement to try to heal the conflict. It shows traces of the older ways in its recognition of the Spirit poured out on all and the right of the whole congregation to decide the matter, but it also shows a far more precise and institutionalized ministry than in Paul's time, and the terminology has much in common with that of household and civic hierarchies. A further important feature in the letter is the way it backs up its condemnation of this 'revolt' by appeal to 'nature' and the order of creation: the new patterns were beginning to be legitimated by theology.[12]

This tendency has run through church history: when the

institution meets a new situation or problem it not only uses theology to think through its response but also often tries afterwards to legitimate what it has done in theological terms. The Bible has been used to support a vast variety of church structures, and modern biblical and historical scholarship has helped to expose the self-interested and ideological character of many such legitimations. It is a fallacy to suppose that there was any single New Testament church order, and many factors other than imitation of biblical models have contributed to the forms of authority through history. Time and again what may have been a creative or at least acceptable response in a particular context has become rigidified, and theology has been used as an ideology to justify it.[13]

Through this history Paul's letters have been interpreted both to support and disturb particular forms and practices. He himself was both an innovator in relation to tradition (Jewish and Christian) and the initiator of a new tradition. He is an uncomfortable bedfellow for most patterns of authority in the later Church. This is partly due to his period of church history and its different circumstances, but partly it is also due to the intrinsic connection of his way of authority with his gospel. This is a continuing challenge to a faith that gives normative status to his writings. He has often, as Maurice Wiles says of him in the patristic period, been domesticated.[14] But he has frequently broken free, most notably since the Reformation. This chapter is an attempt to help this to happen afresh.

It is clear that any fundamentalist attempt to reduplicate a first-century model is impossible and also contradicts Paul's own theology of the Spirit. The main challenge of Paul for a modern Christian understanding of authority is to work it through as thoroughly and in as intrinsic a relation to the gospel as he did. The six principles that we gathered from 2 Corinthians are a helpful starting-point both for scrutinizing and for working out the form and content of church authority.

How does an authority embody the gospel in the ambiguities of a situation? Perhaps the most common divergence from Paul's practice has been to formalize authority, disconnecting it from quality of discipleship and from the need for constant adaptation.

Second, how is authority distributed? How is respect paid to

the Spirit shared among believers? Paul's 'authority for building up' made it inseparable from a new pattern of social relations
which is only imaginable through the power of the Spirit,
common faith and mutual forgiveness and trust. This need by
no means be inconsistent with the development of, for example,
the episcopate. That could be seen as an appropriate means of
ensuring both continuity through time and a combination of
mutual dependence between churches (because each bishop had
to be consecrated by a neighbouring bishop) with a wide
measure of local independence. In other words, bishops
represented the distribution of authority in the wider Church.
But the question still needs to be pressed about how far the
patterns that emerged in fact distributed power and enabled
trust.

Third, how vulnerable is it? How far does it resist the many
temptations to choose security based on domination, distrust, or
other forms of self-protection? Perhaps in no other area has
church authority been more *kata sarka* than this.

Fourth, how does it interpret the gospel, the tradition and its
own role? What is the quality of its communication in word and
act? Theology has often been blatantly ideological in this area,
partly because the personal status of those doing the theology
has usually been at stake; and the practice of those in authority
has often communicated a message about power that has been
hard to distinguish from the rest of the powers that be.

Fifth, how does this authority relate to the Christian hope?
Because the gospel is about a promise being fulfilled and the
Holy Spirit is a foretaste of things to come, authority needs to
be constantly open to transformation in the light of that future.
Legitimation in terms of past or present is not decisive. The
future acts as a critical and constructive factor in the face of
authority's tendencies towards absolutism or perpetuation of the
status quo. In the conflicts between churches eschatology relativizes all their claims. All are measured against the criterion of
the Kingdom of God, which may not in itself be very clear
guidance but at least can help to expose the idolatries, legalisms,
misinterpretations and bondage to the past so common in this
area.

Finally, in what way does this authority derive from and
continue to relate to God? This question puts the matter in its

fullest context. Here is the very essence and source of authority, and all forms of it have implications for the nature of God, which we will discuss further in the final chapter. It is of the utmost importance that Paul and his God are in communication. There is a scandalous particularity about Paul's authority in the Spirit, stemming from the fact that he is under orders himself: 'Or do you imagine I make plans at the human level so that it is in my hands that yes be yes and no be no?' (1.17). This is the basic theme of living in the Spirit or living *kata sarka* which we have found running all through the letter, Paul's claim that 'we have conducted ourselves in the world with the single-minded commitment and straightforwardness of God, not in human wisdom but in God's grace, most of all in our dealings with you' (1.12). This too could be seen as, from the Christian standpoint, the main theme of authority in church history, requiring discernment at every point and often going against the conventional wisdom. At root it is the theological issue of the providence of God and how to recognize it. The task of assessment in turn poses a challenge: is the assessor living in the Spirit, conforming to the gospel so as to be open to the sort of illumination about power that enables Paul to combine confident use of 'weapons that are not human but full of God's power' (10.4) with 'delight in weaknesses, insults, constraints, persecutions and pressures, on Christ's behalf; for when I am weak, then I am powerful' (12.10)?

Such questions are part of the contribution of 2 Corinthians to the process of vision and discernment that can enable healthy authority in the Church and elsewhere. But the seriousness or otherwise with which they are taken cannot be separated from response to the set of writings of which they are part.

(ii) THE CANON OF SCRIPTURE

The Church was never without Scriptures. Chapter 3 has shown how Paul 'lived in the Bible' of Israel, but also how his use of those Scriptures was distinctive. His key was the gospel seen as the fulfilment of what was promised, and so his stress was on prophecy rather than the content of Torah. As the Church moved into the second generation and beyond, it increasingly used writings of its own members to sustain the continuity of its faith. In a complex and gradual process these were sifted, their reliability decided upon and the authoritative set of them became the New Testament.[15] Letters ascribed to Paul were part of this from the time of the earliest references to such a collection in the second century, as were the first three Gospels, but disputes about some books continued for centuries. The earliest list corresponding exactly to what is now in the New Testament is given by Athanasius in AD 367, but he himself also quotes other writings outside his list as having similar weight.

The formation of the canon of Scripture was, along with the development of creeds and patterns of authoritative ministry, part of the Church's way of determining its identity and maintaining its social duration, and crucial stages were often provoked by internal and external threats.[16] One such threat was perceived in the second century in the teaching of Marcion, who wanted to reject the Jewish Scriptures and much of what became the New Testament. The decision to have the twofold canon was crucial to Christianity. It was in continuity with its origins and, as we have seen, the Jewish Scriptures were the main influence on Paul's mind and the way he conceived the gospel. 2 Cor. 3 has often been used to support a Marcionite position, but this is against its intention, as we have argued in Chapter 3 above, where we discuss the way in which Paul sees the gospel superseding but also fulfilling the covenant with Moses. For Paul the Church was the people of God (*ekklēsia*, the word for church, is used of the assembly of Israel in the Septuagint, the translation of the Hebrew Scriptures used by most of the early Church) in the new age of fulfilment brought by Jesus the Messiah. There were not two people but only one. Israel's story was the Church's story, and the main categories of the Church's self-understanding were drawn from Israel.[17]

So Paul had to relate Jesus to Moses and he did it by means of typology. This was the main Christian way of relating Old and New Testaments. It has come under severe attack since the eighteenth century, but it is arguable that that has been only a temporary eclipse and that it is possible, in suitably modern form, to continue to use it.[18] Paul's use in 2 Cor. 3 interprets Israel's covenant through the gospel by relating the faces of Moses, Christ and Christians. These are key points in Paul's narrative framework of interpretation, and in 4.6 he stretches it even further back to creation, which can also be a type of what has happened in Christ (5.17). It is clear how intrinsic to Paul were his Jewish Scriptures, and how appropriate their inclusion in the same canon as his letters. Yet, partly because they were so fundamental to him as to be largely taken for granted, there was the danger of misinterpreting his relationship with them. As the Church changed to become almost completely Gentile and tensions with the synagogue sharpened, Christians no longer understood themselves to be one people with Jews. It was easy for Paul's stress on the newness of the gospel to be separated from its fundamental continuity with God's history with Israel, and for Christians to see the Church as the replacement of Israel rather than themselves as called to share with Israel in the new age of the Messiah. There were extenuating circumstances for this when it began, but its results have been horrific.

So the Christian canon came to embrace the Jewish Scriptures, but often the Church appropriated them in ways alien to Paul and his gospel. What of the role of Paul's letters in the canon? The most obvious fact is that their inclusion let them become a key constitutive element in Christian identity, read at worship, drawn on for doctrine, hymns, ethics, sermons, interpretation of the rest of the Bible, prayer and much else. Their authority was not as individual writings but as part of a body of literature used in worship and other activities. The parts of Scripture were used to interpret each other and the overarching function of it was as the norm for Christian faith.

There were great advantages in having this canon, but there were also dangers. The most insidious through Christian history has been the one that Paul's letters in particular should have ruled out: the tendency to take Scripture formally as authority in a legalistic sense, flattening every part into equally inspired, inerrant statements of unchanging truth.[19] The irony of this is that it so contradicts Paul's way of handling his own Scriptures and ignores his central principle of having the gospel as criterion and key. This was re-emphasized in the Reformation by Martin Luther, who was willing to question the inclusion of the books of James and Revelation in the canon because he did not consider they conveyed the gospel. But in much of later Protestantism the doctrine of Scripture became an iron rule far from the spirit of both Paul and Luther. The rigidity was such that the rise of modern biblical scholarship provoked a crisis in which faith was held to depend on the 'scripture principle', and the divisions over this deepened.

Another danger was that the use of the letters as canonical would ignore their original setting and reference. 2 Corinthians was not made part of the New Testament because the issue of Paul's authority in Corinth continued to be important; but to forget the historical particularity of the letter could lead to misunderstanding or inappropriate generalizing. The loss of context and original intention was partly a freeing of the letter for wider relevance, but, as we argue in Chapters 4 and 5, new applications still need to be in right relationship with Paul's intention and the Corinthian situation. In this area too modern scholarship challenged traditional habits.

The particularity of the individual text could be lost in other ways too. To be included in the canon amounted to a change of genre from occasional letter (in the style of a legal defence) to Scripture. It was read in a new context, and even though this could be quite appropriate it could also suffer from the loss of the original way of taking it. This was one aspect of the general tendency to homogenize the variety of the writings. As regards authority in the Church, a key factor was that the Pastoral Letters to Timothy and Titus were ascribed to Paul and the statements in his genuine letters were often subsumed under a later form of church order. The contribution of scholars has again been important here, to such an extent that the unity of the canon became very problematic. The stress on diversity and contradiction in the various documents, together with discoveries about authorship, earlier forms, and parallels outside the canon put great pressure on traditional uses and justifications.

Is it possible to have a post-critical understanding of canon? This is the subject of some debate at present, leading participants on either side being Brevard Childs[20] and James Barr.[21] Our position is nearest to those of Charles Wood[22] and David Kelsey.[23] One important element is the distinction and relationship between Scripture as 'source' (for history, sociology, literature, meditation, wisdom, etc.) and as 'canon' or norm for Christian faith and witness. As source it contains a wide variety of types of material and needs the varied approaches that we have adopted in our chapters. As canon it is being used by a particular community in a certain way. In Christian history there have been many ways of understanding and justifying it as canon, and these are rightly assessed both according to 'the gospel of God' and the results of the various inquiries. Many ways are suspect by both criteria. But there are also many which can claim both scholarly and Christian integrity. For us the canon is best seen formally as a collection of many genres whose primary one is narrative. The main content is its identification of who God is, with the gospel story of Jesus Christ as the chief criterion of this. The canon therefore functions primarily as testimony to the God of Jesus Christ. Its authority is as testimony to the 'authorizer', God. But part of this testimony is to the importance of particular events, relationships and contexts – hence the necessity of listening to the various disciplines that use it as a source. Its testimony is also to the involvement of God himself in the process of understanding and applying the Scriptures as knowledge of God; so the presence of God is, as Kelsey convincingly argues, intrinsic to the function of Scripture as Christian canon. Wood sums up such a position by reference to the distinction between 'letter' and 'spirit' in 2 Cor. 3.6:

> The same text which is indisputably the work of a particular human author with particular views, insights, and limitations may also become the vehicle of God's word; the text that appears most transparent to a revealed word may become 'letter'. This does not mean that we are at the mercy of the text as it strikes us at any moment. It means that we cannot simply locate the canon in any particular form of words, henceforth exempt from criticism. To be sure, the canon is bound to the words of scripture. But scripture is activated as canon only in the coincidence of letter and spirit. The canon subsists in scripture, to be realized in the event of its explication.[24]

What is the role of 2 Corinthians in the canon understood in this way? Its primary role is as witness to the God of Jesus Christ in the context of the rest of the canon. This is why our final chapter is an 'event of explication' called 'God and 2 Corinthians'. It also has other roles relevant to this testimony: relating the Old Testament to the New (Chapter 3), vividly portraying the 'economy of God' (Chapter 6), showing something of the possibilities and problems of the new social reality enabled by the gospel (Chapter 7), and giving an example of a particular conflict of authority being worked out by reference to the gospel. Through all this we have been using and trying to do justice to the scholarly and hermeneutical disciplines, as discussed in Chapters 4 and 5, for which the canonical status is simply one aspect of the transmission of the text. Finally, all this is in the service of the fresh appropriation of 2 Corinthians by the readers, and to assist this we conclude with a translation of the canonical text.

4 THE AUTHORITY OF PAUL TODAY

Why take Paul seriously as an authority at all today? The claim is not that he should be an authority as an individual but as the author of one section of the Christian canon. This means that one reason is that the Christian community has been formed through his letters and continues to be so. But the most fundamental reason is because what Paul took seriously deserves to be taken seriously – the gospel, Jesus Christ, God. If the same question is asked about them then we are at the limit of such inquiry, because there can be no independent grounding of such authorizers.

Yet the situation is not so stark or irrational. Granted that it is inappropriate to expect certain sorts of proof or demonstration (see Chapter 9 for more on this), there are still many more limited arguments and considerations which will tell in a contemporary assessment of Paul's authority. The best that can be claimed for them is that they converge in supporting the case and in removing difficulties that are raised.

There is first of all our attempt to redescribe the nature and quality of Paul's own concept and exercise of authority so that it can be seen as both in harmony with the gospel and relevant to perennial issues in church and other social life. Allied with this is the effort to explain the background in the Church in Paul's time and the way ministry in the Church developed later so that the fate of Paul's concept and practice is clearly a matter of importance. The result is not supposed to be a resuscitation of a supposed 'Pauline authority structure' but a call to take seriously his example and principles in other situations.

As regards the canon, Paul's way of exercising authority in Corinth is secondary in comparison with his testimony to the gospel and its author, God. That testimony is supported by the rest of the New Testament and its relevance today is something that is, for better or for worse, an obvious fact in the lives of many millions of people in every country of the world. In the world-wide network of churches the one tangible thing common to nearly all is the Bible, so to talk about Paul is to start with a large possible audience already committed to his relevance. As for the truth of his testimony (for he could be taken seriously in the sociology of Christianity as a world faith without his gospel being believed), that again is, on the one hand, impossible to ground or demonstrate neutrally but, on the other hand, is properly the subject of a wide variety of discussions about the plausibility of the Christian faith. These are not within our scope here, but the very fact that they are opened up is a reason for taking Paul seriously, and the most a witness can ask is that he be listened to with a determination to know the truth.

Arising out of all this are many practical challenges. His gospel appeals for a complete response, 'that those who live should no longer live for themselves, but for the one who died and was raised' (5.15). His exercise of authority in the service of a new pattern of social relations questions much that goes on in churches and elsewhere. His interpretation of Scripture according to the Spirit is likely to distress both conservatives and liberals and to lead to dissatisfaction with those common alternatives. Principles such as the embodiment of the gospel by those who claim its authority, or the need for distribution of authority, with accountability and vulnerability in its use, or the eschatological critique of all church claims: these are both radical and widely relevant.

But besides the practicality, and sustaining it, is a *vision* of authority. Paul never romanticized or idolized authority. He suffered too much at the hands of religious and political authorities to do that. His chief concern in 2 Corinthians might be described as theological purification of authority through the gospel. Is it possible to have a specifically Christian concept of authority which, in community, unites the freedom 'where the Spirit is' (3.17) with 'the love of Christ constraining us' (5.14)? Only, Paul suggests, if the vision informing that is of the

authority of God, his glory known 'in the face of Christ' (4.6).
We conclude with a reflection on this face.

5 A CADENZA: THE FACE OF CHRIST

The main features of Paul's idea of authority can be related to
the face of Christ. This face represents the gospel and the
revelation of what was hidden by Moses' veil.[25] Its authority is
relational, interactive and non-coercive. It is both an embodiment of ultimate authority, the glory of God, and also is distributed, 'shining in our hearts'. It has been vulnerable to the
point of actual death. It is an interpretative authority, communicating knowledge, and is eschatological, a vision imper-
fectly grasped by faith until the final 'face to face'. To live in
faith before this face is to have a criterion for all authority and
a liberation from the idolatries of power. Above all it is to live
in freedom and love, in which the very issue of authority, which
is always secondary for Paul, is swallowed up in the reality it
serves, 'transformation into that self-same image, from glory to
glory' (3.18). That is the Church being built up, which is the
only purpose of Paul's authority.

NOTES

1 For a detailed discussion of the complex meaning of 'gospel' in
   Paul's letters see John Howard Schütz, *Paul and the Anatomy of
   Apostolic Authority* (Cambridge University Press, Cambridge,
   1975), Chaps. 3—6.
2 For the account that follows the most helpful studies have been
   those of Meeks, op. cit., Ch. 4; Schütz, op. cit.; and Bengt
   Holmberg, *Paul and Power, the Structure of Authority in the
   Primitive Church as reflected in the Pauline Epistles* (Fortress Press,
   Philadelphia, 1980).
3 Schütz, op. cit., 152f.
4 Meeks, op. cit., Ch. 4.
5 D. W. Oostendorp, *Another Jesus. A Gospel of Jewish-Christian
   Superiority in 2 Corinthians* (J. H. Kok, Kampen, 1967), Ch. 2.
   Our agreement on this issue does not imply acceptance of Oostendorp's whole thesis.

6   op. cit., 14.

7   Quoted in Schütz, op. cit., 13.

8   SCM, London, 1983.

9   For a summary of specific criticism of the book see a review by Frances Young, *Theology* LXXXVI No. 713 (Sept. 1983), 378–82.

10 op. cit., 139.

11 *The Church with a Human Face. A New and Expanded Theology of Ministry* (SCM, London, 1985), 132.

12 See Schillebeeckx, op. cit., 69f., 125f.

13 The studies of Yves Congar have helped to give historical and theological perspective in this area. For a summary of points relevant to this chapter see his essay, 'The Historical Development of Authority in the Church. Points for Reflection', in *Problems of Authority*, ed. J. M. Todd (DLT, London, 1962).

14 'The Domesticated Apostle', in *The Writings of St Paul*, ed. Wayne A. Meeks (Norton, New York, 1972), 207–13.

15 See Robert M. Grant, *The Formation of the New Testament* (Harper & Row, New York, 1965); Hans von Campenhausen, *The Formation of the Christian Bible* (Fortress, Philadelphia, 1972).

16 See Edward Farley, *Ecclesial Reflection. An Anatomy of Theological Method* (Fortress, Philadelphia, 1982), especially Chaps. 2—3. Farley's comprehensive critique of the authority of Scripture, Church and dogma is one well worth grappling with in order to carry the concerns of this chapter further. A fruitful dialogue partner for his work would be George Lindbeck, *The Nature of Doctrine. Religion and Theology in a Postliberal Age* (SPCK, London, 1984), and his essay 'The Church as Messianic Pilgrim People', in the forthcoming volume celebrating the centenary of *Lux Mundi*, ed. Geoffrey Wainright. Our overall position has more in common with Lindbeck, but Farley's work shows decisively why preliberal or antiliberal positions will not do.

17 See Lindbeck, 'The Church as Messianic Pilgrim People', op. cit.

18 This is the position of Hans Frei in 'The "Literal Reading" of Biblical Narrative in the Christian Tradition', *The Bible and the Narrative Tradition*, ed. Frank McConnell (OUP, Oxford, 1986), as further developed by George Lindbeck, 'The Story-Shaped Church: Critical Exegesis and Theological Interpretation', in a forthcoming Festschrift for Hans Frei.

19 See Farley, loc. cit.

20 See especially *Introduction to the Old Testament as Scripture* (SCM, London, 1979).

21   See especially *Holy Scripture. Canon, Authority, Criticism* (OUP, Oxford, 1983).
22   *The Formation of Christian Understanding. An Essay in Theological Hermeneutics* (Westminster Press, Philadelphia, 1981).
23   *The Uses of Scripture in Recent Theology* (Fortress, Philadelphia, 1975).
24   op. cit., 109.
25   See A. T. Hanson, 'The Midrash in II Corinthians 3: A Reconsideration', *JSNT* 9 (1980), 2–28, who argues that Paul understood Moses' veil to be hiding the glory of the pre-existent Christ, and that Christ represented for Paul the visibility of God. The midrash is overall, as Hanson shows, an example of typological use of the Scriptures, which became the main way of relating the Old to the New Testament and of embracing later history within the authoritative history of salvation.

9

God and 2 Corinthians

2 Corinthians is shot through with reference to God. The word *theos* occurs seventy-nine times, and God is also referred to in several other ways. Each chapter above has in its own way shown the God-centredness of the letter; this one goes further in reflecting on the content. It is a theological essay, a fragment of the sort of theology that can be done through engagement with 2 Corinthians.

1 THE TASK

The difficulty of treating God and 2 Corinthians is acute. This is not primarily because of the problems dealt with in the previous chapters, though the discussions there are necessary and presupposed in what follows. Too often questions of meaning, method, historical distance, cultural relativity or epistemology have taken most of the energies of interpreters, leaving little for the theological content. The climax of the task of reading 2 Corinthians must be to take Paul seriously as a theologian in the sense of one who speaks of God. This involves the intensity of his language and its message coming into dialogue with our way of conceiving reality. The principal difficulty in this proves to be in the content of what Paul says. That content challenges and stretches all our capacities if justice is to be done to it. If one's whole self and horizon are not radically questioned by this way of referring everything to God then one has missed the point or has bracketed or neutralized it.

The existence of God is not an issue here, though in a

complete theology it would of course be discussed. The letter
takes it for granted, and is not likely to yield much of value to
theology on this subject. The nature of God is also not a separate
theme. It is possible to start abstracting attributes of God from
the letter: God is seen as living, knowing, encouraging, promising, loving, judging, reconciling, humiliating, guiding,
creating, providing, raising the dead, speaking and acting in
various other ways; he is also affirmed to be holy, powerful,
faithful, glorious, righteous, merciful and a God of peace. It is
important to note these, but it is dangerous if the aim is to grasp
the distinctive thrust of the letter's theology. A listing of such
attributes confirms the obvious: that Paul's God is that of a
faithful Jew deeply rooted in the Scriptures and in contemporary
Pharisaic belief. Isolating attributes and combining them all
into a concept of God is a tempting short cut which leaves the
primary interest of the letter in other areas. But in fact the letter
has a great deal more to contribute to a theology of God.

The problem is that what it has to say is so indirect, it is so
taken up into metaphors, events, relationships and direct
address that it seems impossible to abstract. This in itself says
something vital: that recognition of God is, according to the
mode of reference in 2 Corinthians, indirectly communicated.
God cannot be isolated, immediately known or objectified. Yet
that is itself too general. 2 Corinthians invites us to enter into
those metaphors, events, relationships and forms of address in
order to be in a position to affirm the particularities it acknowledges of God. There is no knowledge of God apart from
acknowledgement. God participates in a relationship and way of
living in which knowledge of God is located in a dynamic
mutuality marked by prayer, thanks, obedience, free speech,
generosity and a variety of other kinds of active receptivity in
community.

This gives rise to two issues that are especially sharp in
modern theology, one relating to the form of theology, the other
to the problem of knowledge of God.

As regards the form, most theology is discursive – systematic
or philosophical or historical theology, doctrinal statements,
essays, commentaries and so on. The features of 2 Corinthians
mentioned above are very hard to express effectively in discursive form. A letter, on the other hand, can embody the relation-

ship and the mutuality. Paul has a close if painful relationship with the Corinthians and the theology of the letter can indicate how God is intrinsic to that relationship and is himself well characterized in relational terms. The genre of the letter proves irreplaceable for theology. Other genres of theology can comment on the letter, draw on it and illuminate it, but its content can never be assimilated without remainder. One danger of doctrine in the past has been a tendency to imperialism, attempting to do justice to the truth of all the other genres (poetry, narrative, letters, law, proverbs, prophecy etc.) in itself. What we meet in trying to grasp 2 Corinthians on God is the irreducible pluralism of genres.

Yet reaction against doctrinal imperialism is sometimes carried to the point of isolation of the genres from each other or even new imperialisms. Isolation happens when the effort to transcend one genre and all its particularities is abandoned, and doctrinal use of other genres is seen as inauthentic ideologizing, theorizing, generalizing or abstraction. And in recent theology oppressed genres (especially poetry and narrative) have sometimes not only sought liberation from doctrinal imperialism but even new domination for themselves. We find the best approach is interaction for mutual benefit. The pluralism of genres is a source of endless enrichment to theology. No one mode has a capacity which can do away with the need for continual close attention to the others, and in relation to God this acts as a safeguard against forms of totalitarianism and idolatry. So it is worth continuing with our attempt to allow 2 Corinthians to inform the doctrine of God, while recognizing that, like the attempt to paraphrase a good poem, the task is infinite and never produces a substitute for the original.

The second issue, that of knowledge of God, goes to the heart of many modern theological debates. Clearly the sort of knowledge claimed in 2 Corinthians is not that of a neutral, value-free spectator (as discussed in Chapter 5), and even many of the 'harder' sciences are suspicious of universalizing that type of objectivity.[1] There are many other ways of trying to bind theological knowledge to criteria, language or models that are inappropriate to the God who is being affirmed or questioned, and there are numerous debates about these. Let us take just one of the fundamental problems prominent in recent theology:

how can we have knowledge of God that both allows for his complete initiative (or prevenience) in our knowing of him and also genuinely treats human beings as responsible active recipients?[2]

In 2 Corinthians there is no sense of competition between these two requirements. The initiative of God is clear throughout (e.g. 1.1,3,4,9,10,20–2; 2.14; 3.5; 3.18; 4.7; 4.14; 5.5; 6.1; 7.6; 8.1; 8.5; 8.16; 9.8–15; 10.8; 10.13; 11.31; 13.4; 13.13), but the whole letter is a plea for an active response to Paul and to God. The letter embodies the union of the two. As regards knowledge, it helps to focus on the category of 'promise', which embraces both the initiative of the promiser and the need for free acceptance of it, with truth and full knowledge inseparable from future developments. This comes to the heart of the structure of knowing God in 2 Corinthians. It is a knowing in which the future is the definitive location of knowledge. As discussed above (p. 156), a knowing that is oriented to truth with a future dimension differs from the knowing of what is totally past or present. Paul calls this sort of knowing faith: 'for we walk by faith, not with the vision before our eyes' (5.7; cf. 4.13–14), and it is rooted in living by the Spirit (5.5). The Spirit is supremely the guarantee of that future face to face knowing (5.5; 1.22; 1 Cor. 13.12), which is of course not just a spectating but a full participation in the glory of God (3.4—4.6; 4.17–18).

It is the fact that there is this future which creates the space for Paul's urgent appeals and for the Corinthians' response. In the letter, God's priority is in no competition with the need for participation in God's glory being by people who freely believe, obey, speak, pray, love, suffer, share, work, praise and thank. For Paul, affirming God's priority goes with strenuous efforts to persuade, to move hearts and minds. The clue to how this is possible is in the nature of God's initiative in Christ: this is a 'Yes' to the promises of God which involves the historical time for appeal and response – 'Look! Now is the acceptable time. Look! Now is the day of salvation' (6.2). In line with this, Paul sees his whole mission being to spread 'the incense of (God's or Christ's) knowledge in every place' (2.14). We want to explore the content of this knowledge further.

2 POWER, CHRIST AND GOD

Genre, knowledge and freedom are not problems for Paul in this letter, but preconceptions about them may cause problems for us. It is different with a further aspect of knowing God, that of power: here Paul is explicit.

In 2 Corinthians the relationship between knowledge and power is most vividly expressed in military imagery:

> For we may operate as human beings, but we do not campaign with human means, for the weapons of our campaign are not human, but full of God's power for the destruction of fortresses, tearing down arguments and every battlement raised against the knowledge of God, and taking every design captive to the obedience of Christ, and ready to punish every disobedience when your obedience is complete (10.3–6).

In this spiritual warfare knowledge and power go with a radically relational freedom which has such definite content that what could earlier be called freedom (3.17) is here seen as captivity. It is the nature of Christ that determines this 'captivity' as freedom. Paul is referring to the fundamental opposition between living *kata sarka*, according to the world's way, and *kata pneuma*, according to the Spirit. He is well aware that what is wisdom in the latter appears as foolishness in the former, and that this is related to a parallel reconception of power and weakness (1 Cor. 1.24–5). 'The Spirit' in Paul combines in itself both the integration of knowledge, freedom and power (all with a crucial future dimension), and also the transformation of those concepts. In 2 Corinthians, with its focus on authority, the leading concept is that of power. We have already discussed this in Chapter 8 as it relates to authority but now we will go further into its meaning for who God is. Under the pressures of the challenge to his authority Paul says things that change not only the notion of power but also of the God who is the ultimate power.

How does Paul give substance to this transformation? The answer is simple: by means of the gospel. He can call this 'the gospel of God' (11.7), and it is this that gives the decisive content to his understanding of God and the Spirit, including his transformed concepts of knowledge, freedom, power and the future. All that has been said above has been formal preparation for the examination of this content. It would be possible to affirm a knowledge of God that maintains his prevenience and comes through active receptivity and relationships in particular events and contexts, and yet to have a radically different understanding of God from that in 2 Corinthians. The reason is that 'particular events and contexts' is not specific enough. It is striking how vibrantly full of events the letter is. The gospel is a proclamation of events and their central character; its transmission generates new events of suffering, conflict, foundation of communities, generosity, praise, prayer, and much else; and there is an urgency about its communication which is powerfully productive of new history. The letter itself is a 'language event' aiming to affect this history. But the substructure of all these events is the narrative of the gospel, pivoting around the death and resurrection of Jesus Christ.[3] This alone is specific enough, and it resists incorporation in any wider framework or being subsumed within any general scheme of reality. It is making an open bid to *be* the framework, to challenge all available schemes of reality in the name of the new creation, and orient all thinking by that. The universality of the claim comes from the fact that God is seen as intrinsic to the events of the gospel and to its continuing eventfulness. The gospel is in turn crucial to the identification of God.

In exploring what this means for God a useful concept is that of contingency. It is remarkable how deeply God is involved in the contingent events of history. The crucifixion was contingent upon what people did to 'the Son of God', Paul's ministry is contingent upon the varied responses to his message and way of living, and the spread of the gospel is inseparable from appeals, decisions, encounters, and sufferings. Paul's more specific word for a key feature of this contingency is weakness. If one's idea of God's power united to knowledge is that it should be able to bring about its purposes with maximum results and minimum vulnerability than Paul would call that *kata sarka*. He sees examples of such worldly notions of power in his opponents (chaps 10—12). Paul's gospel relates power and weakness differently. It is not that he simply replaces power with weakness. Rather, both are reinterpreted through the crucifixion and resurrection of Jesus Christ. Any general notions of them are bound to be drawn from general worldly experience, the 'old creation'. Paul's straining with ordinary language underlines his basic conviction that the new creation must primarily be communicated as testimony to events, both in the gospel and in his own life. But the events themselves identify afresh who God is and in particular they embody the relationship of God to Jesus Christ. So it is concepts not only of power or knowledge that are being transformed but of God too.

The reconception of God in relational terms runs through the letter. The most striking aspect of Paul's way of referring to God is his co-ordination of God and Jesus Christ. The opening address brings 'grace to you and peace from God our Father and Lord Jesus Christ' (1.2). The opening prayer is, 'Blessed is the God and Father of our Lord Jesus Christ...' (1.3). Other examples include: 1.19; 2.17; 3.4; 4.4,6,14; 5.18,20,21; 11.31; 12.19; 13.4,13.

This is the most distinctive feature of Paul's way of referring to God in contrast with his Pharisaic origins. What does it mean? Two main directions of interpretation are possible. On the one hand, God can be seen as predefined, either through the Old Testament tradition and its key events seen as finally definitive, or, in a more philosophical way, as a fixed entity, self-enclosed, autonomous, and known in general terms through various attributes. Such a being might enter into relationships, but they would by definition be extrinsic to what he essentially is, and it is inconceivable that new events might be allowed to affect our conception of who he is. On the other hand, our position is that Paul's gospel has led him to speak of God in relation to Jesus Christ and the events of his crucifixion and resurrection in such a way that his concept of God is transformed. God and Jesus Christ are spoken of as intrinsic to each other. Something ultimate has happened which will not allow either to be conceived without the other, and this goes to the heart of who each is. The logical pressure of Paul's language is towards this relationship being seen as intrinsic to the being of God. There is no simple identification of Jesus with God, but the differentiation is such that there is a unique, intrinsic relationship constitutive of who God is. To put it starkly, if Christ 'is the image of God' (4.4), and Christ was weak, poor, 'made into sin' (5.21), and dead, then we must try to think the almost unthinkable. The relationship of God's very being and glory to weakness, poverty, sin and death must be rethought.

The resistance to doing such thinking in the Christian

tradition has been immense. Spirituality and such genres as hymns, poetry and drama have often been more open to the risks involved. Some modern theology has gradually been forced to face the issues as it has tried to come to terms with the disastrous aspects of the inheritance it has received from the tradition of theism. Those include the tendency to ascribe to God power and freedom which contradicted all weakness and contingency, and an absoluteness and immutability that seemed to rule out mutuality and real involvement in history. The overall sense of God was one which made it especially difficult to think of him being a God of love who is intrinsically related to Jesus Christ in his weakness, his poverty, his identification with sin and his death. The massive Trinitarian synthesis of the patristic and medieval periods held these dimensions together in various ways, but the conception of God's necessary absoluteness was dominant and that became the notion of God that was rejected by modern atheism.

The atheist critique has finally helped to show much Christian theology the unchristian nature of its habitual conception of God. Throughout the post-medieval period there have been many attempts to bring home more radically to the doctrine of God the implications of the gospel. The Reformation tended to specialize in thinking through the problem of sin in relation to God; in terms of Paul's theology this meant a primary concentration on his letters to the Romans and the Galatians. In the nineteenth century the issue of weakness was most systematically handled in kenotic Christology, whose main Pauline text was Philippians 2.5–11. In the twentieth century some influential theologies have tried to conceive 'the death of God' and 'the God of the poor'. All of these theologies have been helped by wider developments which have made available more appropriate concepts of knowledge, power, freedom, event, contingency, the future and relationship, as discussed above. This is the horizon within which the interpretation of 2 Corinthians is situated. It means that this is an especially opportune time for that letter to be heard. The ground has been prepared for us to appreciate its theological content in a way which was not usually possible in the past, and its message can be freshly related to current issues.

Paul is in the Jewish tradition in which knowledge of Yahweh is a practical matter, and believing is inseparable from obedience and a whole way of life. So when he links knowing God to the gospel, he shares and even boasts of his own knowledge learnt through experiencing weakness, poverty, sin and 'being handed over to death for Jesus' sake' (4.11). Knowing God needs to correspond to the gospel, and that requires the practical transformation of the knower. It is not that weakness, sin, poverty or death are in themselves good things. But in the light of the gospel, receptivity to God involves accepting suffering, glorifying God involves glorying in weakness, obedience to God goes the way of the crucifixion, and 'the grace of God' means that the Macedonians in their 'extreme poverty' can risk becoming even poorer (8.1–2). This is at the opposite extreme from neutral knowing, and at its heart is the knowledge of a particular love which transforms the ego of the beloved:

> For the love of Christ constrains us, in that we have come to this verdict, that one died for all – so all died; and he died so that those who live should no longer live for themselves but for the one who died and was raised for them (5.14–15).

The self of the one who truly acknowledges this God has been 'de-centred', its new identity coming through a death which has ended its independent existence and given it a life wholly qualified by relationship to Jesus Christ in a new community of 'us'. This is life in faith. It is a knowing which only corresponds to its object through the active receptivity of living the gospel. If the concept of God is divorced from this then it is not authentic knowledge.

Yet for all its practicality it is still a knowledge which has to be thought. 2 Corinthians does this in a way that rightly engages the doctrine of God in the sort of fundamental reassessment suggested by his involvement in what is usually considered most alien to him. One way of summing up the consequence of this in theological terms is that it radically affects the idea of God's transcendence. Bonhoeffer's dictum, 'Only a suffering God can help', was worked out by him in relation to this issue.[4] Transcendence must not be understood primarily in spatial terms, as distance, remoteness, or other versions of 'beyondness'. Nor is it the maximizing of our ordinary notions of power, knowledge, presence, etc. Nor is it to be identified with a dimension of human interiority, in consciousness, spirituality or any such form of self-transcendence. Rather, transcendence is defined through love, through being for others. This is 'the beyond in the midst', or 'ethical transcendence', in a broad sense of ethics.[5] It means that, when we think of God's transcendence in the light of the gospel as the key to his self-definition, we do not, every time we affirm God's loving involvement in the messy contingency of history, immediately think: But really he is essentially different from all that (unchanging, unable to suffer, etc.). Rather we must do the opposite: every time we affirm a general transcendent attribute of God we must place that concept in the context of the gospel and allow it to be transformed accordingly. God's transcendence is not in his dissimilarity from what history can indicate, but rather in the depth of his loving involvement in history. As Eberhard Jüngel has argued at length, this need not at all remove the difference between God and human beings:

> The difference between God and man, which is constitutive of the essence of Christian faith, is thus not the difference of a still greater dissimilarity, but rather, conversely, the difference of a still greater similarity between God and man in the midst of a great dissimilarity.[6]

Even the language of similarity and dissimilarity does not do justice to the reality of love in which there is both union and differentiation, but with the differentiation always in the service of being for the other and leading to ever new events in the life of love.

This is a concept of transcendence in line with that at the roots of the tradition of Israel. In Exodus 3 God is identified not only from the direction of the past ('I am the God of your father, the God of Abraham, the God of Isaac, and the God of Jacob', v.6) and from his compassionate involvement in the present ('I know their sufferings, and I have come down to deliver them...', vv.7–8), but also by his name Yahweh. Yahweh means 'I am who (or what) I am', or 'I will be who I will be'. This is a God free to identify himself in new ways and so to lead people to rethink who he is. For Paul this is what has happened in the crucifixion and resurrection of Jesus Christ. He is also a God whose characteristic way of revealing his transcendence is by sharing it. He does this through promises which respect the freedom of others to shape the future responsively, and make him vulnerable to rejection. For Paul all the 'promises of God' are realized in Christ (1.20), and the history of rejection also reaches its climax there. In the light of this Paul explicitly goes beyond the tradition of Exodus. He does this primarily through the idea of God's glory. God's glory, which is perhaps the nearest one can come in biblical terms to the more general concept of transcendence, is reconceived through the gospel (3.4—6.10). Now God's glory embraces Jesus Christ as its very definition (4.4-6). A ministry that reflects this glory conforms itself to the death of Christ (4.7-12).

So what has happened to the conception of God? That tradition of Exodus was deeply concerned about idolatry and rejecting images of God. In the gospel we have both the negative and positive sides of that. Negatively, the cross acts as a continual idol-smasher. It wages war on ways of seeing God that have not passed through the inconceivable, this death. To insulate God from weakness, suffering, sin, poverty and death is no longer possible. This is rightly the springboard for spiritualities, artistic work, political practice, theologies and much else that allow their concept of God's glory and will to conform to the gospel. The importance of the intellectual labour in this should not be underestimated. A great deal of theology has been held captive by concepts of God that need to be exposed as idols in this sense. The insidiousness and falsehood of such concepts go very deep, and the task of discerning and combating them is well described by Paul as a military campaign (10.3-6). In this century one recalls Bonhoeffer's final explosive prison writings after a lifetime of intensive thought and action. In Britain there has been the awkward challenge of the theology and life of P. T. Forsyth, and, in a more philosophical mode, the agonizing of Donald MacKinnon over the need for a Christian realism that does justice to the crucifixion. In contemporary Roman Catholic theology the massive corpus of Hans Urs von Balthasar pivots around the day Jesus was dead, Holy Saturday; while the liberation theologians work through with more political relevance the implications of a freedom and a God characterized through a crucified liberator. Asian theology has been particularly attentive to 'the pain of God' and its meaning for a continent that includes the prosperity of Japan and the poverty of many other countries.

And back in European protestantism, in Tübingen, one of the most influential faculties of theology, two of the professors, Eberhard Jüngel and Jürgen Moltmann, have made 'the crucified God' central to their work.

All of the above theologians have in various ways been concerned to let God be God in accordance with the message of the cross, and it has required constant iconoclasm. Theology itself is always in danger of turning into an ideology that domesticates or manipulates God, or renders him as transcendent in false ways. The cross negates such developments. But what does it mean positively? All of the above theologies are constructive. They explore the meaning of the crucifixion in many directions and positively transform concepts and practice. But their engagement with the cross of course opens them to suspicion from the tradition, which asks the simple and central question: What about the resurrection? 2 Corinthians is especially helpful in pressing this home.

The resurrection might seem to make nonsense of all talk of the death of God or death in God. Especially here it seems we have the demonstration of God's transcendence over all weakness and mortality. 'God who raises the dead' (1.9) is a key name for God in the light of the gospel. He is supremely 'the living God' (3.3; 6.16), and never appears to be at risk. Paul's wording needs to be watched closely: typical of his careful distinctions is his statement that 'out of weakness he (Christ) was crucified, but he lives out of God's power' (13.4). There is a direct attribution of the resurrection to God but never of the crucifixion. But we too need to be careful here. The danger is that the content of the resurrection, this crucified man, is separated from the event of resurrection. Christianity has always been tempted to interpret the resurrection in the sense of a happy, victorious ending through which God sets everything right from the outside. This can lead to the sort of triumphalism that Paul met in Corinth and dealt with in 1 Corinthians by such downright statements as: 'For I decided to know nothing among you except Jesus Christ and him crucified' (1 Cor. 2.2). Likewise in 2 Corinthians it is easy to see how the nature of God's power is at stake in Paul's authority, and how the main threat is to conceive power and success in terms that divorce the resurrection from the content of crucifixion. Resurrection is not simply a reversal of death, leaving death behind it. The resurrection does differentiate God from death – his life, sovereign creativity and power are vindicated decisively and his transcendence and prevenience demonstrated. But the differentiation happens through an event which identifies God, including all those attributes, afresh. The directness of the attribution of resurrection is inseparable from the indirectness of the cross.

It could sound paradoxical: God differentiates himself from death in such a way that he is identified through the death of this man. Søren Kierkegaard did frequently use the language of paradox to describe this whole event. In his *Training in Christianity*[7] he penetratingly analysed the fundamental problem with Christendom in terms of a wrong relation of crucifixion and resurrection. Christendom, Christianity triumphant, wants to start with the resurrection, and does not see that the resurrection is only reached through the cross. It conceives God in an idolatrously direct way, and believes that he can be acknowledged apart from going the way of the cross: the happy ending is the good news. Yet perhaps a more appropriate category than paradox is one which Kierkegaard also uses, that of order. Paradox is too static a tension, whereas order allows for a dynamic with direction. The order of the gospel story is irreversible and its contents are cumulative. In a God who 'will be who he will be' is it not possible to conceive of order? If he identifies himself through contingent history is he not allowing the sequential nature of time to be part of his being? Yet such a linear identification is also unsatisfactory, as it seems to submerge God in contingency. The Christian solution is to characterize God through a story whose climactic events defy any simplistic linear description (as if one could have the 'result' of the resurrection without the continuing content of the cross), but which also resist any elimination of the order. It is the logic of this story that presses Christian theology towards the complex talk of unity and differentiation in God that later developed.

If God is understood in this way there can, on the one hand, be no playing down the reality of death, but, on the other hand, death cannot be absolutized. The story means that the reality of death has been relativized in this particular way. The general meaning of death (just like the general meaning of weakness, sin, poverty, freedom, etc.) is challenged, and it is now defined by its relationship to Jesus Christ: 'one died for all – so all died' (5.14). The most dramatic example of the meaning of death being transformed in this way is in what Paul says about his own experience. In chapter 1 he says that

> we even doubted our survival; but for ourselves we have accepted the death sentence, so as not to put confidence in ourselves but in God who raises the dead, the God who rescued us from such brushes with death and will rescue us, the God in whom we have come to hope...(vv.8–10).

In Chapter 4 he describes the working of the power of God in his ministry:

> ...always bearing the killing of Jesus in the body, so that Jesus' life too might be made apparent in our body. For always we who live are being handed over to death for Jesus' sake, so that Jesus' life too might be made apparent in our mortal flesh. So death is at work in us, but life in you (vv.10–12).

Those two quotations frame the section of the letter that is most helpful in showing Paul's concept of transcendence in operation, and in that section we also find the most original contribution of the letter to theological thought. The abundance and overflow of God's economy are represented through a historical transcendence that never ignores or bypasses the negativities. Paul brings it to a densely-packed climax in 4.6. Just as 4.5–7 was the most useful interpretative key to the letter's approach to authority (above pp. 212, 232), so now the central verse 4.6 condenses the theology of God in the letter, while also offering the letter's most distinctive idea for identifying God. It is no accident that the thrust of the letter on authority should converge with that on God, and it is of the utmost theological importance that this should be recognized and thought through.

3 THE FACE OF CHRIST

How does 4.6 summarize what we have been saying about God? 'For the God who said, "Out of darkness light will shine"...' is a decisive statement of God's prevenience and freedom as creator. In seeing God as speaker it allows us to think of God's relationship with creation as linguistic, structured with the possibility of address and response. And in conceiving light shining out of darkness it sees the order of crucifixion and resurrection reflected in the dynamic of creation. The next clause, '...is the one who has shone in our hearts...', is about the transformation of subjectivity that is needed to participate in knowing God, involving active receptivity and mutuality, in a freedom (as described in 3.17–18) which is inseparable from the initiative and capacitating of God. It is also a freedom which is relational and directional, as the final clause of the verse makes clear. The light that is given focuses on God through the particular face of Christ, and that embraces the whole gospel. It also is given for a purpose, so that we might bring 'the enlightenment (which is) the knowledge of God's glory in the face of Christ' to others. This indicates the historical, contingent process of communication in which the Spirit is the eventfulness of God appealing for response in ways which undermine the world's ideas of power and effectiveness (which is the subject of 4.7–14).

But the most important phrase to note is 'the face of Christ'. This is the culmination of the verse and can be seen as the theological heart of the letter. What does it mean that the knowledge of God's glory comes in this face?

Clearly the face of Christ is a symbol for the gospel. This is 'a face that is heard'. It is visual but conveyed in the word and reflected in those who believe the word (3.12–18). The actual vision is eschatological when it will be 'face to face' (cf. 1 Cor. 13.12). So the future dimension of knowledge is stressed, but at the same time its continuity with past and present. But that means a continuity that has been radically interrupted. This face comes from death as well as from God. So far we have talked a good deal about events, but now we have the crucial factor in the unity of the events. The face of Christ represents the subject of the events of crucifixion and resurrection. It transcends paradox but yet inconceivably holds together suffering, sin, death and God. These have to be thought together, according to this gospel, but there is no concept or image that can do it except this name and face. It is something new, it is news, and all previous ways of thinking are bound to be inadequate, but here is a pointer to the way for future thought. It is no accident that precisely this word for face (*prosōpon*) was at the centre of future developments in Christology.

What can we learn theologically from this seminal use of the

word in 2 Corinthians? It leads us beyond a functional understanding of the gospel events. We cannot be content with
speaking of God doing something through these events. We
have to speak also of the person of Jesus Christ and then to
follow through the implications of this face which could be both
dead and the revelation of God's glory. The implications seem
to be that this face is intrinsic to who God is, and that that
revolutionizes our understanding of death and God and all
reality. We have already found that the climactic events of the
gospel led to a transformation in key concepts; now a further
transformation needs to be carried through because of the
centrality of this face, and concepts as yet unquestioned will also
be drawn in.

Knowledge is given its true focus and criterion in this face.
Before the face of one who embodies and reveals knowledge
there can be receptivity without passivity. Mutuality is essential,
and in the face to face relationship neutrality is not an option.
And the face of Christ, as we have said above, is an eschatological
concept and so gives the future dimension of knowledge of God
its decisive content, anticipated now. The power that goes with
this face is that of the non-violent appeal, communicated with a
respect for others which dies rather than coerces. The face that
shows love is vulnerable to rejection, but also has a power that
need not diminish even when most violently rejected. It has an
authority that is more than just indicated by the face: the face
is itself intrinsic to the authority and both undergoes the violent
rejection and manifests the quality and truth of God's power.

In the light of this face the Christian meaning of contingency
and freedom becomes clearer. It is a face that has been shaped
through the contingencies of history and bears their marks. Its
way of transcending them has been to undergo them. Now too
it does not have a life separate from contingencies: a living face
represents continuing sensitivity and responsiveness to events
and people. Indeed for Paul this face sharpens contingency to its
most penetrating urgency, a life or death decision. This is where
directional and relational freedom are oriented, to an encounter
with the face of Christ. With this content, freedom is seen
fulfilled face to face with an other whose appeal to us allows for
the ultimate freedom of acceptance or rejection. The love that
compels (5.14) in this face does not ensure an inevitable happy

ending, but can envisage tragedy – 'to some a stench from death
to death' (2.16). But the invitation is to a free transformation
'from glory to glory' (3.18) as one receives in one's heart the
knowledge of God's glory in this face. To conceive the ultimate
in the form of a face enables one to imagine the possibility of
endlessly interesting free conversation and interaction with one
who is the image and face of the God of all creativity.

This glimpse of a new creation leads us beyond the practicality
of the letter. Paul's theology is of course practical, and a basic
principle is the union of word and act. But both word and act are
taken up into a new dynamic unity in relation to this face. Their
fulfilment is not in any achievement or necessary task but is in
the free overflow, the superfluity and more than necessary abundance of glorifying God: 'So because of him, the Amen is raised
to God to his glory through us' (1.20); 'for everything is for
your sake, so that grace abounding through more and more of
you may cause thanksgiving to overflow to the glory of God'
(4.15). This is the secret of Paul's ministry as he sees it:

> For if the ministry of condemnation is glory, even more will the ministry
> of righteousness overflow with glory. For that which has been glorified
> is not glorified at all in comparison with this extraordinary glory. For if
> what is fading away was born in glory, even more does the ongoing one
> exist in glory. Having that kind of hope, then, we boldly exercise the
> power of free speech (3.9–12).

The boldly exercised power of free speech is *parrhēsia*, the
utterly confident expression possible before one who has given
this freedom. Faith is living before the face of Christ in free
thanks, prayer and praise, and ministry is this *parrhēsia* overflowing in speech and life.

All of this questions our use of the concept of 'identity'
referring to God, Christ and ourselves. If identity implies something self-same, with a permanent centre and discernible boundaries, then that is inadequate. If God's glory in the face of
Christ shows who God is, and if this glory is shared with us in
a way that 'transforms us into that self-same image, from glory
to glory' (3.18), usual notions of identity need to be transformed
too. This 'self-same image' denies any individualism or autonomy in being a person, but constitutes identity in a new way,
through being part of God's sharing of his own glory. This
changes the very idea of the boundaries of self in favour of

concepts such as coinherence, exchange, mutual indwelling and living for others. Above all, the new identity is summed up in the face, which is at once the mark of unique personality and the embodiment of receptivity to others. The welcome of the face is not a threat to other selves but is the supreme sign of the possibility that we can live in free, non-competitive mutuality. Yet this is a freedom that is in its very essence responsible, because it only exists face to face with the other who continually puts the self in question and calls us to live responsively.

The face of Christ is also the clue to the idea of truth most appropriate to this letter's theology. Why have we not been arguing for the plausibility of this theology in terms of criteria of truth, or coherence with historical, philosophical and other positions? Such considerations are relevant, and we will suggest below the contemporary philosophy that gives the best context for affirming the truth of the conceptions explored above. But such general apologetics are bound to be secondary because of the sort of claim to truth made by Paul. He knows well that general wisdom, whether Jewish or Greek, will not give a framework for justifying his gospel. As already argued, he is wanting to change the framework, to introduce a new criterion of truth, It is of the utmost importance that this truth is conceived as a particular person's face. This means that the gospel is testimony. Paul is witnessing to this person, giving news of events and a face. His presupposition is that God is free to do new things, and when they happen the primary form of truth appropriate to them is inevitably testimony.

More precisely, if the truth has a name and a face which belong to one who is living then the urgent thing is to make an introduction and allow the relationship to develop from there. Faced with a face – a face identified through events, rendered in words, reflected in those who know it, and expected to be fully manifested in the future – one is not encountering a proposition to be proved or disproved. The category of contradiction is less relevant than that of rejection. One is being presented to someone whose claim to truth confronts one as a face does, and there is the possibility of acceptance or rejection. The testimony is irreducible: its content is this person who poses a challenge, but whose truth cannot be ultimately justified by any more general considerations.

The vital matter as regards truth of testimony is the authority of the witness, and that is of course at the heart of 2 Corinthians. Paul's authority can be questioned from many angles, as discussed in Chapter 7 above, but he consistently maintains that the only appropriate criteria are those which test him in line with the content of his gospel. What else can a witness do when his testimony is distrusted except to try in every way to establish trust and reaffirm his message? And when that message is about a person, the best way is so to speak and act as to allow people to understand the truth of the person as fully as possible. That is the logic of Paul's claim to truth and it continues to be the logic of Christian truth. Testimony is primary because these events and this person must first be indicated in that way. The embodiment of the message is secondary ('we have this treasure in earthenware pots', 4.7) but yet a sign that can authenticate and communicate it.

So our approach to the truth of 2 Corinthians is primarily to elucidate the message in such a way that it can continue to confront readers with the face of Christ and all that is meant by that. There can be no neutrality here, and we ourselves are searched to the depths as we explicate what is meant. Our presuppositions, world-views, hopes, values, vocations and relationships are all questioned before this face. We cannot get 'outside' the confrontation to judge it and relativize it, for this face is presented as the revelation of the Creator who is not confined within any context or human overview.

Yet that by no means rules out general discussion of reality. Rather, the history of theology, philosophy and other disciplines shows how the gospel can energize the attempt to follow through as broadly and rigorously as possible its implications in many directions. Our immediate question is what understanding can begin to do justice to the face of Christ. We have seen how important features of reality need to be reconceived in the light of this, while at the same time the meaning of the face is further illuminated by the attempt to discern its connections with other areas. We now draw the most embracing conclusion: what is at stake is the most fundamental conception of reality, often called metaphysics or ontology.

So what ontology is consonant with a theology of the face of Christ? Of contemporary philosophers Emmanuel Levinas has contributed most to the above discussion. He is deeply rooted in Judaism like Paul, and in *Totality and Infinity. An Essay on Exteriority*[8] he develops a philosophy that lets the face be the key element in an ontology. More precisely, he criticizes ontology and metaphysics for mostly failing to take account of the priority of the 'face to face' in their understandings of being. Too often they have tried to grasp being through ideas that presuppose the unity of being as some sort of totality of which it is possible to have, at least in principle, an overview. Levinas starts from the face to face relationship and says that there is no overview of that: any third party looking on does not in fact grasp the truth of it. Faces cannot be merged or subsumed under some more general concept. They represent the irreducible pluralism of being itself, resisting all totalities. The other whom I meet has an exteriority, an alterity, that resists all fusion, all comprehension, all inclusion in sameness.

Levinas traces language, responsibility, ethics and reason to the plural reality of the face to face. 'Meaning is the face of the Other, and all recourse to words takes place already within the primordial face to face of language.'[9] The face is an ethical presence, appealing and appealed to, accompanying its presence with speech. Transcendence is to be understood from here, breaking through any idolatry of the face understood as just a visible form:

> If the transcendent cuts across sensibility, if it is openness pre-eminently, if its vision is the vision of the very openness of being, it cuts across the vision of forms and can be stated neither in terms of contemplation nor in terms of practice. It is the face; its revelation is speech. The relation with the Other alone introduces a dimension of transcendence, and leads to a relation totally different from experience in the sensible sense of the term, relative and egoist.[10]

The theological conclusion of Levinas is:

> Monotheism signifies this human kinship, this idea of a human race that refers back to the approach of the Other in the face, in a dimension of height, in responsibility for oneself and for the Other.[11]

God therefore represents, negatively, a critique of any understanding of reality (ontology) that unifies it by ignoring the ultimate pluralism of the face to face, and, positively, the priority of ethics over ontology. This links up with our concern above to bring general concepts of God into line with the gospel. God has supremely been used as a totality, an idol of necessity and omnipotence, and the absolutist ideas of deity continue to have seductive power, both among believers and others. Paul's focus on the face of Christ gives a good lever for shifting this dead-weight, and Levinas' thought is an example of the way a whole understanding of reality, including thorough treatment of philo-sophical problems, might be supportive in this. But our final move must take us through this philosophy into the heart of theology again.

4 WHAT ABOUT THE TRINITY?

At the culmination of Dante's *Divine Comedy*, in the last canto of the *Paradiso*, comes the vision of God. It is a Trinitarian vision, in line with centuries of Christian tradition, but its climax is not the coinherence of Trinity in unity. The most striking thing, which explodes all the poet's categories and leads to the final breakthrough into union with God and 'the love which moves the sun and the other stars', is the vision of the face of Christ, a human face united with the being of God. For 2 Corinthians this raises the vital question of how 'the knowledge of God's glory in the face of Christ' is related to the later development of the doctrine of the Trinity. Dante was only able to begin to do justice to this face by using Trinitarian terms, and even those proved inadequate. We have started from this face and now come to consider the conception of God as Trinity.

It is obvious that Paul would not have held the doctrine of the Trinity as it came to be worked out in the fourth and fifth centuries AD. It is important not to read back into his letters the later conceptions. The 'proof-texting' approach to the Trinity has often been guilty of this, with 2 Corinthians providing some favourite verses, notably 3.17; 5.19 and 13.14. There can be no such naive justification of the doctrine, a point repeated end-lessly by biblical scholars in reaction against the domination of interpretation by dogma.

Yet the matter cannot rest there. There must also be no naive forgetting or rejection of the Trinity when interpreting Paul. This is a naiveté that is far more likely and more dangerous

today. In hermeneutical terms it is an attempt to come to the
text with no presuppositions, pretending that the way God has
been understood for centuries has no effect. Instead, as interpreters of Paul we are in dialogue not only with him but also
with the whole tradition which he helped to form. In Chapter 5
we resisted the tendency to limit meaning to the conscious
intention of Paul or to the context of that time. These must be
understood as well as possible, but meaning is also 'ahead' of
the text. These words can help to generate understanding in
new situations undreamt of by the author or his correspondents.
This is especially important in relation to God, because knowing
him has a crucial future dimension. God is known through the
Spirit given as a downpayment for what is to come. Knowing
God is therefore continually open to further illumination.

This means that we do need to ask about the relation of
2 Corinthians to later doctrine, but that we are not looking for
a deduction of the Trinity from Paul's words. Rather we are
trying to discern whether there is the sort of continuity that the
tradition affirmed in claiming that Paul's letters and the whole
Bible is most adequately understood in Trinitarian terms.

The analogy of grammar is helpful here. It is possible for
someone to speak perfectly grammatically without ever consciously knowing any grammar. Grammatical terms and systems
are a late development in any language. So it is conceivable that
the 'grammar' of Paul's talk of God might have been correctly
understood by later doctrine even if their terminology seems
alien. Paul spoke the language; they both spoke it and analysed
it systematically. It is even possible that the later analysis might
be correct while including inappropriate methods of argument
and proof. So the right question to ask of 2 Corinthians is: does
the 'grammar' of Paul's ways of referring to God accord with
the 'grammar' of the doctrine of the Trinity? Various modern
theologians have looked at the development of the doctrine of
the Trinity as the attempt to work out the proper 'grammar' of
Christian talk of God, deciding the rules intrinsic to the way
God is referred to in Scripture, worship and other articulations
of Christian faith.[12] The result can be put in negative or positive
terms.

Negatively, one could see Trinitarian forms as a way of
guarding against idolatry. The temptation to identify God

simply with a concept of absolute transcendence, or with Jesus of Nazareth, or with 'spirit' understood either cosmically or as indwelling human beings is negated by the requirement always to include each element. The rule is: never refer to God in one way without intending also each of the others. To ignore this rule is to be in danger of fixing God in one mode and having a concept which 'idolizes' that mode and fails to do justice to the differentiation and unity appropriate to this God. Positively, the being and transcendence of God are expressed in three ways. The negative rule is turned around to become: always identify God through Father, Son and Holy Spirit, and intend this even when only one is mentioned.

When this is applied to 2 Corinthians it is possible to see the rules being observed. We have already seen how Jesus Christ has become intrinsic to Paul's way of referring to God, and the threefoldness of his reference to God can also be illustrated (1.21–2; 3.2–3; 13.13). Perhaps the most important verse (now that it has been reflected on at length and connected with the theology of the rest of the letter) is 4.6, in which the Trinitarian pattern is clear (for the Holy Spirit in relation to 'shining in our hearts', compare Rom. 5.5). It is of course possible to construe 2 Corinthians in a non-Trinitarian way as well, and far more than this letter was needed for the development of the later doctrine. Yet our conceptual analysis of it has tried to show that the way Paul was led by his gospel to refer to God does have in it what might be called the 'deep structure' of the Trinity. His gospel exerted a pressure on his talk of God which he himself did not analyse but which is consonant with a differentiation and relationality in God. The prevenience of the Father and Creator, the death and resurrection of Christ, the eventfulness and transforming power of the Spirit are all both inextricably involved with each other and yet to be distinguished. The very form that this chapter has taken in order to try to follow the meaning of the letter's reference to God exhibits the logic of the Trinity: the need to transform concepts 'according to the Spirit', opening them up to the thrust of the gospel on knowledge, freedom, the future, power, contingency and death; the priority of God's prevenience in all this; and the ultimate focus on the face of Christ.

Was this perhaps just a case of presuppositions determining

the analysis? Of course it was, but that does not invalidate it. The further question to be asked is whether, in view of the fact that no one is without presuppositions, these are the most adequate for the task. 2 Corinthians does refer to God in a way that challenges our presuppositions about God and much else. It also contributed to the communal faith, language and behaviour whose basic 'grammar' was later judged to be Trinitarian. It should not be surprising that this concept of God is fruitful as a hermeneutical key to the letter. It amounts to saying that the God indicated by Paul is least inadequately related to when one bears in mind the 'summary grammar' of God[13] that was made explicit after several hundred years of engagement with him.

The analogy of grammar is fruitful and is perhaps the best way to expose the continuity between the God of 2 Corinthians and the God of Trinitarian orthodoxy without being committed to any one particular theology of the Trinity. The same 'grammar' might be seen in radically different developments of the doctrine. Yet the analogy has considerable limitations. The main one is the other side of its usefulness: it is language about language, and makes a firm distinction between primary and secondary discourse. In doing theology this soon becomes an artificial distinction. Our method throughout this book is better described in John Milbank's terms:

> Neither theological concepts, *nor* 'original' narratives and images are foundational, but a constant movement between the two ensures a mutual enrichment.[14]

The thrust of our discussion now calls for something more than an argument that the 'grammar' or logic of 2 Corinthians is compatible with the doctrine of the Trinity. We need to risk coming to conclusions about the relation of the content of 2 Corinthians to particular ways of understanding the Trinity.

One obvious conclusion is implied by our discussion of ontology and the face of Christ. We argued there for a pluralism of being, in line with the philosophy of Levinas. It is clear that the doctrine of the Trinity is well suited to such an ultimate and irreducible pluralism in which otherness is never lost in a totality, although it is also true that many actual doctrines of the Trinity have seemed more like totalitarian systems. Our focus on the face of Christ makes our ontology more 'particularist' than that of Levinas, for whom no particular person or events are decisive for the conception of God. That this face is the main truth about the future is also important for ontology. Reality is a matter of possibility and contingency as well as of actuality, but the future is not random or emptily open. Rather, our destination is best imagined as a face to face meeting; our freedom in history is answerable, relational and directional, and there is the possibility of tragic rejection.

Above all, our previous discussion led us to see the need to go beyond any purely 'economic' doctrine of the Trinity, which sees the threefoldness of God only as the way he chooses to be in relation to the world and human history rather than saying anything about how God is to be conceived in himself. In later theology this became known as the question of the relation of the economic Trinity (God revealed in his relations with us) to the immanent or doxological Trinity (God as he is in himself). The word 'doxological', from *doxa* meaning glory, is the clue to the relevance of 2 Corinthians. In Chapter 6 we saw how 'the economy of God' in 2 Corinthians stretched the metaphor of an economy to its limits, or to the point of changing our ideas of what an economy might be. In this chapter we have been rethinking the 'self' or identity of God in such a way that the very idea of him being 'in himself' is allowed to be determined by his involvement in history. The two chapters converge from different angles in questioning the boundary between the economic and the doxological Trinity.

This is especially evident in the concept of God's glory. This is supremely an attribute that belongs to God 'in himself', yet it is also uniquely present in Jesus Christ and distributed through the Holy Spirit. It is not only the identifying mark of God but is shared by him. It is defined through the crucifixion and resurrection of Jesus Christ in the context of the whole economy of God including creation and the Sinai covenant through Moses. It is the dynamic of transformation in Christian life and it is intrinsically social, to be participated in through a community of those who reflect it together. It has the most radical implications for Church and society and their notions of status, value and authority. Above all, it is a glory imprinted so utterly with the face of Christ that it is wrong to conceive of any other sort of God 'in himself' behind or apart from it. That is the really decisive matter, and it is no accident that two of the leading theologians of this century, Karl Barth and Karl Rahner, have in different ways made the same point: the economic is to be identified with the doxological Trinity, and there is no 'hidden God' different from Jesus Christ. This by no means eliminates the mystery of God – who can comprehend Jesus Christ fully? But it does insist that the glory of God is none other than that in the face of Christ.

5 CONCLUSION

The Glory of God was our working title for this book because we see all the main themes and issues of the letter converging there. Gospel, Old Testament, Church and society, authority, ministry, eschatology and the whole economy of God are essentially related to and interpret the glory of God. It is also the criterion of the fundamental distinction running through the letter between living *kata sarka*, according to human or worldly standards, or *kata pneuma*, according to the Spirit (expressed in a variety of ways, such as *en chariti theou*, in God's grace, 1.12), discriminating between various ultimate concerns, commitments and ways of living.

We have taken the doctrine of God and his glory as the main area for more theological reflection. We might also have taken reconciliation through Christ[15] or the doctrine of ministry[16] or of the Church[17] or of revelation,[18] and the whole letter could have been explored from those standpoints. The sheer density and fruitfulness of the letter tempted us in many other directions too.[19] But the glory of God seemed the right primary focus, as it points to the letter's theological profundity as well as its practical purpose, and offers both the widest horizon and the central image at the heart of gospel, the face of Christ.

In line with that combination of universality and particularity in the content of the letter, our interpretation has tried to elucidate both the meaning in its original context and its wider significance. As Paul says, 'Who is adequate for these things?' But the test by which we would wish to be judged is whether the reader of 2 Corinthians finds the meaning and truth of the letter illuminated by our efforts. To encourage this experiment we conclude with our translation of the text.

NOTES

1 For a survey see Stephen Toulmin, *The Return to Cosmology. Postmodern Science and the Theology of Nature* (Univ. of California Press, Berkeley, Los Angeles and London, 1982), Part 3.

2 For a good discussion of this and of the concept of promise used below see Ronald F. Thiemann, *Revelation and Theology. The Gospel as Narrated Promise* (University of Notre Dame Press, Notre Dame, 1985).

3 Richard B. Hays, in *The Faith of Jesus Christ. The narrative Substructure of Galatians* 3.1—4.11 (Scholars Press, Chico, California 1983), has done for Galatians what could also be done for 2 Corinthians.

4 Especially in *Letters and Papers from Prison* (SCM, London, 1971).

5 cf. Bonhoeffer's *Ethics* (SCM, London, 1978).

6 *God as the Mystery of the World* (T. & T. Clark, Edinburgh, 1983).

7 Princeton University Press, Princeton, 1967.

8 Duquesne University Press, Pittsburgh, 1969.

9 ibid., 206.

10 ibid., 193.

11 ibid., 214.

12 e.g. George Lindbeck, *The Nature of Doctrine. Religion and Theology in a Postliberal Age* (SPCK, London, 1984); Nicholas Lash, 'Considering the Trinity', *Modern Theology* 2 No. 3 (April 1986), 183–96.

13 Lash, op. cit., 183.

14 'The Second Difference', *Modern Theology* 2 No. 3 (April 1986), 222.

15 For a discussion of atonement in relation to 2 Corinthians see David F. Ford, 'Tragedy and Atonement', in the forthcoming *Christ, Ethics and Tragedy. Pursuing the Thought of Donald MacKinnon*, ed. Kenneth Surin (Cambridge University Press, Cambridge, 1988).

16 Chapter 8 has many of the elements for this.

17 Chapter 7 has a few of the elements for this.

18 Chaps. 3, 4, 5, 6, 8 and 9 would do most to contribute to this.

19 One chapter written but not included due to lack of space was on the relationship of 2 Corinthians to Romans, arguing that the usual centrality given to Romans in understanding Paul's theology should be corrected by reference to 2 Corinthians.

10

Reading the Text:
Paul's Second Letter to the Corinthians

Paul, apostle of Christ Jesus through the will of God, and Timothy the brother, to the church of God in Corinth, with all the saints who are in the whole of Achaia, grace to you and peace from God our Father and Lord Jesus Christ (1.1–2).

Blessed is the God and Father of our Lord Jesus Christ, the Father of compassion and God of every encouragement, who encourages us in all our affliction, so as to enable us to encourage those in every affliction through the encouragement we ourselves have received from God (1.3–4). For just as the sufferings of Christ overflow onto us, so through Christ even the encouragement we receive is overflowing (1.5). So if we are afflicted, it is for your encouragement and salvation; if we are encouraged, it is for your encouragement, encouragement that produces endurance of the same sufferings which we also suffer (1.6). And our hope is firm in your case, knowing that as you are partners in the sufferings, so also you are in the encouragement (1.7).

For we don't want you, brothers, to be unaware of the affliction that happened to us in Asia; for we were extraordinarily oppressed, more than our power could stand, so that we even doubted our survival; but for ourselves we have accepted the death sentence, so as not to put confidence in ourselves but in God who raises the dead; the God who rescued us from such brushes with death and will rescue us, the God in whom we have come to hope; for he will yet again rescue us, as you too join as collaborators in efforts on our behalf in prayer, so that from many persons thanks may be offered on our behalf for the favour granted to us through many (prayers) (1.8–11).

For our pride lies in the witness of our conscience that we have conducted ourselves in the world with the single-minded commitment and straightforwardness of God, not in human wisdom but in God's grace, most of all in our dealings with you (1.12). For we do not write to you anything other than what you read and acknowledge; and I hope that – even as you partially acknowledge us now – so you will fully acknowledge that we are your pride and joy, even as you are ours, on the day of our Lord Jesus (1.13–14).

And in this confidence I was intending first to come to you so that you might receive a double pleasure, from my going via you to Macedonia and again coming to you from Macedonia and being given your send-off to Judaea (1.15–16). Surely I wasn't behaving inconsistently in having this intention? Or do (you imagine) I make plans at the human level so that it is in my hands that yes be yes and no be no (1.17)? Yet God is faithful, for our word to you is not yes and no; for the Son of God, Christ Jesus, proclaimed among you through us, through me and Silvanus and Timothy, was not yes and no – the yes is realized in him (1.18–19). For however many the promises of God, the yes to them is realized in him. So because of him, the Amen is raised to God to his glory through us (1.20). God is the one who gives us our guarantee with you in Christ and has anointed us, and has also sealed us and given us the downpayment of the Spirit in our hearts (1.21–2).

I call upon God to witness against me: it was to spare you that I didn't come to Corinth. Not that we lord it over your faith; rather we are fellow-workers for your joy – and you stand (on your own two feet) in faith (1.23–4). But I decided this for myself, that I wouldn't come to you again while there was still (mutual) hurt (2.1). For if I hurt you, who is there to cheer me up, except the very one I've hurt (2.2)? I wrote that (notorious letter) to avoid coming and being hurt by those who should make me rejoice, confident in you all, that my joy is (the joy) of all of you (2.3). For I wrote to you with many tears, out of much affliction and anguish of heart, not that you should be hurt, but that you should know the love which I have overwhelmingly for you (2.4). If someone has caused hurt, it isn't me he's hurt, but to some extent, not to exaggerate the point, all of you (2.5). That rebuke from the majority is sufficient for a man like him, so you ought rather to forgive and encourage him, in case a man like him should be swallowed up by overwhelming hurt (2.6–7).

So then I encourage you to confirm your love for him (2.8).

For the reason I wrote was this: to know (how you would respond) to being put to the proof, whether you were obedient in everything (2.9). But now whoever you forgive, I do too; for the forgiveness I offer, if any forgiveness has come from me, is for your sake in the presence of Christ, so that no advantage may be taken of us by Satan; for we are not ignorant of his intentions (2.10–11). Coming to Troas (to preach) the gospel of Christ, and finding a door open for me in the Lord, I had no rest in my spirit because I didn't find my brother Titus; taking leave of them, I came on to Macedonia (2.12–13). Thanks be to God who in Christ drags us around everywhere in his triumphal procession, and through us makes apparent the incense of his knowledge in every place; for we are Christ's aroma to God among those being saved and those perishing, to some a stench from death to death, to others a scent from life to life (2.14–16a).

Who is adequate for these things (2.16b)? For we are not traders in the word of God, like most of them, but in a straight-forward manner, as from God, we speak in Christ in God's presence (2.17). Are we beginning to commend ourselves again? Surely we do not need introductory letters like some (to present) to you or (take on) from you (3.1)? Our letter is you, a letter written in our (or your) hearts, recognized and read by all men, making apparent the fact that you are Christ's letter delivered by us, (and) written not with ink but with the Spirit of the living God, not on tablets of stone but on tablets which are human hearts (3.2–3).

Such is the confidence we have through Christ in God's presence (3.4). Not that of ourselves we are adequate to count on anything (issuing) from ourselves, but our adequacy is from God, who made us adequate as ministers delivering the new covenant not (based) on the letter but on the Spirit; for the letter kills but the Spirit makes alive (3.5–6). If then the ministry of death engraved in letters on stones was born in glory, so that the sons of Israel could not gaze upon the face of Moses because of the glory of his face, (glory which was) fading, how (could it) not (be that) the ministry of the Spirit will even more exist in glory (3.7–8)? For if the ministry of condemnation is glory, even more will the ministry of righteousness overflow with glory (3.9). For that which has been glorified is not glorified at all by comparison with this extraordinary glory (3.10). For if what is fading away was born in glory, even more does the ongoing one exist in glory (3.11).

Having that kind of hope, then, we boldly exercise the power of free speech, not like Moses who put a veil on his face so that the sons of Israel might not gaze upon the outcome of what was fading away (3.12–13). But their minds were hardened. For until today there remains over the reading of the old covenant the same veil, unlifted, for in Christ it fades away; but until today whenever Moses is read, a veil lies over their heart (3.14–15). Yet whenever one turns to the Lord, the veil is stripped away (3.16). 'The Lord' (here means) 'the Spirit'; where the Spirit is, (there is) freedom (3.17). We all with unveiled face, reflecting the glory of the Lord, are being transformed into that self-same image, from glory to glory, the source (of this transformation being) the Lord, (that is), the Spirit (3.18).

For this reason, having this ministry, as we have received mercy, we do not lose heart, but we have forsworn shameful secrets, we refuse to take the smart way or cheat with the word of God, but we commend ourselves by the transparency of the truth to every human conscience before God (4.1–2). If our gospel is veiled, it is veiled among the perishing, among whom the God of this world has blinded the minds of the unfaithful to prevent them being illuminated by the light of the gospel of the glory of Christ who is the image of God (4.3–4). For we do not proclaim ourselves, but Christ Jesus as Lord, ourselves as your slaves for Jesus' sake (4.5). For the God who said, 'Out of darkness light will shine', is the one who has shone in our hearts to (bring) the enlightenment (which is) the knowledge of God's glory in the face of Christ (4.6).

We have this treasure in earthenware pots, in order that this extraordinary power may be God's and not (come) from us (4.7). Afflicted in every (way) but not crushed, at a loss but not totally without resources, persecuted but not left in the lurch, struck down but not destroyed (that's how we are), always bearing the killing of Jesus in the body, so that Jesus' life too might be made apparent in our body (4.8–10). For always we who live are being handed over to death for Jesus' sake, so that Jesus' life too might be made apparent in our mortal flesh (4.11). So death is at work in us, but life in you (4.12). Having the same spirit of faith (as the Psalmist), according to the text 'I believed, therefore I spoke', we too believe and therefore also speak, knowing that the one who raised the Lord Jesus will raise us also with Jesus and stand (us) up with you (before him) (4.13–14).

For everything is for your sake, so that grace abounding through more and more (of you) may cause thanksgiving to overflow to the glory of God (4.15). So we do not give up, but even if our outer self is being destroyed, yet our inner self is being renewed day by day (4.16). For this immediate trifle of an affliction produces for us, in extraordinary quantities, an eternal weight of glory if we keep our eyes not on visible but invisible realities; for visible realities are temporary whereas the invisible are eternal (4.17–18). For we know that if our earthly tent-home is taken down, we have a building from God, an eternal home not made with hands in the heavens (5.1). In this (state), after all, we groan, longing to put on the dwelling supplied us from heaven, if only by putting it on we will not be found naked (5.2–3). After all, we who are in the tent groan at being weighed down, not that we want to shed our covering but rather put on more so that the mortal is swallowed up by life (5.4). But the one who prepared us for this very (destiny), is God, who has given us the down-payment of the Spirit (5.5).

So we are always full of courage even knowing that being at home in the body we are away from the Lord – for we walk by faith, not with the vision before our eyes (5.6–7). We are full of courage and would rather be away from the body and at home in the Lord (5.8). So we strive all the more vigorously, whether at home or away, to be pleasing to him (5.9). For we must all be made transparent before the judgement-seat of Christ so that each may receive his due for deeds done through the body, whether good or bad (5.10).

Knowing then the fear of the Lord, we persuade men, but to God we are transparent; I hope to be transparent to your consciences, too (5.11). We are not commending ourselves to you again, but giving you a base for taking a pride in us, so that you may have (ammunition) against those who take a pride in outward appearance and not in the heart (5.12). For if we were beside ourselves, (it was) for God; if we are in control of ourselves, (it is) for you (5.13). For the love of Christ constrains us, in that we have come to this verdict, that one died for all –

so all died; and he died for all so that those who live should no longer live for themselves, but for the one who died and was raised for them (5.14–15).

So from now on we know no one at the human level; even if we know Christ through getting to know him at the human level, no longer do we know him so (5.16). So if anyone is in Christ, he is a new creation; (or: If anyone is a new creation in Christ,) the old state has passed away, – look! the new has come into being (5.17). The whole thing comes from God, who has reconciled us to himself through Christ and has given to us the ministry of reconciliation, (the proclamation) that it was God reconciling the world to himself in Christ, not counting their sins against them, and (it is God who has) put the word of reconciliation in us (5.18–19). On Christ's behalf, then, we act as ambassadors, God (himself) encouraging your response through us; we beg on Christ's behalf, be reconciled with God (5.20). On our behalf he made into sin the one who knew no sin, so that we might become the righteousness of God in him (5.21). And we as his fellow-workers encourage you not to receive the grace of God in vain – for he says, 'At the acceptable time I heard you and on the day of salvation I helped you' (6.1–2a).

Look! Now is the acceptable time. Look! Now is the day of salvation (6.2b). (We appeal to you, we who) put no obstacle in front of anyone in case the ministry should be faulted, but in every way recommend ourselves as God's ministers, with great endurance, in situations of affliction, constraint or pressure, through floggings, imprisonments, lynchings, in labours, lack of sleep and lack of food, with dedication, knowledge, patience, goodness, Holy Spirit, genuine love, with the word of truth and with the power of God, by means of the weapons of righteousness in the right hand and the left, through glory and dishonour, through bad reputation and good, as false and true, as unknown and acknowledged, as dead yet – look! – we live, as punished yet not put to death, as hurt but always rejoicing, as poor but enriching many, as having nothing yet possessing all things (6.3–10).

Our mouth is open towards you, Corinthians, our heart is wide; there's no pressure on you from us, but you are pressurized by your own feelings (6.11–12). So you too open up in return – I speak (to you) as to (my) children (6.13). Don't be harnessed up all lopsided with the unfaithful – for what common goal is there between righteousness and wickedness? What partnership has light with darkness (6.14)? What harmony is there between Christ and Beliar, what common lot do faith and unfaith share (6.15)? What agreement can a temple of God have with idols? For we are a temple of the living God; as God said,

> I will dwell in them and walk with them
> And I will be their God and they shall be my people.
> Wherefore come out from them
> And be separated, says the Lord,
> And don't touch the unclean;
> And I will receive you,
> And I will be a Father to you,
> And to me you will be sons and daughters,
> Says the Lord Almighty (6.16–18).

So having these promises, beloved, let us purify ourselves from every stain of flesh and spirit, bringing dedication to fruition in fear of God (7.1).

Make room for us; we have wronged no one, we have ruined no one, we have defrauded no one (7.2). I do not say this to condemn; for I stand by what I said before – you are in our hearts so that we die together and live together (7.3). I speak to you freely with great frankness, and take great pride in you; I am filled with encouragement, I am overflowing with more and more joy in all our affliction (7.4). For since we came to Macedonia, our human self has had no rest, but is afflicted in every way (or: at all times); outside there are battles, inside, fears (7.5). But God, the one who encourages the downcast, has encouraged us by the arrival of Titus; and not merely by his arrival, but by the encouragement he received at your hands – for he reports to us your longing, your grief, your enthusiasm for me, so that I rejoice even more (7.6–7).

For even if I hurt you with my letter, I do not regret it; even if I did regret it, I see that even if that letter hurt you for an hour or so, now I rejoice, not because you were hurt, but because you were hurt in such a way as to produce repentance. For you were hurt under God (or: in God's way) so that you might in no way be damaged by us (7.8–9). For hurt under God brings about the repentance which leads to salvation and can never be regretted, but the world's hurt brings about death (7.10). For look! the very fact of having been hurt under God has produced in you such great enthusiasm, such self-defence, such indignation, such fear, such longing, such jealous zeal, such an act of reprisal. In every way you have commended yourselves as pure in deed (7.11).

Consequently, even if I did write to you, it was not for the sake of the one who had done wrong, nor for the sake of the one wronged, but simply that your enthusiasm for us should be made transparent to yourselves before God (7.12). For this reason we are encouraged. And in addition to our encouragement we rejoice all the more especially at Titus' joy, because his spirit has received refreshment from you all (7.13). For if I have indicated to him any pride in you, I was not let down, but as we told you everything in truth, so also our pride has been confirmed as true as far as Titus is concerned, and his feelings are overwhelmingly engaged on your behalf as he remembers your obedience, how you received him with fear and trembling. I rejoice because in every way I can depend on you (7.14–16).

We (write to) let you know, brothers, about the grace of God granted among the churches of Macedonia, that through a considerable testing affliction the overflow of their joy and their extreme poverty have flowed out into the wealth of their single-minded commitment (8.1–2). For as far as lay in their power – in fact I can testify, even beyond their power – they have taken the initiative, encouraging us urgently, begging us for the grace of partnership in ministering to the saints – not merely as we hoped – indeed, they have given themselves first to the Lord and then to us through the will of God, with the result that we can encourage Titus to continue what he has begun and perfect in you this same grace (8.3–6).

But as you overflow with every (grace) – faith, speech, knowledge, whole-hearted enthusiasm, and the love between us – see that you overflow with this grace too (8.7). I do not speak by way of command, but to test the genuineness of your love by comparison with the enthusiasm of others; for you know the grace of our Lord Jesus Christ, that for you he became poor though he was rich, so that you might become rich through his poverty (8.8–9). On this matter I give my opinion: it is in your interest, you who a year ago began to act on this – in fact even to want to do so (8.10). So now, complete the doing of it, so that the completion (of the collection) out of your resources may match your original willing purpose (8.11). For if that purpose comes first, whatever fits your means is appropriate, not anything that puts a strain on them (8.12). For there is no intention that relief for others should bring affliction to you; but for the present time, on the basis of equality, your overflow should make up their shortage, so that their overflow may make up your shortage, that equality may prevail, as it is written: 'The one with a lot did not have too much, and the one with a little did not go short' (8.13–15).

Thanks be to God who puts the same enthusiasm for you in the heart of Titus, because he received encouragement, and with greater enthusiasm he takes the initiative in setting out to you (8.16–17). We send with him the brother whose standing in the gospel is recognized through all the churches, and not only that, but he has been elected by the churches as our fellow-missionary in this gracious task that is being administered by us to the glory of the Lord himself and to (promote) our purpose (8.18–19). Our intention (in sending him) is this – that no one should find reason to blame us with respect to the large sum of money we are administering (8.20). For what we intend are noble deeds not only in the sight of the Lord but also in the sight of men (8.21). We send with them our brother whom we have proved on many occasions to be enthusiastic, but now he is much more full of enthusiasm and confidence in you (8.22). On Titus' behalf (I say) he is my partner and collaborator in relation to you; and as far as our brothers are concerned, they are apostles of the churches, Christ's glory! So display to them before the churches the proof of your love and of our pride in you (8.23–4).

So, as regards the ministration to the saints, it is superfluous for me to write to you. For I know your purpose. To the Macedonians I take a pride on your behalf that Achaea has been prepared for a year, and your energetic involvement has stirred up the majority of them (9.1–2). I am sending the brothers so that our pride in you may not be proved empty on this point – (I am rather afraid) that after having insisted that you were prepared, if the Macedonians come with me and find you not prepared, we – not to mention you – may be humiliated in our assurance (9.3–4). For I think it necessary to encourage the brothers to go ahead to you and get ready in advance your publicized open-handedness, that it may be collected as a free offering and not as an extortion (9.5). The fact is the one who sows with a closed fist, will also have a niggardly harvest, and the one who sows with an open hand will be blessed with a generous harvest (9.6). Let each obey the promptings of his own heart, and not act out of hurt or compulsion – for God loves a cheerful giver (9.7).

In fact, God enables every grace to overflow into you, self-sufficiency to overflow into every act of goodness, as it is written: 'He has scattered, he has given to the poor; his righteousness remains for ever' (9.8–9). The one who provides seed for the sower, will also provide bread for the consumer, and will multiply your seed-corn, and will increase the off-shoots of your righteousness (9.10). In every way you are enriched for that single-minded commitment which through us brings about thanksgiving to God (9.11). For the ministration of this service is not only making up the shortages of the saints, but is even overflowing through the multiplication of thanks to God (9.12). By the test of this ministration, they glorify God for the obedience of your confession of the gospel of Christ and the commitment of your partnership with them and everyone, while in prayer for you they yearn for you because of the extraordinary grace of God upon you. Thanks be to God for his inexpressible gift (9.13–15)!

I myself, Paul, encourage you through the gentle restraint of Christ (to respond to my appeal), I who am humble face to face with you, but bold towards you when absent: I beg you not to make me act when I am present with the bold confidence which I think I shall dare to use against some who regard us as operating at the human level (10.1–2). For we may operate as human beings, but we do not campaign with human means, for the weapons of our campaign are not human, but full of God's power for the destruction of fortresses, tearing down arguments and every battlement raised against the knowledge of God, and taking every design captive to the obedience of Christ, and ready to punish every disobedience when your obedience is complete (10.3–6). Just look at what is before your eyes. If

anyone is confident he belongs to Christ, let him again take this
into his reckoning: that as he is Christ's, so also are we
(10.7).

For even if I take a bit too much pride in our authority,
authority the Lord gave to build you up and not tear you down,
I will not be shamed into seeming not to terrify you with my
letters (10.8–9). For someone says: 'The letters are weighty and
powerful (enough), but his physical presence is weak and his
speech contemptible' (10.10). Well – let that kind of person
reckon on this, that as we are verbally by letters in our absence,
so we shall be actively when present (10.11). For we do not dare
to class or compare ourselves with some who commend themselves – they in measuring themselves by themselves and judging themselves by themselves have no understanding (10.12).

But we will not boast with a pride lacking criteria, but according to the criterion God has allotted us, namely our reaching
as far as you. For it is not as though we didn't reach you, and
overextended our claims – for we did reach you first with the
gospel of Christ; and it is not as though we've taken a pride in
other people's efforts – rather we have hopes, as your faith
increases, of expanding as far as our limit and of overflowing
beyond, of evangelizing in areas beyond your region, not of
taking a pride in what has been prepared in a region allotted to
someone else (10.13–16). 'Let him who prides himself on anything, pride himself on the Lord'; for the person who commends
himself, is not the one approved, but the one whom the Lord
commends (10.17–18).

I wish you'd bear with me in a little foolishness – surely you
are bearing with me. For I am jealous for you with God's own
jealousy – I engaged you to one man, to give you away to Christ
as a pure virgin; but I fear that just as the serpent deceived Eve
with his cunning, so somehow your minds may be distracted
from their single-minded commitment (and dedication) to
Christ (11.1–3). For if the person who turns up proclaims a
Jesus other than the Jesus we proclaimed, or you receive a spirit
other than you received, or a gospel other than the one you
accepted, you bear with that well enough. I reckon I'm not a bit
inferior to such 'super-apostles'. If my speech is idiosyncratic,
my knowledge is not, and we have been utterly transparent to
you in all matters (11.4–6). Or did I make a mistake in humbling

myself so as to exalt you? For I did preach the gospel of God to you free, gratis and for nothing. In fact I robbed other churches, getting my keep from them so as to minister to you; and while I was with you, if I went short I didn't burden anyone; my shortage the brothers who came from Macedonia made up; and in every way I kept myself from burdening you, and I will continue to do so (11.7-9).

The truth of Christ is in me: I will not let my pride in this be bottled up within me in the regions of Achaea (11.10). Why? Because I've no love for you? God knows the truth... (11.11). What I am doing, I will go on doing, in order to chop away the base of those who want a base, so that the object of their pride may be the same as ours (11.12). For such people are false apostles, workers who cheat, passing themselves off as apostles of Christ. And no wonder – for Satan himself passes himself off as an angel of light (11.13-14). So it's no great thing if his ministers pass themselves off as ministers of righteousness; their end will befit their deeds (11.15).

Again I say, don't let anyone think I'm a fool; but if that's impossible, accept me even if as a fool, so that I too can pride myself a little on something (11.16). What I say now, I don't say as the Lord's spokesman, but as one indulging in foolishness, making a confident assertion of pride (11.17). Since many take pride in achievements at the human level, I too will pride myself (11.18). For you bear with fools gladly being wise yourselves (11.19). You even bear with anyone who enslaves you, or devours you, or captures you, or sets himself up (in your way), or even strikes you full in the face (11.20).

To my shame I say we have been weaklings; but whatever anyone else dares (to take a pride in) – I speak as a fool – I dare too. Are they Hebrews? So am I. Are they Israelites? I am too. Are they the seed of Abraham? So am I. Are they ministers of Christ? I am out of my mind when I say this – but I am even more so – more so in my labours, more so in imprisonments, supremely so in the beatings I've sustained, and in my frequent brushes with death (11.21-3). From the Jews I've received the thirty-nine lashes five times, three times I've been thrashed with rods, once I was stoned, three times I was shipwrecked, night and day I've spent in the deep; often on journeys, in danger from rivers and robbers, in danger from my fellow-Jews, in danger from Gentiles, in danger from the perils of town and country-side, in danger at sea, in danger from false brothers, in labour and toil, often sleepless, famished, thirsty, often going without food, cold and naked – quite apart from that constant day-to-day pressure upon me, the care of all the churches (11.24–8). Who is weak, and I'm not weak? Who is sent sprawling and I'm not burned up about it? If it is necessary to take a pride in things, I will take a pride in the things that belong to my weakness (11.29–30).

The God and Father of the Lord Jesus Christ, God who is blessed for ever, he knows that I do not lie (11.31). In Damascus the ethnarch under King Aretas set up a guard round the city to arrest me, and I was lowered in a basket through an outlet in the wall and escaped his clutches (11.32). It is necessary to take a pride in things – it's not very beneficial – but I will come on to visions and revelations of the Lord (12.1). I know a man in Christ who fourteen years ago – whether in the body or out of the body I just don't know – God knows – (anyway) the kind of man (I speak of) was snatched up to the third heaven. And I know that that kind of man – whether in the body or apart from it I don't know, but God knows – was snatched up to Paradise and heard unutterable utterances, things that a human being may not speak (12.2–4).

I will take a pride in that kind of man, but for myself, I will take a pride only in my weaknesses (12.5). If I wish to take pride, I will not be a fool since I will be speaking the truth; but I refrain, in case anyone should reach an estimate of me based on more than he sees of me or hears from me, indeed on the basis of extraordinary revelations (12.6–7a). For this very reason, that I should not get above myself, (at the human level) a sharp splinter got under my skin, a messenger from Satan, to knock me about and prevent me getting about myself (12.7b). I prayed to the Lord three times about this, urging him to take it away from me (12.8). And he has told me, 'My grace is sufficient for you; for power is perfected in weakness' (12.9a).

Gladly then will I take a pride in weaknesses, that the power of Christ may be pitched like a tent over me (12.9b). For this very reason I delight in weaknesses, insults, constraints, persecutions and pressures, on Christ's behalf; for when I am weak, then I am powerful (12.10).

I've been a fool – but then, you compelled me. In fact I ought
to be commended by you. For I am not a bit inferior to the
'super-apostles', even if I am nothing (12.11). The signs of the
(genuine) apostle were performed among you, with all perse-
verance, with signs and wonders and acts of power (12.12). For
what is there which makes you inferior to the rest of the
churches, except that I did not make myself a burden to you?
Forgive me this injustice (12.13).

Look – this is the third time I've been ready to come to
you – and I won't burden you this time either. I don't want your
goods, but you. Children ought not to make a fortune for their
parents, but parents for their children (12.14). But I will gladly
spend and be spent on your behalf. If I have overwhelming love
for you, am I to be loved less (12.15)? All right, granted I didn't
burden you, yet being the smart operator I am, I got you by
cheating (I suppose)! Surely I haven't exploited you through
any one of those I've sent to you (12.16–17)? I encouraged Titus
and sent the brother with him; Titus didn't exploit you, did he?
Haven't we walked by the same Spirit? Haven't we trodden in
the same tracks (12.18)?

All along you've been thinking that I was making my apology
to you. Before God we speak in Christ: everything is for your
building up, my beloved (12.19). For I'm afraid I'll come and
find you not as I wish, and I'll be found not as you wish; (I'm
afraid there'll be) strife, jealousy, passions, disputes, slanders,
tale-bearing, posturing, rebellion (12.20). (I'm afraid) when I
come, my God may humiliate me in your presence, and I will
mourn many who've sinned and not repented of committing
impurity or adultery or perversion (12.21).

For the third time I am coming to you; everything is established on the word of two or three witnesses. I said in advance
when present the second time, and I say in advance again, now
I'm absent, to those who sinned before and to all the rest, that
if I come again, I will not refrain (from judgement), since you
seek proof that the one speaking in me is Christ. He is not weak
in (encountering) you but is powerful among you (13.1–3). For
out of weakness he was crucified, but he lives out of God's
power. So we are weak in him, but we will live with him out of
God's power in (encountering) you (13.4). Examine yourselves
(to see) if you are in faith, prove yourselves; or do you not

acknowledge that Jesus Christ is in you? – unless you've not been subjected to proving (13.5). I hope you will find that we have been subjected to proving (13.6). We pray to God that you do nothing evil, not so that it is apparent that we are proved right, but so that you may do the right thing, even though we seem to be proved wrong (13.7). For we have no power against the truth, only for the truth (13.8). We rejoice when we are weak and you are powerful; and our prayer is for this, for your renewal (13.9).

For this reason I write these things in my absence, so that when I'm present I may not act drastically according to the power which the Lord has given me to build you up, not tear you down (13.10). For the rest, brothers, rejoice, be renewed, be encouraged, have the same intentions, be at peace, and the God of love and peace will be with you (13.11). Greet one another with a holy kiss. All the saints greet you (13.12).

The grace of the Lord Jesus Christ and the love of God and the partnership of the Holy Spirit be with all of you (13.13).

Commentaries on 2 Corinthians

John Chrysostom, *Homilies on 1 and 2 Corinthians*, ET in NPNF series. Text in F. Field, ed., *Johannis Chrysostomis Interpretatis Omnium Epistolarum Paulinarum* tom. iii (Bibliotheca Patrum, Oxford, 1845).

Allo, E.-R., *Saint Paul: Seconde Épitre aux Corinthiens*. Paris 1937, 1956.

Bachmann, P., *Der Zweite Brief des Paulus an die Korinther*, Zahns Kommentar. Leipzig 1918.

Barrett, C. K., *A Commentary on the Second Epistle to the Corinthians*, Black's New Testament Commentaries. London 1973.

Bruce, F. F., *1 & 2 Corinthians*, New Century Bible. London 1971.

Bultmann, R., rev. E. Dinkler, *Der zweite Brief an die Korinther*, Meyers Kommentar. Göttingen 1976.

Furnish, V. P., *II Corinthians*, The Anchor Bible. New York 1984.

Goudge, H. L., *The Second Epistle to the Corinthians*, Westminster Commentaries. London 1927.

Héring, J., *The Second Epistle of Saint Paul to the Corinthians*. ET London 1958.

Hughes, P. E., *Paul's Second Epistle to the Corinthians*, New London Commentary. London 1962.

Lietzmann, H., rev. W. Kümmel, *An die Korinther I–II*, Handbuch zum Neuen Testament. Tübingen 1949.

Menzies, A., *The Second Epistle to the Corinthians*, London 1912.

Plummer, A. *A Critical and Exegetical Commentary on the Second Epistle of Saint Paul to the Corinthians*, International Critical Commentary, Edinburgh 1915.

Schlatter, A., *Paulus der Bote Jesu*. Stuttgart 1934.

Strachan, R. H., *The Second Epistle of Paul to the Corinthians*, Moffat New Testament Commentary. London 1946.

Thrall, M. E., *The First and Second Letters of Paul to the Corinthians*, The Cambridge Bible Commentary. Cambridge 1965.

Windisch, H., *Der zweite Korintherbrief*, Meyers Kommentar. Göttingen 1924, 1970.

Index of Biblical References

Index of Names and Subjects